The Essential Guide to
Managing Teacher Stress

The Essential Guides series

Thorough, practical, and up-to-date advice on the core aspects of teaching and classroom strategies.

The Essential Guide to
Successful School Trips
John Trant

9781408204474

The Essential Guide to
Using ICT Creatively in the Primary Classroom
Steve Woods

9781408224977

The Essential Guide to
Classroom Assessment
Paul Dix

9781408230251

The Essential Guide to
Shaping Children's Behaviour in the Early Years
Lynn Cousins

9781408225028

The Essential Guide to
Secondary Teaching
Susan Davies

9781408224526

The Essential Guide to
Teaching 14–19 Diplomas
Lynn Senior

9781408225493

The Essential Guide to
Understanding Special Educational Needs
Jenny Thompson

9781408225004

The Essential Guide to
Taking Care of Behaviour
(second edition)
Paul Dix

9781408225547

The Essential Guide to
Primary Teaching
Susan Davies

9781408225042

The Essential Guide to
Managing Teacher Stress
Bill Rogers

9781408261743

The Essential Guide to
Tackling Bullying
Michele Elliott

9781408264836

The Essential Guide to
Coaching and Mentoring
(second edition)
Judith Tolhurst

9781408241721

The Essential Guide to
Lesson Planning
(second edition)
Leila Walker

9781408253366

Practical Skills for Teachers
www.pearson-books.com/essentialguides

The Essential Guide to Managing Teacher Stress

Bill Rogers

PEARSON

Harlow, England • London • New York • Boston • San Francisco • Toronto • Sydney • Auckland • Singapore • Hong Kong
Tokyo • Seoul • Taipei • New Delhi • Cape Town • São Paulo • Mexico City • Madrid • Amsterdam • Munich • Paris • Milan

Pearson Education Limited

Edinburgh Gate
Harlow CM20 2JE
Tel: +44 (0)1279 623623
Fax: +44 (0)1279 431059
Website: www.pearson.com/uk

First published in Australia in 1992 as *Supporting Teachers in the Workplace*
UK first edition published 1996 by Pitman Publishing
This edition published 2012

Pearson Education is not responsible for the content of third-party internet sites.

ISBN: 978-1-4082-6174-3

British Library Cataloguing-in-Publication Data
A catalogue record for this book is available from the British Library

Library of Congress Cataloging-in-Publication Data
Rogers, Bill, 1947-
  The essential guide to managing teacher stress : practical skills for teachers / Bill
Rogers. -- 2nd ed.
       p. cm.
  Includes bibliographical references and index.
  ISBN 978-1-4082-6174-3 (pbk.)
  1. Teachers--Job stress. 2. School management and organization. I. Title.
  LB2840.2.R64 2012
  371.1001'9--dc23
                                    2011038683

10 9 8 7 6 5 4 3 2 1
15 14 13 12 11

Typeset in 10/12pt Frutiger LT Std by 3
Printed by Ashford Colour Press Ltd., Gosport

Contents

About the author

Dr Bill Rogers read theology, psychology, philosophy and education at Melbourne University. His doctoral research addressed the nature, extent and utility of colleague support and the significant difference that colleague support can make to the management of teacher stress and coping on the one hand and the effect such support has on building effective and workable whole-school approaches to the teaching and leadership of our students.

He is a regular visitor to the United Kingdom (and Europe) conducting seminars with schools, local education authorities and universities. He is a Fellow of the Australian College of Education, an Honorary Fellow of the Graduate School of Education at Melbourne University and an Honorary Life Fellow at Trinity College (Leeds University).

Bill has worked in schools in Australia, Britain and Europe for over twenty years now as a mentor-teacher, in challenging schools. His approach to teacher stress is solidly grounded in the practical reality, and demands, of day-to-day teaching. He does not shirk the hard questions and difficult issues teachers face as they seek to make a difference in the lives of children and young people.

Acknowledgements

There are many colleagues whose accounts of the day-to-day stresses of our profession are recorded here – I have taught alongside many of them as a mentor-teacher (Chapter 10). I want to thank them for inviting me to work alongside them, team-teaching in what were often very challenging classes. I want to thank them for their professional honesty and goodwill in (at times) very stressful teaching contexts.

I want to thank Andy Schofield for his very generous review of the first edition of this book I also want to thank my colleagues who have reviewed this major second edition (see later). This book is much more than a second edition – it is a substantially new text. It has retained the central premises, approaches and skills – particularly the essential emphasis on colleague support and a whole-school approach to behaviour management and discipline. The text is extended in areas such as the challenging class, bullying of teachers and mentoring support for professional development in behaviour leadership.

I want to thank the team at Pearson Education who encouraged me to pursue this major new work. My particular thanks go to Katy Robinson, Catherine Yates, Priyadharshini Dhanagopal and Tony Clappison. I want to thank them for the support extended to me over the miles from Australia to England. On my regular trips to Britain (to work) they have been generous and kind hosts to my wife and myself.

To the ever efficient typist and translator of *handwritten* drafts (yes – I know it's hard to believe that some of us still write longhand – remember? pen on paper?) Thank you again Felicia Schmidt for your skill, patience and support.

My wife and eldest daughter (also teachers) have certainly had countless hours of 'moan bonding' about our profession, as well as the good humour and satisfaction that teaching can bring. I thank them for their patience and encouragement over the years.

Reviews

The *Times Educational Supplement* review

It is written with that touch of pragmatism with which teachers will at once identify … practical, jargon-free guide to making one's work more acceptable, it makes excellent reading.

Above all else, it is realistic. It isn't sentimental about pupils and the advice on dealing with what Rogers calls the *reputation class* or *reputation individual* could be put into practice straight away.

The chapter on staff development underlines the responsibility that senior management have for sustaining a climate within the school which actively reduces, rather than increases, the amount of stress that teachers experience. Rogers concludes that *we live in a marginally sane world*. Blaming others or moaning that life shouldn't be like this will not help us cope.

The author's humane and realistic ideas are about dealing with the world as it is, not as we would like it to be. As such, this book has the potential to make our working lives more meaningful and hopefully more enjoyable.

Andy Schofield (deputy head teacher of Varndean School, Brighton).
Times Educational Supplement

Bill Roger's text offers a comprehensive analysis of the phenomenon of teacher stress and its management. He writes in a clear succinct style thereby making the text entertaining, informative and accessible to all.

This text is relevant to those in involved in educational management, teacher training programs, and policy making. New entrants to the teaching profession and teachers at all levels in the educational system will specifically benefit from reading this book.

The author challenges educational practitioners to engage in an interactive dialogue with the issue of teacher stress management. He acknowledges that stress is central to the teaching profession. He argues that teachers need to be skilled practitioners in behavioral leadership in order to successfully address this. This book in part could be implicitly considered to be as much about classroom management and discipline as it is about the management of teacher stress.

In the early chapters of the book, the author identifies the various dimensions of teacher stress, and its consequent negative effects on teacher health and well-being. Critically he offers numerous practical and well thought out strategies designed to address these issues.

In this context, chapter seven is pivotal. The author's greatest contribution is the advocacy of a class behavior management and discipline plan, which he argues, ' is also integral to a whole school approach to behavior management and discipline'. The author argues that such a plan properly implemented can 'significantly moderate the natural stress occasioned by our role in behavioral leadership'.

In discussing various strategies designed to prevent the escalation of teacher stress in the classroom, the author also highlights the fundamental importance of collegiality and various other mechanisms of teacher support.

This is a truly masterful piece of work. It is scholarly, comprehensive well structured and above all thought provoking. It is well illustrated by numerous pertinent case studies, which elucidates the relevant themes being discussed. It is an enjoyable lively text to read and a difficult one to put down.

Dr Suzanne Parkinson, Mary Immaculate College, SCR, Limerick

This text should be *compulsory reading* in both teacher-training and professional development courses for senior teachers and school executives in topics such as Teacher Well-being: Preventing Burnout, or Collegial Whole School Approaches to Managing Classroom Behaviour. In it, Dr Rogers provides a solid backdrop of highly appropriate international research and theory into anxiety and stress from which educators can learn to recognise the triggers for their negative emotions, thoughts and behaviours. Next, he explains, through detailed real-life school examples, how these symptoms can be alleviated by gaining personal awareness of the nature of stress and anxiety, and by being supported in and out of the classroom by respectful, collegial coaching/mentoring, preferably occurring together. Throughout this rich resource book, Dr Rogers draws on his professional lifetime of face-to-face teaching and coaching/mentoring behavioural leadership in highly challenging classrooms in two continents (UK and Australia). In doing so, he provides page after page of tested, successful, and highly practical strategies for teachers at all levels of experience to use to manage the multiple sources of anxiety and stress that are inherent in their profession. With compassion, respect and humour, he shows how these strategies can work in the context of educational settings such as those with difficult students, angry parents and unsupportive fellow teachers and executives. Most importantly, he acknowledges and provides solid guidance for managing the stress of the seemingly endless rigours of preparing well-organised teaching materials in order to lead, by example, frequently unmotivated students through the stages of effective learning to deep understanding.

Valentina McInerney, Associate Professor of Educational Psychology,
School of Psychology, University of Western Sydney, Australia

This is a thoroughly well informed and engaging analysis of teacher stress that will be of immense practical help to those seeking to understand and deal with their own stress or support colleagues to do so. Bill Rogers' focus on the role of mentoring and colleague support within schools makes a significant contribution to the development of effective approaches for dealing with stress in the teaching profession. This is a book I can whole heartedly recommend.

Chris Kyriacou, Professor of Educational Psychology,
University of York, UK

This book is a treasure trove of practical advice, based on sound psychological principles, on minimising classroom stress. The text is brought alive by the writer's engaging style and examples drawn from his extensive experience of working with some very challenging youngsters – and helping their teachers.

It is far more than a book on stress reduction. Develop your teaching, and your relationship-building and behaviour management skills and your life as a teacher will become easier and more rewarding. Following this advice, Bill revisits the essential micro-skills possessed by the best teachers – in particular the appropriate use of the spoken word, of the meaningful silence, of the use of classroom layout, of 'tactical ignoring' and much else.

For the middle manager or school leader there are timely reminders of their responsibilities, particularly the need to promote a collegiate, mutually respectful and helpful school ethos.

Highly recommended – particularly for teachers and teaching assistants new to Bill Rogers' impressive work and for staff specialising in working with children and young people with social, emotional and behavioural difficulties.

Dr Ted Cole, SEBDA, UK

Bill Rogers is arguably the leading international authority of behaviour management in schools. In this revised and updated edition of *The Essential Guide to Managing Teacher Stress* he brings his vast knowledge and practical experience to bear on the much neglected social-emotional needs of teachers. All policy makers and school managers should use this book as a manual for helping them to fulfil their responsibilities for fostering socially and emotionally climates in their schools. Rogers shows how when this happens not only are teachers happier and more effective, but students benefit too. As with all of his writings, *The Essential Guide to Managing Teacher Stress* is firmly rooted in scholarship, full of practical suggestions and insights and written in a direct, warm and engaging style. This excellent book deserves a wide readership among teachers and teacher managers.

Professor Paul Cooper, PhD, CPsychol, School of Education,
University of Leicester, UK

Introduction

The thousand natural shocks that flesh is heir to ...

Hamlet (Act III: v.1: 56–91)

In Shakespeare's most famous soliloquy – in Hamlet – the young prince of Denmark is musing long and hard on what he has just learned. He is deeply troubled by the appearance of the ghost of his recently deceased father (the king). In those ghostly appearances his father reports, to his son (Hamlet), that his death was no accident[1]. That it was the king's brother who had dispatched him and who, now, has married Hamlet's mother. Hamlet is riven with grief, confusion and anger. What will he do? To be or not to be? – that is the question (III: 1).

These are the most famous lines in the soliloquy, perhaps in the Shakespearian canon. The question is more than a mere philosophic *c'est la vie*. 'To be or not to be that is the question.' But it isn't the only question. He continues to muse, 'whether 'tis nobler in the mind to suffer the slings and arrows of outrageous fortune or take arms against a sea of troubles ...', 'who would bear the whips and scorns of time ...', 'who would fardels (burdens) bear to grunt and sweat under a weary life ...'?

There are several flashes of insight in this long musing of Hamlet – particularly how we address and cope with the question of suffering *'in* the mind ...' and *'with* the mind'. Whether, and how, we 'take arms against a sea of troubles ...'. I'm particularly intrigued with the lines towards the end of the soliloquy: 'The *thousand natural shocks that flesh is heir to ...*' because this is the reality of our humanity – to be human (flesh) is to know, and experience, 'the thousand *natural* shocks ...' (also the 'slings and arrows of outrageous fortune ...'). He could almost be writing about teachers!

The first point I want to make about stress, any stress in life, but particularly here in this book on *teacher stress* is that much of the stress we experience is *natural*, normal to the nature of our profession. Stress is frustrating, irritating, annoying – but natural. We'll come back to these themes later.

I get by with a little help …

In 1985 I had the privilege of visiting Britain as a recipient of a travelling scholarship[2]. During that visit I met with the Elton Committee who published the Elton Report *Discipline in Schools* (1989). This seminal report addressed a wide range of concerns and issues relating to discipline in British schools. It is *still*, in my opinion, one of the most thorough and sensible reports addressing behaviour and discipline concerns in British schools. Many of its recommendations have become core features of policies, and programmes and plans in our schools. One of the key issues discussed (in the committee) concerned colleague support and how such support affects what we do as teachers – particularly with the stress occasioned by challenging students and classes. The evidence I gave to the committee related to the ideas, concepts and practices that were outlined in the book *Supporting Teachers in the Workplace* (published in Britain as *Managing Teacher Stress*). That work was further developed within 'the whole-school approach to behaviour' we were – then – developing in Australia (see Rogers, 2006).

Within the context of colleague support, the Elton Committee noted that there is a tradition of 'isolation' in schools where a colleague who is stressed and struggling with behaviour and discipline issues hesitates to ask for assistance, concerned they may be perceived as ineffective – or 'weak'. This is further entrenched by some senior colleagues' reluctance to approach a colleague who we know is struggling and stressed for fear we may impute they are ineffective, weak or even incompetent.

Thankfully, that 'climate' (noted in Elton, 1989) is changing – it has to change if we are going to develop safer and more positive learning communities that minimise the natural stress occasioned by the demanding nature of what schools are (by definition and social existence).

One of the more disturbing letters I received relates to how an unsupportive school ethos can affect an individual. It is quoted below, with my colleague's permission:

> It still makes me angry that if you are 'going under', the perception is there must be something wrong with you. Also, admitting you need support usually is seen by peers and some principals as admitting that you are in some way failing, rather than seeing the problem 'separate' from the teacher. I remember finally admitting to one principal that I was having trouble (with

some of my students) and he asked me how my marriage was – as if to say there was something wrong with me!

That particular school had such low morale, buoyed by insensitive comments (like that) that teachers operated virtually individually, in fear that if they opened up their reputations would be shot. For two years a general unhappiness escalated to severe stress reactions – my symptoms were so physical and alarming; insomnia, nausea, vomiting – but the unwritten, unspoken law meant that I spoke to nobody. Weekends and holidays were no longer a time when I could recoup or revitalise, or even turn off. My assessment stated had that I was a gifted and progressive teacher, but for three years I lived like a pressure cooker – the fear of failure sent me to a psychiatrist. He gave me medication that dulled all my feelings so I could cope with my everyday job. This psychiatrist had spent a lot of time working with Vietnam War veterans and now specialises in teacher stress because both syndromes are similar. The troops felt as if they had no control, being in a war zone, and didn't have faith in the generals.

It strikes me as comic, on reflection, how many times I have sat on committees and written up lovely ideals about student self-esteem, encouragement of students and effective conflict resolutions – often this was done in a staffroom where people were divided by fear or resignation. We were meant to develop these positive aims for students in an atmosphere of destructive staff morale.

Joy

I happen to know that this person was an effective and positive teacher but that the particular school she describes had a wearing and stressful effect on her and others there. When she finally moved to another school, that effective and positive attitude and approach eventually came back. Colleague support – particularly senior colleague support – made the difference (Chapter 9). It's not only the natural challenges of our profession that affect how stressed we feel but also the collegial culture (Chapter 11).

Where you work *does* have an effect on how you cope.

Exhaustion

One arises from lonely battles and unappreciated efforts, losing ground and growing a gnawing feeling of hopelessness that you cannot make a difference. The other type of exhaustion is the type that accompanies hard work as part of a team, a growing recognition that you are engaged in a struggle that is worth the effort and a recognition that what you are doing makes a critical difference for a recalcitrant child or a discouraged colleague. The former type of exhaustion ineluctably takes its toll on the motivation of the most enthusiastic teacher. The latter has its own inner reserve that allows us to bounce back after a good night's sleep. Indeed the first type of exhaustion causes anxiety and sleeplessness, while the second induces rest and regeneration of energy.

School cultures make a difference in what kind of tiredness we experience.

Fullan and Hargreaves, 1991 (page 107).

What stress can do to us

I've worked with colleagues whose physical symptoms (like Joy's) were real – recurrent headaches, anxiety attacks, even chest pains (page 21). In almost all those occasions my colleagues had reported that their doctors had noted that their general health was fine – it was stress that was the contributing factor to the real physical symptoms they were experiencing. More correctly it was *stressors* – the daily experience of facing very demanding situations and contexts every single day; very difficult classes and challenging students; work demands and deadlines; relationships at work (working with unsupportive, difficult or demanding colleagues).

It will help – always help – to get professional medical advice and counsel for any unusual or recurrent physical symptoms (such as those noted above). It may also help to seek out professional psychological support where the ongoing demands of work are significantly affecting one's ability to cope and manage on a daily basis (see page 28).

One of the ways in which the issue of stress is explored in this book is through personal and collegial responsiveness to stressful situations (the stress*ors*). Our coping abilities are naturally (at times severely) challenged (particularly if we cannot 'escape' the stressful situation). The primal 'fight or flight' is rarely a simple option (page 20). What colleague support can do is give us that moral and professional support essential to reorient and refocus possibilities of coping and management of those inherent stressors. This is the central tenet of the text. Nowhere is this more important than in the area of classroom management and discipline. Several chapters of this book are specifically devoted to the support we can (and need) to give one another in this area of our professional life.

Our individual response to stress

Not all individuals respond to the *same stressors* in the *same way*. It is this difference that has intrigued psychologists – particularly in the field of cognitive-behaviour psychology.

As well as variations in one's health, the effect of one's life experiences; varying environmental factors; personality factors (more 'driven', more competitive, more relaxed and sanguine) there is also *one's perception and characteristic beliefs about that which occasions their stress*. I don't know how I'd perceive – and cope – with years in prison, but there are cases where the mental and psychological perspective of the individual was able to moderate (even positively moderate) their stressful prison experience (take Boethius, John Bunyan and Nelson Mandela, for example).

The *way we perceive* stressful events not only varies – widely – but according to cognitive-behaviour psychologists also has a significant effect on *how* stressed we feel and how we cope and manage during and after stressful arousal. Our perceptions are not merely a personal and individual contribution to stressful reality, they too are affected by the kind of colleague support we receive and give in our teaching community. This is the second major theme of this text – we have to balance the social and relational aspects of living and work with our individual responses and responsibilities (to self and others). Chapter 4 is the seminal chapter addressing this crucial aspect of stress management.

What this book is essentially about

There are a number of theories about stress – they are not addressed in this text (apart from the seminal works of Hans Selye (1975, 1978) and the more recent work of those in the field of cognitive-behaviour therapy, particularly Martin Seligman (1991).

There are reams of statistics about stress in the workplace generally, and copious statistics about stress in the teaching profession. The fundamental 'causes' and 'contributions' to *teacher stress* haven't changed a great deal in the last 30 years – nor do they vary greatly across the Western world. While I've made some comments about recent statistics – and contributing causes to teacher stress – this is not a research document about those statistics.

What I'm really concerned about in this book is how we as teachers perceive and manage our *normative* day-to-day stress as well as the critical areas of stress in our profession – 'the thousand natural shocks ...' (page xvi).

While acknowledging that our personal lives, our perceptions and beliefs, and our health profile all impact on how we manage stress, this book addresses *the practical realities of our workplace stress* and how we can – collegially – address such stress.

I am concerned when I see (in popular magazines), even in in-service programmes for teachers, the common suggestion that if only we would 'meditate more', 'exercise right', 'eat right', 'take up a hobby' and 'have a good mental attitude' (we'll get to that later) then we'll cope. An underlying message in such themes is that dealing with our stress may *simply* be up to us, as individuals. While exercise, diet (etc.) are crucial to our individual well-being, there are inherent stressors in our schools *that have to be addressed at that level.* It is unfair and unreasonable to tell teachers to go on such courses to 'de-stress' themselves only to return to a workplace that may well have inherently stressful factors, quite apart from the imposed, mandated pressures from the Department of Education. The experience of stress and coping resources – in any one school culture – vary considerably and are in large part condi-tional not just on one's attitude (important as that is) but also on the nature, kind and degree of colleague support available at that school (Rogers, 2002).

My colleagues and I have consistently noted that the nature, quality and extent of practical and dependable colleague support has a significant effect on normative stress in our profession. Such support goes well beyond the necessary moral support to practical and structural solutions to issues of stressful concern in our profession.

The solutions we have developed are shared in this book.

Mentoring support

I have been engaged in colleague mentoring (and teacher mentor-coaching approaches) in schools in Australia and the United Kingdom for over 15 years now. This approach to mentoring is an *elective* model based in collegial trust (Chapter 10). The research, the approaches, practices and skills drawn from that mentoring approach are the substance of this book. The purpose of such mentoring is to offer colleagues the opportunity to genuinely team-teach in challenging classes. In this way the mentor-colleague can see, hear and feel (existentially as it were) what their colleague experiences and feels in that normative classroom context. Then later, over tea or coffee, we debrief, share our experiences and draw from that shared reflection an approach, a plan, to enable and support that colleague as they continue to lead their class and build workable relationships with their students. Such plans have a direct (and highly beneficial) bearing on one's management of stress (Rogers, 2002 and 2011).

My colleagues and I also use formal and informal teaming approaches to identify the common stressors in 'our local workplaces'. We focus on our personal management and discipline (within our individual teacher leadership) as well as the management 'structure' within our local school. We also engage in stress auditing to address the organisational and even physical environment (flickering lights, noisy science stools – get those solid rubber stoppers on – squeaky doors, lack of cupboard space) (page 186).

I have noticed a significant reduction in the management of occupational/ work-related stress in those schools that have consciously – and purposefully – developed a *whole-school approach* to areas commonly associated with stress in our profession – discipline and classroom management, students with diagnosed or symptomatic behaviour disorders, time and workload pressures (particularly those mandated from the Department of Education), curriculum planning and teaching practice. Differences – in schools with a whole-school approach – are noted as having more positive working relationships with their students, more consistent work practices expressed in whole-school policy and practice (page 112), better working conditions (physical and organisational), a more confident sense of professionalism *and* less stress-related illness (Rogers, 2002 and 2006). Such whole-school approaches need to be based on collaborative practice and maintained generationally within the local school culture.

I have included case examples and case studies (and some correspondence) drawn directly from colleagues I have worked with as a mentor-teacher. As ever my colleagues have helped me to understand stress in the workplace and have convinced me that a conscious commitment to colleague support is the way ahead. I want to thank them for their understanding, commitment and support.

Lastly this is not a book about blame – or even *who* to blame (that's self-defeating). It is designed to address and positively confront the normality of stress in our profession.

Notes

1. 'Murder most foul ...' (I : 5: 27)

2. My original research interest in teacher stress began with a scholarship to the UK (from Australia) in 1988. As an English ex-patriot I soon noticed that the causes/effects of teacher stress in Australia are fundamentally the same as what you will read in reports from Australia, the UK, America or Europe. During my time in the UK (then) I also gave evidence to the Elton Committee on *Discipline in Schools* (in Westminster). That research scholarship became the genesis for my PhD research at Melbourne University (in the mid-1990s) on *Colleague Support,* addressing the link between the kind – and nature – of colleague support in schools, and how such support is able to mitigate stress, enable coping and build confident, professional, educational communities. A programme for schools was developed out of this long-term research project. (See Rogers, 2002).

The dimensions of teacher stress

What this chapter will explore and develop:

- The all too familiar dimensions of stress and its frustrating 'normality'
- What we can and can't directly control in the parameters, and dimensions, of stress
- The need to move beyond an isolationist mentality about coping with stress. How to develop a meaningful collegial response to what we all face regarding the dimensions of stress

The dimensions of stress

The statistics

You probably don't need me to detail the current statistics on teacher stress and burnout. Teacher stress is the most cited factor in work care and illness claims.[1]

For many teachers, stress is the *natural* physical and psychological wear and tear of daily teaching. Twenty-five to thirty children (or adolescents) in a small room, sometimes with inadequate and uncomfortable furniture, and a lack of air-conditioning. I've taught in portable classrooms, with poor ventilation, facing west on 40°C days in Australia! And poor or inadequate heating in the colder weather. I've also taught in sweltering classrooms *in winter* in the UK!

I'm not trying to be negative – I'm citing the 'normality' of it all (page xii). It is under these conditions – in many schools – that we have to teach, lead, guide, encourage and support a positive teaching and learning climate. We do this five or six periods a day, five days a week, three (or four) terms a year. *We're entitled to say it's a challenge, no matter how optimistic a view we take of our profession.*

> *I read this on a school notice board:*
>
> *If a doctor or lawyer had 30 people in his/her office at one time, all of whom had different needs, and some of whom didn't want to be there and were causing trouble, and the doctor or lawyer, without assistance, had to treat them all with professional excellence for 42 weeks every year, then they might have some concept of the classroom teacher's job.*

Contributing factors

The contributing causes to teacher stress are well established in the literature:

- *The daily role demands* of curriculum, lesson-planning and homework, following-up with students – as well as teaching itself five or six periods a day, day after day after ...

- *Discipline concerns* – this issue is always in the top two or three concerns in every report I've ever read. While discipline is essential to effective teacher leadership in our schools, it is *frequent* distracting and disruptive behaviour, and argumentative and challenging students that increase the stress that such discipline necessitates (page 45).

- *Inclusion* policy – for 30 years in Australia and the UK (and most Western democratic countries) schools have been required to have inclusive policies – equal opportunity – for students with learning disabilities, socio-emotional behaviour disorders and diagnosed disorders such as ASD and ADSD (autism spectrum disorders and attention deficit spectrum disorders).[2] It is right, proper and just that we have such a policy – what creates stress is the inadequate resources of teacher/integration aides and specialist support.

- The natural demands of mixed ability teaching and differentiation – particularly with students with challenging and severe behaviours, and students diagnosed with behaviour disorders. As with inclusive policy, teachers frequently cite challenging students in any stress review. We need only one challenging student in a class – let alone several – to make teaching stressful.

The issue of challenging behaviour and behaviour disorders is addressed in Chapter 8 and hard-to-manage classes in Chapter 9.

- The demands of formal accountability (such as OFSTED) and the increasing demands from external mandates from the Department of Education. I've also spoken with many colleagues in challenging schools in England who rightly wonder if some OFSTED inspectors really know what the challenges of teaching in some schools is *really* like. It's one thing to watch it all from the back of a classroom (from the safety of 'Inspectorate') but it's quite another to be able to 'do it' – day in, day out!

- The demands for high retention rates for students at post-primary level. In years past we had technical schools – a provision for students who did not easily work with, or respond to, an 'academic curriculum'. This helped ease the demands of formal schooling and overfocusing on academic provision for *every* student. Fortunately (in Australia at least) there is a return to alternative formal schooling pathways at post-primary education in Year 9 upwards. This reduces the stress many students experience from an overly skewed academic, and testing, approach to daily schooling.

What we can and can't 'control'

One of the factors in our understanding and managing of stress in school contexts is that of perception of 'control' in what we are called to do and be. Beyond the formal requirements of the national curriculum (and national testing regimes), beyond the physical environment of our local school and beyond the recurrent mandates of the Department of Education, our primary professional calling is the welfare and well-being of our students within the formal expectations of schooling.

A school is more than a mere 'learning factory' – it is a local learning community where parents entrust their children to staff care, protection, support and leadership, guidance and counsel – *as well as their formal learning.*

In this leadership role there are natural stresses that will – at times – tax our goodwill and resources to the limit as we seek to meet the disparate needs of our students.

It is important to remember that there are many factors about *some* of our students' lives we cannot control – substance abuse, inadequate diet, long-term unemployment, generational poverty, inappropriate TV and internet, sexist, racist and homophobic attitudes within family conditioning, parental expectations and attitudes to schooling and family dysfunction. While we cannot control these factors, we can significantly affect, and support, such students in our schools (Rogers, 2009). Since the early work of Professor Michael Rutter et al. (1979) the research clearly shows that supportive schools can, and do, enable and support at-risk students. And where there is a whole-school approach to behaviour management generally – and the development of dedicated case supervision with at-risk students specifically – that natural stress of working with challenging students is significantly reduced. This, in turn, reduces the stress for colleagues who work with at-risk students (Rogers, 2002).

Public perception of teachers

I find frustrating – and naively pathetic – the view that somehow teaching is an 'easy profession', a second choice if you can't make it 'somewhere else'. As George Bernard Shaw's annoying throw-away line puts it, 'He who can does. He who cannot teaches.'[3]

I've challenged similar facile comments from non-teaching colleagues (over the years). I've invited them to teach one day – *just one day* – with me in a school. There's often a hasty retreat – no one has yet taken up the offer.

Galton and McBeath (2008) noted in a primary study they conducted that teachers didn't own up to being a teacher when asked at a social gathering what they did for a living. This was because admitting to being a teacher usually drew a response such as, 'Oh! Aren't you the lucky one with a nine-to-three job and all those lovely long holidays' (page 13). I've heard this drivel countless times in my teaching career. It has been my experience, however, that when you speak directly to the parents of primary-aged children they do normally value the teachers' contributions to their children's lives. Many also recognise the demanding nature of teaching, leading, guiding and supporting so many students for a third of their waking day. Imagine for a moment closing all schools – unilaterally. There would be a national riot of parents!

The pace of policy change

Galton and McBeath (2008) also noted that a rise in stress correlates with the 'speed with which policy changes have been introduced' – what I have also heard called 'reformation fatigue'. National and regional changes in a wide range of areas happen without due consultation, reasonable implementation time and – particularly – time for professional development. Decentralisation and the competitive nature of the market economy also bring a need to work harder in addressing the many demands increasingly made on schools beyond the so-called 'core curriculum'.

They further note that 'principals/head teachers have more responsibilities than power, carry on their own shoulders responsibility for the success or failure of their schools and deliver success in the currency of test scores within a prescribed period [sic] and in a turbulent socio-economic context, where few things stand still enough to be measured' (Thompson et al., 2003, pages 8, 9).

Harder than they think

Some years ago, on British TV, I watched a documentary (a 'reality' TV show) detailing an exchange between a senior teacher working in what I perceived as a 'leafy' – and very pleasant – outer London suburb and a senior teacher in a rather gloomy high-rise suburb in London that (at first sight) looked like the *Lubyanka*.

When the TV cameras 'observed' the senior teacher in her own 'middle-class' school she looked confident, cheerful and – often – relaxed. She was clearly well-liked, and respected by her students.

When she arrived in the challenging London school she was met – quickly – by raucous, fractious, highly attentional students in her classes. Within a very short time (on day one) she began to shout, even threaten students in ways that (she admitted later) were uncharacteristic to her normal teaching style . As I watched this harrowing reality TV programme I really felt for that teacher as she tried familiar and tested teaching and discipline practices on students who rewarded her with laughter, even derision at times, and – often – argumentative and challenging outbursts. She just managed to cope that week, and all in front of TV cameras! Thankfully the teachers at the challenging school gave her moral support and (when asked for) supportive advice. I was – yet again – encouraged by the willingness of colleagues to non-judgementally 'step into the breach'.

She breathed a sigh of relief when she returned to her 'own' school and was very honest on camera that she would have found it very, very difficult to continue working at *that* London school. Of course the producers (dare we say) contrived the context and characters – a teacher in a prestigious girls' school now ensconced in this unfamiliar 'bleak house' as a newcomer (however experienced that teacher is in their own setting) is 'exciting' TV! That week – in that challenging London school – showed that experience, alone, is not enough.

There was a similar 'reality' TV show (in Britain) where a well-known British journalist and 'soap star' chose to teach in primary schools for a week. A week – easy? It wasn't long before the journalist and the soap actor's perception about teachers clashed vigourously and stressfully with the reality of day-to-day teaching (at least for a week!) There were frequent loud voices, and shouting, from these new 'teachers' as they tried to control children and the learning process. Of course it wasn't fair, of course they would probably come undone. It was – after all – 'reality' TV. But something could be learned by any viewer with a half attendant eye. Good teachers don't merely 'control' and 'tell' students what to do and how to behave. They lead – they guide and they motivate, engage, enthuse and encourage children to own – and be responsible for – their own behaviour *as they relate to others*. No mean feat – it takes certain predispositions and skills to do that well day after day after day after …

Areas of potential risk in work-related stress

The Health and Safety Executive identify six key areas (as 'risk' factors) that can be causes of work related stress:

- the *demands* of your job (and its *unique* local setting as well as its *general* demands)
- the *control* over your work (in that *local* setting)
- the *support* you receive from managers and colleagues
- your *relationships* at work
- your *role in the organisation*
- *change* and how it's managed (both at the individual and at the collegial level).[4]

When addressing these areas, collegial consultation is – to my mind – the anchor variable. That consultation needs to occur across all members of the teaching fraternity in a school (including teaching assistants and long-term cover supply colleagues).

As the Health and Safety Executive note, there is a difference between stress and pressure. They define stress as 'the adverse reaction of person to excessive pressure or other types of demand placed upon them'.

In their booklet, Working Together to Reduce the Stress at Work, they make the essential point (made over and over in this book) that work-related stress can be realistically tackled by working with one's employer to identify issues at the source, and agreeing on realistic and workable ways to tackle them. They note that this is 'a right' (ibid.).

While we have the right to a safe workplace, there are natural demands and tensions in the teaching profession. Our right to have our say – particularly when it affects others' behaviour and their decisions – will create natural tension. Senior colleagues need to be willing, and able, to work with those natural tensions to realise those rights and the responsibilities that follow from the rights. A right to something (say, a safe workplace) also implies a responsibility on the part of the 'line managers' and the employee – the individual.

An isolationist culture – history? design? culture?

What do you remember about colleague support in your teaching journey? It is said that our profession has a propensity for professional isolation. We teach with minors (25–30) in a small room (for what is asked of it) hour after hour, day after day. The bell goes and we then rush off to do other duties – and there are the inevitable meetings. We don't always get a chance to spend active, purposeful time with colleagues.

We can probably remember staffrooms where we rushed in to recharge with tea or coffee, whinged, off-loaded, then rushed off to yet another class. What in my day (1970s) we jokingly (?) called 'cells' and 'bells'.

Fullan and Hargreaves (1991) have observed that teaching is a 'lonely profession – the problem of isolation is a deep-seated one. Architecture often supports it. The timetable reinforces it. Overload sustains it. History legitimises it' (page 6). One of my colleagues has noted that 'education is among the last vocations where it is still legitimate to work by yourself in a space that is secure against invaders' (Ruddock, 1991 page 31). Ruddock's use of the word 'invader' highlights how some teachers feel in schools without a strong collegial culture (Rogers, 2002). That physical locus, that psychological-relational locus, that small room where we work with 25–30 students day in and day out. And is my colleague across the corridor a better, more effective teacher than me? Do they know what it's *really* like for me?

> ... *loneliness and isolation are high prices to pay but teachers willingly pay them when the alternatives are seen as exposure and censure ... by following the privacy rule [sic] teachers forfeit the opportunity to display their successes but they also gain the security of not having to face their failures publicly and losing face ...*
>
> Leiberman and Miller (in Miller, 1996, pages 94, 95).

Admittedly that was in the 90s – the collegial climate in schools is now changing, particularly in primary schools. However, it is not uncommon in secondary schools to still find this 'architectural premise' to *professional* isolation. When I first read the quote above, I recalled many schools that aptly fitted that description. Some still do.

'Open classrooms' are not the answer either. I've taught in schools where four classes worked in a larger, open space – the noise (from some groups) made it extremely difficult to teach. Within six months, even the 'progressive' teachers were asking for partitions and even doors to be put up between the four class groupings. The issue is not architecture *per se*, it is *professional isolation* – this occurs where teachers are effectively 'left alone' to cope as best they can, and if they're struggling (and we almost always 'know' when a colleague is struggling) we don't intervene because of 'some ludicrous code' (as one teacher remarked) that says it's 'their room – their class.' It's stupid [sic] especially when we know they need help ...' (cited in Rogers, 2002, page 15).

The anomaly is that the very people – our colleagues – who know *our* challenges in *our* school, who know *our* students are surely the very people who can help us.

What may hinder us, though, are the attitudes – still prevalent in our profession – that if we ask for assistance we may be perceived as 'not coping', 'ineffective', 'weak' – perhaps a failure. If a senior teacher does offer support (however) some teachers may feel that this offer is suggesting that their colleague cannot cope and is – by implication – a failure (or, worse, incompetent). I have had that 'feeling' (as a senior teacher). I hope I would never impute that to a colleague. But that overconcern about imputation of 'failure' can stifle the offer of necessary support, or even the request for support. I believe we need to *build* a supportive colleague culture that allows a confident sharing of concerns; that encourages colleagues to seek support; that allows honest professional discourse. It rarely happens naturally. It depends – in significant part – on the kind of leadership team within a given school. This is a challenge within the range of personalities in any one school. It is possible when there is a commitment to:

- Moral and professional empathy that arises from a common source of mission, purpose and – yes – *shared struggle* at times.
- *Building the opportunities and occasions* for appropriate, normative, professional disclosure in our shared practice, and particularly in circumstances and situations that occasion stress (Chapter 11). For example, the hard class-issues addressed in Chapter 9.
- Non-confrontational problem-solving in *useful* teams and even *ad hoc* teaming and peer support groups designed to focus on direct solution-oriented outcomes.
- Building approaches, 'forms', practices even policies that factor in – by their very nature – the opportunity for colleague support. Obviously a school cannot order colleagues to support one another. A school can, however, build processes that enable the likelihood that the moral and professional needs of staff are met (pages 12–16).
- Behaviour management and discipline and a management policy and practice that enables us to cope with our most challenging and at-risk students (Chapter 8).

This kind of collegial climate has to be *factored into our team planning, it has to be developed within a school culture*. Where it does – and where it has – teachers consistently report less stress, higher motivation, more professional assurance and more confident professional development (Rogers, 2002, 2006).

Bullying of teachers by students (beyond the silly, the attentional and the 'bad day')

This is a difficult and unpleasant topic to write about. Raising this issue in print, however, is necessary. Bullying of any kind at any age is a harrowing experience. I saw bullying as a student, I saw it in the army (as a National Service conscript in the late 1960s). I saw appalling and disgusting bullying. Our NCOs and commissioned officers turned a blind eye – the common view being that it was 'character building'.

I saw bullying as a teenager working on building sites in Queensland ('initiation ceremonies') – I always fought back with words and (at times) with fists. It stopped. I saw others, however, 'go under' – disillusionised, demoralised, betrayed by those responsible for their welfare.

I have also seen the bullying of teachers by students and even (on occasions) by other teachers. The kind of bullying I'm talking about here is not the off-word, the snide comment, the excuse of humour by some teachers – it is the intentional, calculated, repeated psychological harassment that cannot be tolerated or excused (page 155).

A survey by NASUNT addressing working conditions of teachers shows that student behaviour is the major cause of excessive workload and stress. In 2006 NASUNT's Advancing Health and Safety Report (a survey of 5000 teachers) indicated that over 60% had experienced harassment by students.

Their definition of harassment is 'any situation where a person is abused, threatened or assaulted in circumstances relating to their work.'

(See A Guide to Risk Assessment of Violent and Abusive Behaviour).

The issue of bullying of teachers is addressed at length later, in Chapter 9.

Case study

Patrick is in his late twenties, he's just started as a newly qualified high school teacher of humanities. He's been told that his Year 9 class is 'challenging' – he's already also heard some 'horror stories' on the grapevine.

He'd done reasonably well on his teaching practice (but it wasn't in a school like this . . .). It's his first period with Year 9C. He's got a lot of goodwill and is keen to make a good impression.

The class file into the classroom noisily – they are quite restless and take some time to settle in and settle down. Several students ask him his name as they enter the classroom. He starts conversing with them – at the classroom door. They 'bunch up', several students start to loudly complain, some are jostling, a few are pushing their way in. 'Get out of the way idiot!!' Eventually he raises his voice to get some quiet, some settling and focus. He raises his voice loudly – he's almost shouting now. 'C'MON GUYS! LISTENING UP *PLEASE*. CAN YOU PLEASE SETTLE DOWN? COME ON EVERYONE, WILL YOU PLEASE JUST GET A SEAT!?' He's smiling – trying to look positive, though he's visibly quite nervous. Several students (mostly girls) are calling out, 'What's your name sir?' He responds by saying, 'It's Patrick, but can you *please* put your hand up?'

The girls continue to call out – some with their hand up. One of the boys calls out loudly, 'Hey sir – just tell them to shut up!' Patrick responds with, 'Come on – PLEASE – language!' The boy leans back in his seat and sighs loudly, '*What*? What did I do? – What?!'

Patrick is not sure what to do now. He soldiers on, 'Look guys – please be quiet for a moment alright? I want us to have a good time together this year but I do need you to be quiet – OK?'

One of the girls (Carly) calls out (with her hand up) and asks, 'Hey Patrick – you got a girlfriend?' One of the boys says to the girl, 'Give it a rest!' She turns and says, 'Shut up – I'm interested – alright?!'

As Patrick anxiously scans the faces of his new class he feels it all slipping away from him – and it is.

Carly calls out – yet again, 'Heeey – Patrick; you got a girlfriend?' Patrick wasn't expecting *this*. He tries to keep it 'light hearted' – but he's nervous and doesn't quite know what to say. 'Yes I have …', before he can finish Carly adds, 'What's she like – is she hot?' Carly turns to see what response her comments are having on the others in her class. Patrick is now both embarrassed and annoyed as well as anxious. He does his best to keep a sense of focus. 'Look I don't really want to talk about this OK? We need to get to work …' Carly adds, as she turns – grinning – to her coterie of girlfriends, 'What you saying, you don't *love* her?' Patrick is now flustered and getting increasingly agitated. 'WILL YOU JUST STOP WITH ALL THIS – *PLEASE*!?' Carly leans back in her seat, folds her arms and says loudly with a calculatedly sulky demeanour, 'You can't say anything here …'

The lesson doesn't get much better. It is punctuated frequently by calling out, talking while Patrick is trying to explain the course of work for the next few weeks, students fiddling with things on their desks … He raises his voice – loudly – many times. He can't wait for the bell for lesson closure. When it comes most of the students race for the door.

What is disconcerting about the stressful genesis of Patrick and 9C is that he believed (at least initially) that this stressful episode was largely his fault – 'I *should* have been able to manage them …!' 'I *shouldn't* have got into all those arguments; I certainly shouldn't have responded as I did to Carly …!'

He starts to worry about what it will be like next lesson with 9C. That worry creates more stress …

Patrick could have been better prepared, and supported *right at the outset* at this school, by:

- Talking through the establishment phase, with a senior colleague and with other beginning colleagues (page 91) and planning for the critical first meeting with a new class (see Chapter 7), particularly a class like 9C.

  The establishment phase, with a new class, is naturally testing. In challenging schools, there is no 'honeymoon period' in leading and managing a new class group. It is important to plan ahead for typical testing behaviours, particularly the probing questions –'What's your private life like …?'. Those annoying personal questions that some students ask, which, in Carly's case, are all about attentional posturing. These skills are addressed at some length in Chapter 7).

- Developing language cues that enable us to be appropriately assertive (pages 81, 79, 104).

- Some early mentoring – even 'in class' mentoring (Chapter 10).

When Patrick and I did eventually discuss these issues (after our first mentoring session in his classroom) we explored the sorts of things one can say when students wave an 'attentional flag'. For example, once we have cued the class about 'hands up *without* calling out' and addressed the incidental chatting (page 95) if we then get the annoying personal questions we can say something like: 'No doubt some of you are interested (the 'girlfriend' or other personal questions asked …). (Wait for the residual laughter to drop.) I'm not answering personal questions now. Let's get back to our lesson.' If any student persists it's enough to repeat the above once – adding, perhaps, 'It's not appropriate now. We're focusing on the work we'll be doing this term.'

Of course our tone and manner need to convey our confidence as a teacher leader and, where necessary, display appropriate assertion (pages 79, 81, 104). Confidence (not cockiness) comes from preparedness *and* skill. The practices and skills of classroom leadership and management are rarely inherent naturally – they have to be learned. Goodwill alone, bonhomie or simply leaving it to the moment are self-defeating behaviours in a teacher (particularly with a class like 9C). You need to be able to convey that you, at least as teacher-leader, *know what you are doing* and what you want the class to be doing.

It would have also helped if Patrick had also followed up with the key 'ringleaders' – particularly Carly. Such follow-up (with a female student) will also need the direct support of a senior female colleague. Speaking to Carly – directly (away from her peer audience) – would have helped her be aware of the total inappropriateness of her behaviour (page 158).

In Patrick's case he had tried to be 'a friend' of his class, a kind of 'big buddy'. He wanted their 'approval'. As it was, Carly continued to tease, taunt and bait Patrick. She got others in the class to laugh along. It became a pattern of bullying. That's when I got involved. We set up an accountability conference to address the bullying behaviours (page 158). The result of that was an apology from Carly and an assurance that this behaviour would stop – and it did.

> Bullying – in the sense illustrated in this case study – is not some ill-thought or silly comment. It is not the distracting and disruptive calling out and chatting.
>
> Bullying is the calculated, intentional, selective and repetitive behaviour of others – designed to intimidate, hurt or control. Most bullying in the workplace is psychological – taunts, 'winding other students up', 'egging them on' to ignore their teacher, name calling, non-verbal suggestive cueing and posturing. (Rogers, 2011a)

Colleague support and teacher stress (locus of control)

In researching the topic of colleague support and teacher stress I have had countless 'structured conversations' with colleagues across a very wide range of schools. A common theme I've noticed is the perception of 'locus of control' regarding our stress – how much, and to what degree, a colleague believes they have some meaningful control over the events, circumstances and relationships that occasion stress in their school. This was as true for groups as it was for individuals.

They tended – *often* – to use language descriptors such as 'winning and losing', 'fighting on too many fronts' and 'we're losing control'. Colleagues in such schools would often list – quickly – the behaviour and discipline issues, the lack of support, too much to do in a day, too much to follow up and tracking of difficult students, as well as the mandated demands from the Department of Education. I also noticed in such schools the formation of 'cliques' as teachers tried to garner some sense of protective support, even if it involved just one or two colleagues.

Case study

As one senior colleague in a very challenging school put it, 'here the culture changes you!' I noted (on my first visit) a common interpretive style when we discussed behaviour issues – 'We'll *never* change this place …', 'The kids here are *always* stuffing around, they never listen …', '*No one* cares …'. When people are very stressed it is not uncommon for them to 'globalise' their perceptions in their *characteristic language* – that language, then, affects mood, behaviour and motivation for change. They often resort to blaming –

'it's (mostly) others' fault' (even other colleagues – hence the cliques). Some teachers begin to blame themselves (like Patrick). This is also, itself, self-defeating (and stressful) as are the stressful conditions that give rise to those perceptions (page 49).

Twelve months later when I revisited the school, I sensed and heard a much more positive tone in staff discussion and a genuine belief in purposeful change. A new head teacher had been appointed and several, new, senior staff. Peer groups had developed for open and frank discussion – among colleagues – about common concerns, including the mandated 'demands' from the Department of Education. Now, though, the talk was, 'We can change the culture here; indeed we have to ...' I noticed – as we talked together twelve months later – how colleagues also felt more supported, more willing to seriously consider new possibilities and to 'try again', and, above all, to start to look at a whole-school approach to issues of common stressful concern. The tenor of collegial conversation had moved from sensing, even believing, that 'all these things' were outside their control, and were the fault of others. They no longer saw their school culture as influenced only by outside events, by these terrible students, 'powerful others' – even 'fatalistic normality' (let alone 'luck'). There was clearly a collegial belief that we, here in our school, can make a difference to how we see, interpret, manage and support one another to enable us to manage our stressful reality. A critical factor was the kind of leadership now present in the school. They listened, they took colleagues' concerns seriously, but they didn't rush into immediate, precipitous and reactive change. The process of being aware of factors that worked against a supportive culture took some time and trust.

The other crucial factor was *the perceptual shift* that enabled *the behavioural shift* of individuals and groups across the staff team. They had realised that they could effect change in perception, beliefs, attitude and collegial behaviour – and that had clearly begun to make a difference in their day-to-day teaching and behaviour leadership. None of this happened accidentally, mind you – the new leadership had tuned into and acknowledged the 'collegial malaise' and started to challenge its assumptions about where the 'locus of control' really was. The questionnaire noted in Appendix 1 was one of several entry points into the change process in the school along with a collegially supportive mentoring model (see Chapter 10).

A *colleague* response to what we all face regarding the dimensions of stress

When my colleagues and I began to sit and discuss these issues in a climate of common concern – addressing the *shared realities* – we began, at first, to realise that while many of these factors were outside our control there was a lot we could do (and had to do) if we were going to have an impact on what we were there for – in *that* school as teachers.

- We accepted, and began to appreciate, that this *was* our reality. It was a stressful reality – like it or not, though, it was *our reality*. There were many students from very difficult home backgrounds, as well as students diagnosed with behaviour disorders. We realised that, so far, we had all tried to do our best as individuals. Was there something – anything – we could do collegially?. I recall several teachers complaining bitterly about 'these kids and their bastard parents!' and that 'they all seem to drift to *this* school!!' 'Why can't other schools take a fair share!' I was not unsympathetic to this *crie de coeur*.

  A colleague asked – wryly – if the department would change its policy in this area! (Chorus 'In your dreams!'); would these difficult, and lazy, parents change overnight? (chorus – ditto!); and the mandates – the recurring mandates from the Department of Education – would they slow down? (A few swear words – translated as highly unlikely!)

  We began to realise – after these first meetings – that any meaningful change would have to originate from us – *we* would need to begin to find ways to do something *here* in this place *and that each department would need to have* a common commitment to the way we're seeking to manage, *and lead*, our students based on shared identification of the common needs, concerns and issues we all faced here (Chapter 11). Some of these commitments were *deceptively basic* – involving class routines such as considerate entry to and settling in classrooms; how to initiate and sustain a positive and calm beginning to lessons; workable seating (see Chapter 7). What really helped was that we started to genuinely talk about our practice – what we were *actually doing* (as teacher leaders) and where we believed we need to change – *and why*.

  It *sounded* simple enough but it took 12 months to get a genuine sense of cohesion around common aims, practices and plans (pages 108, 113 and Appendix 1).

- We accepted that there were many external demands – including recurrent mandates from the Department of Education. While we couldn't stop these mandates coming, we could make sure that we minimised their stressful imposition by 'working those mandates' at the local level, making sure we did what was necessary but not letting those *external* demands overwhelm us. Mostly it meant fine-tuning what was – already – 'reasonable practice' considering the pressure we were under.

- We were especially conscious that *reasonable*, and *fair*, consistency was possible in discipline practice (page 113).

- We also realised that our stress – as individuals and as colleagues – could be moderated by a sense of *shared collegial reality* so we didn't feel overwhelmed. We realised that it was important that we refocus the place of teaming – both the formal faculty teams and the development of peer support groups.

These peer support groups enabled us to gain – afresh – a common perspective about shared concerns. 'We're in the same boat – a bit leaky, a bit rusty perhaps in spots – but at least we're in it together and we'll be going in the same direction' – was a metaphor given by one of our experienced, and very caring, senior colleagues.

These peer support groups enabled us (beyond formal teaming necessities) to gain new insights about our leadership of our students and decrease that sense of professional and social isolation in a busy and demanding place like a school. We did have serious and pressing classroom needs and while we admitted that some colleagues were clearly more adept – more able – at connecting with difficult classes, they too admitted it was a challenging school and that they still found it stressful at times. This common admission was the early prime mover for a mentoring approach that became a feature of ongoing professional development (Chapter 10). Those more able colleagues were willing to utilise their knowledge and skill within a supportive mentoring approach to enable colleagues to address the more challenging students and classes more effectively.

There were setbacks, grumbles and plenty of 'bad-days'. At times it was three steps forward and one step back, but staff agreed that this sense of common purpose based around common needs was making a genuine difference to levels of stress and also to practical outcomes, notably in the area of difficult class groups (page 137). It was from these groups that many colleagues gained a renewed sense of confidence and the willingness to take some risks and try something different. Again, this strengthened our perceptual shift about 'locus of control'. Most of all, we gained a fresh sense of 'professional security' that other colleagues would, and did, back them up as we sought to develop our whole-school approach (Rogers, 2002).

We've chosen a naturally stressful profession

While I have referred to the current research on teacher stress – including that on colleague support and whole-school approaches to policy and practice – I have done so with a predominant emphasis on listening to (the) teacher voice. In terms of any grounded theory about teacher stress, I believe that in terms of 'explanatory power' a theory must resonate with its crucial voice *in context* – the teacher voice. Yes I've listened to academics and researchers but almost all my own work in this area is grounded in a wide teacher voice, working with my colleagues *in their daily place of work* – hearing and trying to understand, interpret and make workable sense of their voice. My colleagues noted that positive collegial environments:

- *lessen* the feeling of isolation and 'it's just me', or 'only me'. This, also, minimises the self-blame that can easily occur in a demanding profession like ours.

- *enable* the feeling that we're 'all-in-the-same-boat', and because of that we can and need to share concerns, problems *and* shared perspectives. Based on a non-judgemental sharing, we can often do something about these concerns and problems.

- *provide* the backup we need in challenging situations with challenging classes and students.

- *nurture* positive professional links between colleagues.

Most of all my colleagues realised that any meaningful change has to be developed within a whole-school approach.

Later (in Chapters 8–12) I will address the kinds of supportive colleague 'forms' and 'structures' that enable such support.

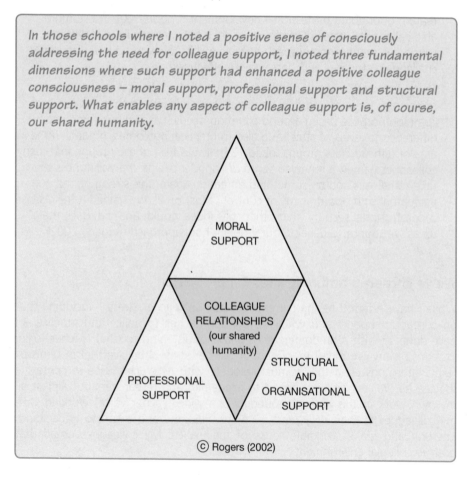

In those schools where I noted a positive sense of consciously addressing the need for colleague support, I noted three fundamental dimensions where such support had enhanced a positive colleague consciousness – moral support, professional support and structural support. What enables any aspect of colleague support is, of course, our shared humanity.

MORAL
SUPPORT

COLLEAGUE
RELATIONSHIPS
(our shared
humanity)

PROFESSIONAL
SUPPORT

STRUCTURAL
AND
ORGANISATIONAL
SUPPORT

© Rogers (2002)

The eminent psychiatrist, Oliver Sacks (1990), has noted that 'the private sphere of individual actions and feelings is everywhere co-mingled with the public sphere, with the human and non-human environment. *We cannot really separate individual endeavours from social endeavours*' (page 268; italics mine).

Martin Seligman (1991), the research psychologist who coined the terms 'learned helplessness' and 'learned optimism', makes the crucial point that 'One necessary condition for meaning is the attachment to something larger than you are ... 'The self, to put it another way, is a very poor site for meaning.' (page 287)[5]

Aristotle – in the *Nicomachean Ethics* (Thompson, trans., 1969) – notes several times that we are *social* beings – this is one essential feature of what it means to be *human*. Aristotle goes on to speak about a conception of concord as 'shared ground', 'where (people) are in harmony with both themselves and with one another, having pretty much the same ground to stand upon' (page 271 in Thompson's translation, 1969). The concept of 'collegially shared ground' is explored later (in Chapter 4).

Meaningful coping, even positive coping, depends on *how* we support each other in ways that affirm our individual sense of dignity as well as our personal and professional dignity.

Notes

1. The Health and Safety Executive INDG 424 11/08 (4 of 4 pages) www.hsebooks.co.uk. Doctors do not always record stress as the cause of (an) illness even though it may be the root cause.

2. This book does not address the management of students with these diagnosed disorders. I commend to you the excellent text of Peter Clough (et al.) *Handbook of Emotional and Behavioural Difficulties* (2005) London: Sage Publications.

3. The Sprinthalls (1974) say of George Bernard Shaw's quote, 'We should revise this quote to, Those who can do, teach!' (p. 13).

4. www.atl.org.uk.publicationsandresources/report 17/06/2010.

5. Seligman's work is addressed later in Chapter 4.

The physiology of stress: what it does to us

What this chapter will explore and develop:

- The physiology of stress: the physical symptoms of wearing stress
- The autonomic nervous system (how it works under stress)
- Eustress and toxic stress – the paradox
- Self and others – how we perceive and rate our own stress
- Self-concept and self-esteem
- The relationship between stress at work and stress at home
- Our health and stress

Stress: the physiology of stress; the wear and tear

The physiology of stress – how we feel under stress – takes a variety of expressions. We've all experienced the psychological, physiological and even physical 'wear and tear' of teaching. Our body adapts to stressful demands in remarkable ways. We have a physiology that is highly adaptable under normal stress and – occasional – extreme stress. The body produces chemicals to alert and affect body systems so that we can meet and address stressful demands. McEwan and Boyce (2010) call this 'allostasis':[1] 'there is this whole network of what we call allostasis, which is the active process by which the body adapts to a challenge – a stressful situation.'

The autonomic nervous system

The autonomic nervous system is a critical feature of our physiology – it enables us to respond and maintain some 'balance' when under stress.

The *sympathetic nervous system* is essential to the 'autonomy' of physiological responses when we experience stress in the degree, and nature, of a threat. It does this by triggering an increase in heart rate, an inhibition of the digestive process and the release of adrenalin. When we are highly stressed the hormone epinephrine is also secreted to mobilise bodily arousal.[2] This hormone raises blood sugar, and enables the tensing of muscles and pupil dilation. Blood pressure is mobilised to pump blood to areas of need (muscles). This physiological response capacity happens instantly to engage the body for 'fight' or 'flight'. When we experience high stress arousal, the autonomic – and systemic – physiological reactions also include how we breathe, often shallow and quick. Where there is a release of too much carbon dioxide this compounds the feeling of real, or perceived, threat. In cases of recurrent anxiety this may become a 'physiological habit' when under stress (page 73). It is at this point that the individual can bring some relative – and helpful – cognitive assistance to the physiological processes of raised heart rate and rapid breathing. This is addressed later (page 70).

The *parasympathetic nervous system* is the corresponding feature of the autonomic nervous system. It enables the heart rate and breathing to slow down and to re-engage the digestive process. The body – now – seeks some homeostatic balance. We calm down, we refocus (hopefully and thankfully).

Our brain, of course, is the essential link between these systems. It engages our perception and processes the unique electrochemistry: the neurological and physiological complexity within these systems. Rightly could Hamlet say, 'What a piece of work ...'[3]

> *This complex feedback mechanism allows our hormones to take us from hyperarousal to quiescence in a relatively short time. It also allows us to adapt to an increasingly high 'resting' level, as it were, while at the same time maintaining some sort of equilibrium. In a sense it's like an ecosystem which is constantly adjusting to changing environmental circumstances.*
>
> Merson, 2001 (page 8)

However, if stressful symptoms are unrelieved and frequent – not ameliorated by the weekend by days off and holidays – they become disturbing, and genuinely affect our ability to do our work as teachers.

The symptoms of wearing and ongoing stress include:

- frequent tension in the neck and shoulders. A very common physical physiological response to stress is an elevated tension in our muscles – particularly the shoulder and neck. This is part of the fight/flight response – our body 'getting ready ...'. Problems occur when that normal tenseness is *elevated and sustained* (check it in yourself now as you read).

- more than the 'normal' share of headaches, or a significant variation in the type of headaches (if, for example, you are a migraine sufferer)

- regular 'churning of the stomach' during (and after) stressful episodes

- frequent tightness in the bowel region

- frequent tiredness and weariness

- being more easily, and frequently, frustrated, and feeling 'on edge' during and after stressful episodes

- difficulty in concentrating and focusing (even *after* stressful episodes)

- feelings of inadequacy and inability to cope with normative demands in one's role – a perceptual frame of mind that sees the situations and relationships as *inherently* stressful.

These physiological symptoms and feelings are real – they're often disturbing and distracting as we seek to do our work as a teacher. When stress is chronic such symptoms, feelings and thoughts can become debilitating. They are a signal that we are not coping with the demands we have to face and address as a teacher. It is *always* worth getting medical advice and support when the physical symptoms noted above are frequent – beyond 'normal' wear and tear.

These feelings and physical symptoms are also compounded by how we think about the stressful situations we have to address. Physiology and emotion are directly connected, as are cognition and emotion – those stressful feelings are nonetheless real and will have to be confronted if we are going to cope with, and manage, our stress. Evolution has, of course, equipped us with the fight-or-flight response which (normally) is neither necessary nor appropriate in our workplace! We can hardly run out of 8D in the middle of a lesson or 'fight' all oncomers (tempting as these options may be at times!) Mind you, I have seen teachers fighting verbally with their students. I've also seen teachers walk out of a challenging and riotous class because it has become impossible for them to cope. This is understandable – this difficult issue is addressed later on page 150. It takes conscious awareness, effort and some discipline to refocus that *emotional readiness* and address the kind of self-talk we use when we are directly under significant pressure and stress (Chapter 4). We can learn to understand the link between our emotional sense and our cognitive sense – this is a skill we have to develop in our profession so that our emotions are not *merely* reactive, but responsive (even within our physiology).

The skill areas addressed in the following chapters address our characteristic cognition and thinking when under pressure and how such thinking and cognition affect how we interpret, and respond, to stressful contexts we face.

Eustress and toxic stress – the paradox

The paradox of stress is well known – stress expressed as a 'positive drive' can keep us focused and attentive (as when we have to address an assembly at school – or teach a challenging class). Eustress is that 'good' stress – the motivational energising of mind and body. Then there's that level of stress – and our response to it – that we find draining or debilitating, distressing even 'toxic'.

As McEwan and Boyce (2010) note:

Positive stress (occurs) when you rise to a challenge and (are) generally exhilarated because you're able to meet that challenge. And it means you have to have a good sense of yourself, a good sense of whether the risk is worth taking, a good self-esteem and a good sense of control. And then there's 'tolerable' stress when something really bad happens, say the loss of a job, a divorce, the loss of a loved one – but you have these internal resources and you have a social support system that can help you out so you can weather the storm (italics mine).

These authors also write about 'toxic stress', where the individual doesn't have the personal resources or the social support systems to enable their coping. It is at this level, and affect, of stress that they write about stress as 'loss of control' accompanied by the 'paradox [sic] about the body (producing) chemicals – hormones like cortisol and adrenalin ... 'The autonomic nervous system are sympathetic in our parasympathetic system – they help keep our heart rate balanced and also affect inflammatory and metabolic processes. The paradox is that when these chemicals are overproduced or underproduced, when this network is out of sync, then the body can show a wear and tear that we call allostatic low – it really is the price that the body pays.' (McEwan and Boyce, 2010)

What intrigues and encourages me about this study is that our sense of self-esteem in stressful situations – our sense of *how* we are perceiving, interpreting and coping – also has a direct impact on the amount of stress we experience and how we cope and manage. That is, we can actually directly affect how *physiological stress* works on us and in us (see Chapter 4).

The work of Hans Selye

Hans Selye, widely regarded as the 'father' of stress research (1975, 1978), describes stress as the wear and tear on one's body (the physiological response) to the demands placed on, or faced by, the individual. He coined the term the 'general adaption syndrome'. When the body detects – and feels – stress there is an adaptive physiological response – blood pumps faster, heart rate goes up, muscle tone is affected (often tensed), breathing *rate* increases, the adrenals (the adrenal cortex) enlarges and starts to work harder, 'stress hormones' go to work, and so on. All this is the 'body's job (as it were). We are mobilised to 'fight' or 'flight' – that primal feature of our evolutionary development at work (page 20).

If our response to the stressful (fight-or-flight) event is able to combat the stress (what Selye calls the 'resistance phase') then the physiological state starts to 'rebalance' (thankfully) – if not then our body (and our response) may range from exhaustion to burnout. It is this kind of stress that the work-care statistics note – this is chronic stress. This state is sometimes called 'burnout' – the exhaustion of our physical, emotional and psychological coping resources.

Selye also coined the term *eustress* – positive stress – everything from looking forward to a pleasant evening at a restaurant to planning for a holiday or sports activities. These events – pleasant though they are – can also, on occasion, create stress in the form of pressure regarding what has to be done – the planning, as well as the 'wear and tear' natural to any effort. However, this is the way we actually work – in this sense *stress is part and parcel of what we have to do*. It is when our coping resources (our own as well as social and collegial support) do not enable us to manage, mediate, cope and work through those demands that stress becomes bad for us. This is regardless of whether these demands are implicit to our profession, or imposed by others or even self-imposed.

Burnout

We know that 'burnout' rates are lower for those professionals who have the opportunity to actively express, share and analyse the concerns and feelings about factors that cause stress in the workplace. The earlier that one can do this in episodic stress, the more effective the support will be. Of course that willingness to seek support needs to be matched by a non-judgemental response (particularly from senior colleagues). Not only are we able, then, to 'get things off our chest' but we also have the opportunity to develop new understandings, perspectives and even opportunities regarding our role and our relationships with students and colleagues. We also have the opportunity to receive supportive and enabling feedback within those new perspectives. Maslach (1976), Etzion (1984), Rogers (2002).

Dean Ornish (1999) (cardiologist and Clinical Professor of Medicine – University of California) notes a well-established correlation in the workplace between loneliness, isolation and even depression and the lack of reliable support. Workers who self-isolate, or by the nature of their workplace feel isolated, are three to five times more likely to get sick than those who have a sense of connection and community.

We also know that *work-related* stress and feelings of depersonalisation decrease as supervisory support is available. Such support is qualified – in the research – as *reliable* support, particularly the reliance available in stressful contexts, for example the challenging class; back-up support with very challenging students; difficult playground management contexts (such as 'mobbing' and fights); challenging and demanding parents. (Russell et al., 1987; House, 1981; Rogers, 2002 and 2009).

Self and others: how we perceive and rate our own stress

We are a unique universe of thought, feelings and emotions, sustained by both physiology and heredity. We are more though, much more, than the *mere* product of our history and our genes.

We can watch, observe and communicate with others – we can, however, uniquely communicate with ourselves. We are *self*-aware and *self*-identified as well as environmentally contingent. It is the *you* in the you that makes one uniquely human.

While experience 'shapes' us (how can it not?) and our physiology engages mood, emotion, feeling and pain, we always have to interact, address and cope with our experience. We always have to process, and make sense and shape meaning within and from our experiences.

Our self-concept, as a *self*, is also strongly sustained by others (particularly those nearest and dearest to us). As we get older, our *self*-concept is also significantly affected by the messages we give ourselves, consciously and subconsciously. Nowhere is this 'shaping effect' of self-awareness more acute than when we are experiencing stress. What we *characteristically* say to ourselves when we are under stress, and – later on – when reflecting about stress, can significantly affect how we shape and manage our reality and our sense of coping. This aspect of stress management is addressed in some detail in Chapter 4.

Self-concept and self-esteem (and other-esteem)

Self-concept is not a fixed construct – neither is self-esteem. As life journeys on we learn to address life in self-enhancing or (at times) self-defeating ways. We hopefully learn that our cognitions (in that universe of self) can be a cross-walk for change. We learn, too, that *what* and *how* we *characteristically think* also affects mood, disposition, emotion and coping ability.

If we are continually beset by a negative and self-defeating internal (and external) discourse in the workplace, it can have a negatively wearing effect. It takes a resilient individual mindset to confront that. That resilience can be learned.

It is a bold assertion to argue for a confident self-identity but it needs to be balanced by the reality that we are also *social* beings – we do need each other. My earlier point, confident self-identity, was one of *self-worth* and not merely *defining* or (worse) *demanding* our self-*worth* only from others.

The research on teacher stress clearly indicates that job-related stress and demoralisation decrease – and become more manageable – whenever teachers identify ongoing supportive collegial relationships within their school. Rogers (2002) and Russell et al. (1987) note that 'thoughtful [*sic*] positive support from supervisors was consistently predictive of measures of physical and mental health, and that when others (in their schools) respected their skills, abilities and contributions (then) feelings of depersonalisation and emotional exhaustion were lessened and they had a greater sense of personal accomplishment and ability to cope and manage the normative demands of stress.'

Etzion (1984) noted that 'burnout rates are also lower (statistically) for those professionals who actively express, analyse and share their personal feelings with their colleagues'. Etzion (ibid.) argued that these are 'needs fulfilling elements'. In my studies on collegially supportive school cultures, colleagues consistently noted that when they 'felt able to share – without criticism, blame or censure', where they received *constructive* feedback from colleagues (notably senior colleagues), this enabled them to 'develop professionally; better cope with teaching (and discipline); gain new perspectives and take risks in new learnings' (Rogers, 2002).

I have noticed in my work in mentor teaching that when we experience the stress of a particularly challenging class (or student) *together,* the 'psychological and physiological stress' is lessened. There is – in that existentiality – a sense of 'we're here, together; we can see, hear, feel, know … *it's not just me'* (page 173). This – when accompanied by positive debriefing and colleague support – can significantly decrease the psychological pain and that *physical* tenseness one sometimes feels when one is 'alone' in a stressful setting (like a classroom) – a kind of 'Dunkirk spirit'. I have noticed this phenomenon more often in challenging schools. The obvious is sharpened now; if we don't actually work together on this then we will definitely feel more stressed, more isolated – less able to cope.

What if my stress is not work related?

It is still important to let your senior colleagues know – within the limits and boundaries of trust – when issues outside school are significantly affecting stress levels and coping ability at work. Assuming you have a supportive 'line-manager' (a senior colleague) there's a good chance they can do something to reduce some of the pressure at work – at the very least they'll (hopefully) understand.

There is often a reluctance to talk about one's stress generally – either work-related or personal. This reluctance is often due to a perception that one will be viewed as 'weak', 'ineffective', 'non-coping' or – worse – incompetent (page xiii).

What stress feels like: managing difficult student behaviour and difficult classes

'Sometimes it's like feeling trapped; of actually losing control; control of myself *as well as the class'.* I've heard this description in many forms from colleagues as they recount the stress of managing very difficult classes.

As if the disruptive behaviour of the students wasn't enough, there are some senior colleagues who will stare through the classroom window at a teacher clearly struggling with a very challenging class (and continue to stare) or even barge into the classroom and shout the class down! (page 151).

I'm not wanting to paint a bleak picture here – I said *some* senior colleagues. Some teachers will not come forward to ask for help in such schools, particularly if they feel they will be perceived as a weak and ineffective teacher. Some teachers won't come forward to ask for help because they feel (maybe inaccurately) that help will be given – of a sort – but it will be 'remembered' in the teacher review interviews. Many teachers have said to me, 'I kept quiet instead.'

We cannot remain isolated from needed support when we are significantly stressed – it will take its toll. I have sat down with colleagues in faculty staffrooms, some in tears, and asked 'Why didn't you ask for help earlier? Tell us, now, what was going on.' Most say they didn't want people to think they couldn't cope. In schools with a low colleague consciousness this phenomenon is more likely to occur (Rogers, 2002). People feel that to 'own up' to one's struggle, one's stress or that they need help is a sign of weakness. Some teachers (in such schools) survive alone – professionally isolated as it were. Instead of experiencing professional dignity and support, there is a degrading survivalism.

I have been in other schools where colleagues feel comfortable in asking for (and receiving) not only moral support (itself essential) but also structural, professional, organisational, problem-addressing and resolving support. Classroom management and discipline practices, skills and plans are addressed in Chapters 7, 8, 9 and 10.

Colleague support is the crucial anchor variable in addressing stress of any sort in our profession. Research has consistently shown that when a school has a consciously supportive culture seeking to address the real (not merely espoused) needs of colleagues, then there is a corresponding reduction in measures of stress noted by staff (Rogers, 2002).

This is a theme we will come back to time and again in this text.

As one colleague noted, in explaining this colleague relationship factor:

> I was feeling down, not making progress, feeling stifled by being unable to get staff support. I couldn't do it all. I felt like giving it away. I saw a colleague (year level coordinator) about a student management matter. After dealing with this I then expressed my feelings, she listened and we discussed a few things. I left already feeling better. Three days later a card appeared on my desk: it said, 'Hang in there, most of us are pulling in the same direction.' I immediately went to her class and thanked her for her support. Later we worked on some behaviour management and organisational strategies for my class. The willingness to give ongoing support like this began to renew my confidence ...
>
> Rogers, 1999

Our health and stress: taking time to reassess

Prolonged negative stress at school can obviously affect our relationships outside school as well as our day-to-day responsibilities. When stress becomes chronic, both home and work become places of stress. There is that draining tiredness, jadedness, irritability and even physical pain (page 121). As noted earlier, those real physical symptoms and pains (associated with stress) may be stress-triggered or stress-related – they can also be frightening.

If frequent shallow breathing, palpitations, headaches and 'different' pains exist, it is worth the peace of mind that a thorough medical check-up can bring. Where the stress is compounding, it is worth taking stress-leave to reassess to regroup. Our physical *and* psychological health sometimes needs a 'breathing space' to refocus and reorient – before we re-engage with our work. It will also be crucial to seek out trusted colleague support, including trusted senior support.

Your union can also be helpful. What is necessary is to enable opportunities to talk things through, in the first instance with a colleague (or counsellor) and *then* set some priorities for how you address the causes and contexts of stress in the workplace. This will enable that sense of taking charge – but trusted colleague support is essential for such enabling to be genuinely helpful.

I think the biggest problem to such a course of action (as above) is the 'shame' some teachers feel in taking time off – 'What will others think?', 'Does this mean I'm a failure?', 'Haven't I let my colleagues, and my students down?' The answer to these questions is – of course – *no*. When stress (distress – even burnout) is so limiting and draining then a break from work is clearly needed.

The Queensland Centre for Mental Health has conducted a major study of workplace depression: *The WORC Project: Valuing Employee Health*. This project originated as a Harvard study (USA) and has been modified to the Australian culture. It surveyed almost 500000 employees and found that almost 7% had symptoms of depression; but only one in three were seeking treatment.

People tend not to come forward to seek assistance because of the stigma still associated with depression in the workplace. And because depression affects people's mood and temperament, it can make it hard for friends, colleagues and loved ones to recognise a condition that can be treated, and a colleague who can be helped.[5]

It's your life, your well-being, and it may be important to take time out before it takes you out. There's no stigma – unless you believe it so. This is your career, your life, and our lives are more important than our work, our profession. Yes, we need an income but that income won't be there without our health – our total health.

It may well be that a change of class grouping, even a new school or a fresh start (after a necessary work break) can be that positive opportunity to reassess and 'regroup'. There are helplines (as well as your union, friends and colleagues) that can start the process. As one colleague noted:

> *When I was at my last school I actually dreaded going in the school gate; I could feel the tension rising even as I drove up. After a day's teaching I'd go home with headaches and have nightmares – I'm not joking!*

> *At my new school (I've been there six months now) I actually look forward to going – I feel different as I drive through the school gates. I look forward to working here – to teaching again. The biggest single difference is the support I have of colleagues here – no bitching, no pushing one colleague against another. I feel valued here and I'm given feedback about how I'm going on. I don't feel criticised or put down.*

To make any decision about our career when we're very stressed is obviously difficult and may be counterproductive. Stress clouds both mood and thinking – that's why a 'breathing space' and trusted advice is essential. That advice may need to involve medical and psychological support as well as advice from one's colleagues and union. But it has to be your choice – it is your career. What is essential is that you do not make such crucial choices in the midst of chronic stress.

Notes

1. Allostasis – from the Greek adjective *allo*: variable, and the noun *stasis*: stability.
2. Adrenalin is a hormone our bodies secrete (via the adrenal glands) – it is colloquially called the 'stress hormone'. The secretion of adrenaline has a stimulatory and excitatory effect on circulation and muscular activity.

   Epinephrine is – biochemically – adrenaline (from the Greek noun *nephros*: kidney); the adrenal glands 'sit' on top of the kidney.
3. Shakespeare's Hamlet: 'What a piece of work is man!' (II: 2: 300).
4. This was a correlational study. It does not address individual variables though it does indicate the importance of colleague support in moderating stress. Cortisol is also termed a 'stress hormone'. As an adrenal steroid it (among other things) causes the liver to release stored sugar so the body has some energy for immediate action.

'The problem with allostatic load … is that we begin to release dangerously high levels of adrenaline and cortisol habitually. To compensate for increased feelings of anxiety we may overeat, smoke or drink more than is good for us, but we do adapt and may learn to ignore an underlying condition of stress, which in turn begins to impact on the crucial neurotransmitters in the brain which affect our mood' (Merson, 2001, page 25).

5. See www.qcmhr.uq.edu.au/worc/

A lesson in London:
stress in the classroom

What this chapter will explore and develop:

- The nature of classroom dynamics and how it affects distracting, disruptive and challenging student behaviours
- How such behaviours can easily trigger frustration and anger (for teachers) and what we can do to address that natural stress
- How our 'thinking styles' also affect our stress levels and our coping in response to challenging student behaviours
- How a conscious plan for discipline can reduce the normative stress occasioned by such distracting, disruptive and challenging behaviours in the classroom

This will be developed by drawing on a major case study of teaching in a challenging London school.

A lesson in London

I was mentor-teaching in a school in London. It had been designated as 'a school in serious weaknesses' needing 'special measures' (OFSTED speak[1]).

It was our first lesson together. As my colleague was standing at the front of the classroom introducing me to a very noisy, restless, kinaesthetic class of Year 8 students, several were calling out to my colleague, 'Oi! Why's *he* here!' They then started calling out to me, 'Hey – what's your name?' 'Why you here?!' 'You going to be our teacher?' I *tactically* ignored the half dozen voices calling out to me – I was giving my main focus to my colleague who was trying to settle the class (my turn would come soon enough) – 'Can you *please* be quiet? I told you a visitor was coming today! Please stop talking.' My colleague was clearly doing his best.

A couple of girls persisted in calling out to me while my colleague sought to settle and focus the class. I continued to *tactically* ignore them (not even looking in their direction). I could see them out of 'the corner of my eye' – They were clearly annoyed that I wasn't immediately answering them. 'Hey I'm talking to you!', one of the girls called out. I continued to *tactically* ignore her. She turned to her classmate and said, 'He doesn't listen – who does he think he is?' I didn't want to address her at this stage, because my colleague was valiantly trying to gain some whole-class attention. She snorted, leaned back in her seat and said – loudly and with clear attentional intent – 'Well I won't talk to *you*!' I recognised (for the umpteenth time) familiar patterns of attentional and posturing behaviours. I also felt for my colleague and transitionally wondered (yet again) how this first lesson would go for both of us. The class settled to a fractious hum with several students chatting while my colleague sought to introduce me as the visiting teacher.

As my colleague was about to 'hand the class over' (in a team-teaching sense) two lads walked in late, coats on, bags 'a swinging' – completely ignoring my colleague (and me). They started walking to the back of the classroom (amidst the noise) calling out to their mates at the back of the classroom, 'Hey! What's happening?!' Several students started cheering – many of the girls called out their welcome, and clapped.

My colleague hadn't addressed this lateness (or the hubbub it produced). I quickly said, 'Mr Smith do you mind if I have a word with the class?' (this was a *planned* cue for 'I'll take the class here at this point ...'). I wanted this cue to look 'natural' (in a teaming sense – not easy). I said to the class, 'Excuse me for a moment class', and raising my voice called out to the two boys – quickly (before they'd got to their seats) – 'Fellas!' (a firmer, *raised*, voice – not shouting). 'Fellas.' They turned, 'What? – who are you!?' (Here I dropped the voice level.) 'Fellas (...) over here by the door.' They protested, 'What did we do?' 'What?!' (I sensed they *knew* perfectly well that I was a teacher and that their behaviour was clearly well 'over the top'). 'Over here by the door – *now*. Thanks.' I turned and walked off towards the door conveying (I hoped) an expectant 'take-up' tone. They came, muttering loudly, 'What did we do – who's he anyway?' (and a few sibilant sh-ts!). I walked out of the classroom with them, quietly closed the door, walked down the corridor and stopped for a *brief* chat. I was hoping this distraction of the boys (out of the class) would give Mr Smith a chance to refocus the class.

I introduced myself and asked them their names (sulkily given). Now – away from direct observation of the class – I described, briefly, what I'd seen. 'Darren (...) Kosta (...) you barged in through the door – loudly. You completely ignored your teacher as if he wasn't there and you then started talking loudly to your mates at the back of the classroom. You did this *while* your teacher was teaching.' I paused. One of the boys said – frowning, loudly – 'You going to be here all day?' 'Too right', I said . I asked the important question – not '*Why* did you come in arrogantly in the way I just said?' (I hoped the *description* I had just given was clear enough for that) – but, rather, 'What's the *fair* way to come in when you're late and your teacher is teaching?' No answer. So I said, 'You knock, wait, apologise for lateness and take your seats without speaking loudly to your mates. Let's try it again.'

I'd wanted to re-establish (with Darren and Kosta) the reasonable, and fair, way to come into class when you're late. Back in the classroom Darren and Kosta sulked back to their seats, arms folded, leaning back (typical *residual* 'secondary behaviours' see page 45). I walked back to the front of the classroom and stood near Mr Smith, trying to look as if we were relaxedly resuming our team-teaching.

My colleague was still trying to settle the class. He was pacing up and down and raising his voice – behaviours that are natural when we're very frustrated and stressed; when we feel as if we're 'losing control'. Within a minute or two of being back in the classroom, Mr Smith 'handed the class over'. 'Thank you Mr. Rogers' (did I see a passing hint of relief in his eyes?). Several students continued to call out directly to me now, 'Hey, you going to be our new teacher!?' 'What you doing here?' I waited for several seconds – looking for any 'break in the psychological traffic' as it were. 'Hands down, thanks – I'll take your questions later,' (some tactical pausing). Scanning the room I made very brief transitional eye contact with each student – even with the sulking Darren and Kosta (the latecomers) and Lola and Chantelle and several others who had been frequently calling out five minutes earlier. I was aware (consciously aware) of seeking to non-verbally (as well as verbally) communicate a sense of calmness (page 103) to the class – it wasn't easy.

Students were still chatting. I directed the class – again – 'A number of students are still chatting –you need to be looking this way and listening – thanks' (more brief, tactical pausing). Several students were fiddling with pencil cases and other *objets d'art* (abstractedly? intentionally? attentionally?). I briefly – and descriptively – cued the class, 'A number of students are fiddling with pencil cases and pens ... it's really distracting' ... (*brief* tactical pause). Most stopped chatting (as I continued to scan the class). Calm scanning of the class group enables us to make transitional, *brief*, even human (!) connection. It also enables us to sense how we are connecting; how we're coming across to the group and to individuals.

NB When giving directions during whole-class teaching time, it can help to use *descriptive* and *directional* cues for behaviours – like calling out, butting in, fiddling with objects etc., talking while the teacher is talking. We briefly *describe* the distracting behaviour, 'A number of students are calling out.' This raises 'behaviour awareness' (Rogers, 2011). Sometimes this, in itself, is enough. If we sense it isn't, we quickly add a *direction* or *rule-reminder*, '. . . hands up without calling out, thanks' or 'Remember our class rule for questions.' (see page 95). A confident and positive tone and manner will enhance this.

This approach is particularly helpful for older primary and secondary classes.

I *re-cued* the class, 'Looking this way, thanks (. . .) and listening. I'll take questions later (. . .) For the moment I need you all to face this way and listen. Thanks.'

I could *feel* (as well as see, sense and hear) the class beginning to respond, to settle and focus. A few minutes – at most – had passed; it seemed longer.

'Good morning everyone. You're much more relaxed now – thanks. My name is Mr. Rogers and I'm visiting your class today as an English teacher – though I'm from Australia ...' Before I could finish several students called out, 'What's on *Neighbours*?', 'Bring any kangaroos?' I waited briefly for the residual laughter to drop and continued. I asked them what they had been studying in this particular class. 'I want you to share with me what you've been studying together these last few lessons with Mr Smith. Hands up, thanks, without calling out. And please give me your first name. Who'd like to start?' Several students called out, I briefly reminded them of the fair expectation, 'Hands up, thanks; without calling out. We'll all get a fair go.' I chatted with them about Australia (there were quite a few questions on that topic). I sensed they were continuing to moderate their group behaviour (re: hands up ... waiting their turn in asking ... facing the front of the room, etc.). I also sensed that returned 'calmness' – across the group – from them, to me. This basic sense of group calmness is essential to whole-class teaching (page 103).

When there was some isolated chatter, I quietly cued the individuals concerned, 'Melissa (. . .) Chantelle (. . .) you're chatting.' Sometimes this brief descriptive cue was enough. Sometimes I'd need to add the brief direction, 'Looking this way, thanks – and listening.' Or, if students called out, the brief reminder, 'Hands up, thanks.' Sometimes I'd need to add 'without calling out.' I was conscious of keeping such directions/reminders brief and positive in tone and of *resuming the flow of the lesson,* thus giving take-up time to the students I'd spoken to. The lesson progressed quite well – considering its very disruptive start. I thanked the class for their sharing, I then 'handed the class back' to my colleague (we were *team* teaching). 'I'll ask Mr. Smith to discuss with you what we'll be doing today

...' The noise level rose, calling out started and there was some chatting. My colleague largely talked *through* the noise (as it were) – was this how he normally taught? I suspected that what I'd observed, already, was 'habituated' behaviour in this class. Many students 'believing' that it was OK to chatter and call out *while their teacher was talking.*

During the *on-task phase* of the lesson my colleague and I had to address several students calling out 'Hey Mr Rogers can you help us!?' 'I don't know what to do.' 'Hey Mr. Smith what do we have to do again?!' I suspected this – too – was habituated behaviour. Students wandered round the classroom (to socialise). Terry had chewed apart a large liquorice sherbet straw and (with a bit of spit) had made a sticky slurry of the sherbet on his desk. Rory threw a pen at Andrew ... twice, during the lesson. I sensed, yet again, this behaviour was probably habituated over the last few months, so that now the students were only half aware (if that) that they were being 'disruptive'. This was what they were used to. We needed a 'circuit breaker'. I went to the front of the classroom to re-cue the class. 'EVERYBODY (said a little louder) (...) stop what you are doing' (a *raised voice* – not shouting). I allowed some tactical pausing to let the group cue sink in. Most of the students did settle, did turn and face the front of the classroom. I re-cued several disruptive students: 'Kirsty, Jackie, Chantelle (...) Looking this way (...) now, thanks. Andrew (...) *leave the pen there.* Rory (...) leave it' (the pen). 'Amy, (...) Lola (...) back in your seats now.' 'But we were just ...' (they protested and whinged that they were 'just getting a pen').

Tactical pausing

You'll note, in all the case studies in the book, that when I'm recording teacher language (say a descriptive cue, a direction, a reminder ...) that after the student's name I've got brackets with an ellipsis (...). This is to alert (and cue) the reader to the use of a conscious aspect of our leadership language – the brief *tactical pause* (...).

We cue the student/s by name, then pause (...) to allow some corresponding attentional connection in the student/s. Until we've got that (including some marginal eye contact) they may not be focused on the following words containing the direction or reminder.

'Back in your seats, now thanks.' They sloped off – sulkily – and dropped into their seats, arms folded and sighing. *Tactically* ignoring this I re-directed the class – again – to 'settle' and 'face the front'. 'Thank you; that's better. Let me tell you what I've just noticed. Several of you were wandering round the class (I didn't name names), some of you were throwing things (there was some residual laughter). We don't throw *anything* in our class – full stop.' I was aware – as I scanned the group – of 'keeping the calmness'; not rushing or *blaming.* 'I'm not saying it's all of you (...) A number of students were calling out, *frequently.* If you need Mr. Smith's help, or mine, it's hands up – thanks – without calling out or clicking fingers. Please check the set work yourself first. Read through and ask yourself 'What am I asked to do here …?' If you need pens/rulers/extra paper – by the way – we've got some here (page 145). Right – we've got 20 minutes or so before the bell. What you need to be doing now is …'

We went back to work. The class was more focused now, though there were still some pockets of task avoiding and social chit-chat. I went across to Terry with some moisturised hand-wipes (for the sherbet slurry) and helped him refocus on the work Mr Smith had set. I began to sense, yet again, we were on that *slow road to re-habituation as a class*.

Later that day Mr Smith and I sat and chatted over coffee. After some shared 'moan bonding' (an elegant form of whingeing) we started to discuss a fresh-start strategy for the class. This class, it seemed, had developed patterns of distracting and disruptive behaviour – a kind of *group habituation*. I didn't believe this was accidental. As my colleague and I debriefed, after that first lesson, I began to realise – yet again – that this 'behaviour habituation' (the repeated calling out, talking while the teacher was talking, the arrogant and 'grandstanding' lateness) had all occurred – and had continued – over the first half dozen lessons in September. It was at the close of term one, that I began working with my colleague as a mentor (Chapter 10).

My colleague shared how he had tried to deal with these kinds of distracting and disruptive behaviours and that he had found it tiring and wearying, and had – at times – 'given in' and 'let things go' – such as not appropriately confronting lateness and not reinforcing fair expectations and rules. In fact he agreed he had not really had a proper *establishment phase* with his class (page 93). He hadn't actually developed – and *maintained* – clear (and fair) routines, rules and expectations (page 92).

We also agreed to chat with other colleagues who taught these students to see if the behaviours we had experienced were 'common' across subjects and teachers. Already my colleague was feeling better and said he had seen something 'different' in the general behaviour of the class that day. (The hard to manage class is addressed later in Chapter 9).

Shared struggle

… from this point of view one might indeed consider that the appropriate form of address between man and man ought not to be monsieur, sir, but fellow sufferer, compagnon de misères. However strange this may sound, it corresponds to the nature of the case, makes us see other men in a true light and reminds us of what are the most necessary of all things – tolerance, patience, forbearance and charity, which each of us needs and which each of us are therefore owed …

Arthur Schopenhauer (1788–1860): Essays and Aphorisms (page 50)

Student arrogance – teacher frustration and anger

A student is late to his first Year 8 maths class – five minutes. The teacher is new to this school (a school with a 'bit of a reputation'). Jayson walks in to class swaggering and grinning to his mates in the back row. It's his first lesson with Mr Smith.

Already the 'hackles are rising' – Mr Smith is visibly annoyed. The lad walks past his teacher, ignoring him. The teacher calls him back, 'Oi ... come here.' The lad continues to ignore him, 'I said *come here*!' The lad turns, 'What? What did I do?' (grinning).

'*Why* are you late?' The teacher is annoyed by the boy's attitude (particularly his insouciant body language and his tone of voice). He thinks, 'How dare he speak, to me like that.'

The boy turns and says, 'People are late sometimes you know. I got here as quick as I could – what's the big deal?!' Mr Smith is angry now. '*Who* do you think you're speaking to?! You walk in here five minutes late – you're arrogant ...'. The boy butts in, 'What! Gees – get a life! I'm here, alright!'

Some of his classmates are laughing and the rest of the class is wondering what is going to happen. After all, it's their first lesson with this teacher. For some it's entertainment – it's better than 'a lesson'; the lad has his audience.

'Where's your late pass?!' The teacher's body language is tense, his voice sharp and stressed. The boy replies, 'I came straight here! What do I need a late pass for!?'

'Right – if you're going to barge into my class late and stand there arguing with me, you can get out of my class – NOW! You go straight to Mr Brown!'

Without batting an eyelid the boy glances at the class, and his mates – 'I'm going – it's a sh-t class anyway!' He barges out of the door – the teacher races after him calling out – 'and you'll be on detention!' Without even halting, the boy mutters a loud swearing retort.

The teacher is visibly angry; it takes him some time to refocus himself – let alone his class. His residual anger stays with him for the rest of the day.

If we could tune into Mr Smith's thinking we'd hear, 'Students *should not* be rude ...; I *must prove* I'm in control; I'm the boss here ...; No student is going to answer me back and get away with it ...'. Is it the boy's behaviour *alone* that causes the amount, and level, of stress he's feeling right now?

Same student, different class, (also Mrs Cassidy's first lesson with this student). The student walks in late – grinning. Mrs Cassidy pauses in her whole-class teaching and says – to the class, 'Excuse me a moment' and turns to face Jayson. 'Welcome; I don't know your name.' Jayson frowns; he wasn't quite expecting this. He mutters his name, a little sulkily. He turns to look at his mates again. 'Jayson (...)' the teacher quickly readdresses him – though she now drops her voice, 'Welcome to the class. I notice you're late – we'll have a chat later. There's a spare seat over by the window.' She doesn't ask him *why* he's late (*at this point* it doesn't matter) – she'll do that later in the on-task phase of the lesson, or even *briefly* after class if necessary.

Jayson turns, 'Look I don't sit *there*. I sit with Craig and Dean' (he points to the back row). The teacher doesn't argue – she partially 'tunes-in' and quickly – positively – refocuses, 'Jayson, those seats at the back are taken.' Mrs Cassidy quickly scans the room to let the class know (non-verbally) how she appreciates their brief 'waiting ...' while Jayson plays out his 'entrance'. She adds, 'We might be able to arrange a seat change later – take a seat, thanks.' Beckoning to a spare seat by the window she turns aside from Jayson to indicate she's finished this *brief* chat – this also telegraphs expectation and 'take-up time' to Jayson. He walks to the seat – sighing – eyes raised to the ceiling. Mrs Cassidy *tactically* ignores this 'secondary' behaviour. She resumes the flow of the lesson as Jayson slumps in his seat, arms folded with practised sulking(?) Her calmness, her sense of confidence (without any hint of bossy arrogance) is quickly picked up by the rest of the class. *Is the difference in Mrs Cassidy's teacher approach mere personality – or is there more at issue here?*

I would argue that while this second teacher addresses a small issue like 'grand-standing lateness' skilfully, she was still irritated by Jayson's behaviour – but *irritated*, not angry. She was significantly less 'stressed' by this event, and not only because of her leadership skill and the language and approach she used. She also did not make the sorts of *cognitive demands* Mr Smith made about the student or her own leadership. She also realises she cannot directly *control* Jayson (or his behaviour) – she can, however, control *her response* to Jayson's lateness. She uses her leadership 'power' not to control Jayson but control events – her response in the emotional moment.

If you tune in to Mrs Cassidy's thinking you hear preference, not demand. 'OK – I don't like grandstanding lateness but I'll consciously welcome him, refocus the student's argumentative stance, keep to the flow of the lesson and follow up with Jayson later' (rather than demand reasons for his lateness in the immediate emotional moment). She was less stressed and more able to lead Jayson, and the class, that morning. I know ... I was there.

A relative, more realistic, belief argues that while a good teacher needs to have confident, respectful leadership of a class, simply demanding compliance and having a controlling style that forces obedience will only exacerbate the already naturally stressful demands of behaviour management and discipline.

The key variable in one's perception here is the underlying characteristic, absolutistic cognitive *demand,* in contrast to a preferential realistic expectation. The previous colleague had argued:

- 'He *shouldn't* be rude!' He was.
- 'He *shouldn't* argue back!' He did.
- 'Children *should respect* their teachers!' Some don't – at least they don't respect teachers easily, quickly, with the sort of deferential respect some teachers demand. Whether we like it or not, respect has to be earned by the kind of teacher–leader we choose to be (page 47).
- 'Children *shouldn't* swear!' They do (page 129).
- 'A good teacher must be *in control at all times.*' Really? Is it possible to control everything and everyone in a classroom – or anywhere for that matter? Control is different from leadership (page 49).

I'm not saying that we should not address argumentative, challenging, rude, arrogant behaviours in our students – of course we should. I am saying that if we characteristically *demand* that things *should,* or shouldn't be – when they are – the social reality we experience has no obligation to simply conform to such 'absolutistic' beliefs. A realistic sense of the word 'should' or 'must' is used as an expectation; a necessary expectation – i.e.: 'I should get a haircut', 'I should get those essays marked by next week'. The problem is not the words 'should'/'shouldn't', 'must'/'mustn't' but the *intensity of demand* that some people invest in them when they seek to explain and manage their daily, stressful reality.

Our beliefs and stress

There are many facets of our teaching life that are *naturally* stressful. We should not delimit or deny this stress. However, we still have to perceive, interpret and evaluate those events hourly, daily. Our perceptions – as patterns of thinking – are not always immediately conscious. Often it's not until later – after a class – that a teacher will sit down and might say, 'I can't stand 8D! – and that little sh-t Jayson! Who the hell does he think he is – *no student should answer back like that …!* Students *should* show respect to their teacher!'

While difficult students and challenging classes are naturally stressful, our emotional stress and coping ability is also affected by how we characteristically perceive, rate, interpret and explain those stressful demands to ourselves.

Cognitive-behaviour theory argues that the degree of stress we experience (in this case frustration – even anger) is significantly affected by the kind, and nature, of insistent demands made about our stressful reality – an *idée fixe,* 'Children *must* respect their teachers; they *should not* answer back and be rude!' Such beliefs may also be stressfully affected by a perfectionist mentality – 'A good teacher *must be* in control of the class at all times.'

Back in the naturally stressful environment of the classroom, such beliefs – running through the head at nanosecond speed – *directly affect* attitude, emotion and behaviour.

Feelings of stress and testing reality

Our feelings – both negative and pleasant – are not merely (or *just*) caused by external pressures and stressors – a noisy class, disruptive behaviours, rude and argumentative children, rude and argumentative colleagues (!). It seems 'natural' that there is a cause and effect here – if we feel that stressed then the stressful event *must* have caused it. However, our thinking processes – our *characteristic* thinking processes – *intervene*, mediate or exacerbate how we feel.

As Albert Ellis[2] has noted, our emotions – to a varying degree – are not simply caused (or only, or merely) by external events. We have certain beliefs, attitudes and *evaluations* we bring to the activating events and situations that contribute significantly to *how anxious, frustrated or angry we feel about these events, people or circumstances.*

How often do we hear others (or ourselves) say, 'He made me so angry'? This is more than a figure of speech – people often believe (sometimes intensely believe) that the behaviour of another person *caused* 'how I feel now'. This is understandable – but this is only part of what happens in day-to-day reality. Low frustration tolerance, for example, is often correlated with a style of thinking that *demands* that others shouldn't behave in ways we don't like. 'I don't like your behaviour and you *shouldn't* behave that way!' If that 'explanatory style' is frequently applied to behaviours such as students calling out, answering back, defiance and swearing; it increases a person's degree of frustration – and anger (Chapter 6). This is more than discomfort frustration – it is a demand that others shouldn't act in the way that I demand they *shouldn't* act. But they do – and that's the social reality. So, now, social reality is seen as the primary cause of one's degree of stress.

When we say, 'I find it annoying when students call out and butt in and answer back …' that's realistic – we've all felt that and reasoned thus. The difference between a preference and a *characteristic demand* (in our thinking and in our evaluation about stressful events) is the degree to which such beliefs connect with our reality and interpret and enable us to manage our reality. One 'style' of thinking, belief and evaluation will better enable our coping – including *how* we feel – and better enable our goals, particularly in our behaviour leadership. In effect it is a difference between preferential – and more realistic – thinking, and *absolutistic, demanding* thinking. This is addressed in some detail in Chapter 4.

When we feel frustrated, anxious or angry – when we are stressed – these emotions are *natural*, they are normal; they tell us something about what's happening. They don't, however, tell us what to think about what has happened to 'make us feel that way', nor do they tell us what to do about what we feel in a given moment. Emotions never tell us what to do.

Cognitive-behaviour theory (and therapy) argues that the *characteristic way* we perceive and process stressful events has a direct impact on *how* stressful we feel and and, secondly, how effectively we cope and manage such events. Kyriacou (1986) notes:

> The most interesting trait linked to stress appears to be that which charac-terises differences between those individuals who believe that things in their lives are generally within their control (a belief in 'internal control') and those who tend to believe such things are generally outside their control – attrib-utable primarily to luck, fate, powerful others or essentially unpredictable (a belief in external control).

> (page 194)

Professional help: caveat emptor[3]

This book is an educator's response to the daily realities of stress in the teaching profession. If you are struggling with chronic stress and if your daily experience of stress in terms of anxiety and intense frustration is such that it significantly affects your health and your work then it is important to seek *professional* medical and psychological support.

There are plenty of people advertising on the worldwide graffiti board (the internet) who claim to be able to 'reduce your stress' in 10 steps ... with *this* program or that. There are counsellors and therapists out there in www land who make all kinds of 'therapeutic' claims – some are clearly outrageous, yet I've seen people taken in by on-screen claims made by clearly unqualified practitioners.

For example, clinical depression needs medical assistance – not only psycho-logical assistance (even clinical psychology). While antidepressants won't 'cure' depression – as such – they can provide that early coping support so that underlying psychological and relational issues can, in time, be more functionally addressed.

When a colleague is stressed and depressed it is insensitive, even heartless, to suggest that all they need to do is think 'more positively' or 'pull themselves together' or 'just get on with it ...'. It is attitudes like these, I'm sure, that contribute to colleagues suffering acute, even chronic, stress for fear they will be judged if they can't adequately 'pull themselves together ...'. It is – sometimes – necessary to take adequate sick leave to seek medical and psychological support; firstly get that professional help for one's health and then, in time, it is possible to regain a sense of perspective and control of one's life (page 28).

You often see self-help books with titles like '10 steps to a stress-free life'; 'The 5 laws of ...'; '8 steps to a healthy body'; 'The 10 principles of wealth creation'. I've even seen books with titles like '50 ways to ...', '100 ways to ...'. I can't (and won't) give you a 5, 8 or 10 step programme. I won't give you some formulaic process.

This book shares principles, practices, strategies and skills that my colleagues and I have used to lead and manage classes and to help students and teachers take control of their behaviour. These principles, practices, strategies and skills are based on sound psychology and pedagogy and are based on the humanitarian tradition of rights and responsibilities.

I also want to encourage you to take stock of how you characteristically interpret, process and rate the stress you experience as a teacher. There are important and well-established skills of thinking that can also enable us to moderate, and realistically refocus, our stress without foolishly denying our stressful reality.

Most of all, I will share that approach to colleague support that enables reasonable sanity, good grace and goodwill to do the work we choose to do – *be a teacher*.

Notes

1. We don't have an Office For Standards in Education (as such) in Australia.
2. Albert Ellis (a clinical psychologist) was one of the original pioneers of a form of cognitive-behaviour therapy called rational emotive therapy in the mid-1950s.
3. Latin: 'let the buyer beware'.

Beliefs, emotion, stress and our daily reality

What this chapter will explore and develop:

- The difference between leadership and control
- The challenge of dealing with a student's 'secondary behaviours' (the sulking, whining, moaning, whingeing, sighing ...)
- The link between emotions, our beliefs, and our behaviour in the classroom
- Challenging faulty assumptions and unhelpful beliefs – our 'explanatory style' when we're under stress
- The skills of positive disputations and *learned* optimism

Teacher discipline and stress and the nature of 'control'

The stress associated with the need to discipline is consistently cited among the top five stressors teachers face every day (page 2). Even if it's 'only' addressing frequent calling out and talking while the teacher is talking (the most common distractions in a lesson). Often we'll also have students who argue, avoid or refuse to engage in learning tasks, who sulk, moan and whine and challenge a teacher's leadership. And there are those students who swear (page 129), defy, challenge, bully and aggress (page 155).

The degree to which we're 'stressed' by our need to discipline depends on a number of factors – some of which are clearly outside our control (such as a student's home background and their behaviour profile in terms of symptomatic or diagnosed behaviour disorders). However, there are many factors we can affect at the school level to reduce the normative stress of managing students. We'll come to those in a moment.

At the outset it's worth pointing out the distinction between 'controlling' situations, as a teacher–leader, and trying to 'control' the student.

Case example

It's on-task learning time (Year 7) and students are supposed to be doing their normal set classwork. Travis has an iPod plugged into his ears. The teacher hears the buzz of the music so he walks over and directs the student to take it off. The student leans back in his seat, frowns and says, 'What!?' Already the student's tone of voice is annoying to the teacher. He asks the boy to hand over the iPod. 'What!?' The boy leans forward, 'that's my iPod. No way, I'll put it in my bag – anyway, other teachers don't hassle us as long as we get our work done.'

On that point Travis was right. Having worked in this school many times as a mentor teacher I've noted some teachers have 'allowed' students to have iPods in class, 'as long as they get on with their class work' – (although there was a stated school rule that students should not use iPods – or phones – in class time.)

The teacher is getting annoyed now. 'Look I don't care what other teachers do – you can hand it over to me *now* please.' He's trying to be civil.

It surprises me, still, that some teachers think they can *just expect* a student to hand over an expensive iPod or phone just because they say so. This is a challenging school, and this teacher – new to the school – was (to be fair) trying to enforce the rules but it quickly got out of hand.

The lad, too, is annoyed. 'No way – if it's that such a big deal I'll put it in my bag if it makes you happy!' What is really frustrating to the teacher is the boy's attitude – by 'attitude' he means the boy's insouciant tone of voice, the ambient sarcasm '... if it makes you happy!', the argumentative stance, the 'look on his face'. (I know – I discussed it all later, with my colleagues, over coffee.)

'Right – if you don't hand it over now, you'll be on detention!'

The boy responds with, 'Get real! A detention! F---, what did I do? I said I'd put it away!'

At this point the teacher is visibly angry. Having heard the swearing, he orders the student out of the class, to a chorus of ambient cheering by some of his mates.

The teacher believed he 'controlled' the student – that he 'won' ...

Who *won*? *Why define it as a contest*? (The issue of swearing is addressed on page 129.)

'Primary' and 'secondary' aspects of students' behaviour

I'm not unsympathetic to how my colleague felt in managing this situation. Knowing this student, I know he can 'argue the leg off a chair if you let him'(as other colleagues have said).

What often stresses teachers in discipline contexts is not the student's 'primary' behaviour alone (the calling out, the task avoidance, the lateness (page 37) or – in this case – having an iPod on in class), it's the 'secondary' aspects of the behaviour – the student's sulky tone of voice, the sighing, the whining, the pouting, the eyes-raised-to-the-ceiling, the argumentation about 'other teachers' and the swearing. My colleague did admit, later, that the student hadn't actually sworn *at* him.

My colleague saw all these aspects of behaviour (in the immediate emotional moment in the classroom) as a kind of compound attitude of disrespect *directed towards him*. This, allied to the teacher's belief about his need to control, and the student needing to show respect, quickly coalesced into the slanging match described above.

The belief some teachers hold about the respect students should show their teachers is often perceived through these 'secondary behaviours'. I have frequently sat with teachers who will say (after such an episode as above) that 'Children *should*, or *must*, respect their teachers' which means that they *shouldn't* pout, sulk, whine, moan or argue when told to do something.

I would argue that the above belief – if held as a *characteristic attitude* – will create as much stress as the behaviour exhibited by the student in this management episode. Such thinking becomes problematic when we rate, interpret and perceive situations and relations beyond the preferential to the absolute. Such thinking also directly affects how the teacher then responds to the behaviour.

Case example

In the same school another colleague (Julie) had approached the same student (different subject class). Her first response was not to even mention the student's partially secreted iPod. Approaching the student's desk, she non-verbally beckoned to Travis to take the ear buds out; he did. 'How's the work going?' (It was 'on-task learning time'). Her first response was to greet him and then focus his attention to the learning activity.

Having taught with Julie I know that her tone and manner is normally positive, expectant – even 'welcoming'. 'Do you mind if I take a look?' The student grunted, a bit of skewed eye contact and sighed, 'It's OK.' She didn't simply pick up the student's work. She asked a few questions, checked if he understood, made a couple of suggestions, and then said, 'I notice you've got an iPod there.' Julie didn't touch it, she merely *described the reality* (as it were). Travis sighed (again) raised his eyes to the ceiling (she *tactically* ignored this) and said, 'Oh come on, what's the big deal? Other teachers let us have them – long as we get our work done.'

'Even if they do Travis,' she replied, 'what's our school rule about iPods?' Travis leaned back, raised his eyes again, frowned and continued his case. 'Well, ask anyone here (he looks around with a frown and then grins) – Vanessa (he names another teacher) she lets us.'

Julie *partially* agreed – she's not going to get into a discussion, *or* argument, about which teachers do or don't allow iPods. 'Even if she does, Travis – the school rule is clear. I expect you to put it on my table (she nods to her desk) or (she drops her voice) in your bag.' Her voice was quiet – she was calm; *it's not a contest*. She was not trying to control him. In fact she was about to walk away leaving him with the *directed* 'choice'. He said, 'All right, I'll put it in my bag if it makes you happy.' He sighed loudly, raised his eyes as if it's 'all so big a deal'. Julie *tactically* ignored all this 'secondary' behaviour. She walked off giving him 'take-up time' (Rogers, 2011) with an *ex parte* comment, 'I'll come back and see how your work is going later' (a task reminder). Travis sulked for a while but eventually got back to work.

In this second example, Julie hasn't taken any longer than her other colleague (page 44) in managing this discipline 'issue'. The difference is she has consciously:

- avoided unnecessary confrontation
- used 'descriptive' cueing and 'directed choice' language (page 95)
- kept the whole transaction *least intrusive* (pages 105, 108)
- not *defined* the transaction as one she needs to 'win' – she knows it's not about 'winning' or 'losing' here; it's also not about controlling the student but seeking to 'control' the situation and enabling the student to own their behaviour
- crucially – kept the focus of the transaction directed to the 'primary' issue of the fair *school* rule and *tactically* ignored the non-verbal sighing (etc.) and *refocused* the student's argumentative stance; she has not been drawn into the 'secondary behaviours' (page 45)
- been aware that her behaviour is *enabling* a workable, even a positive relationship with Travis – she knows that the *way* she disciplines is also affected by the *way* she relates to him
- not demanded respect – she has, however, earned it by the way she leads; and she's not stressed by it all; it's an annoyance, at most – no more.

If the student had refused to put the iPod away she would have clarified the consequence (as she normally does) and followed up one-to-one with Travis later (pages 107, 118).

In such a case she would have said something like, 'Travis, you know the fair rule – if you choose not to put it away I'll have to follow this up with you at recess.' She would have made the consequence clear (in this case, the *deferred* consequence) and left the student to 'own' his behaviour.

When I talked with Julie, and others in the school, about these typical behaviour issues, we also discussed how we *felt* in such 'transactions'. We agreed that we felt irritated and annoyed but not *angry*. Why get angry over such a small issue? We also discussed the difference between annoyance, frustration and anger (page 76). Within our discipline plan approach (Chapter 7) we discussed the importance of avoiding the overservicing of 'secondary behaviours' and pointless argumentation or 'teacher comparisons' (!) (page 45)

Some of my colleagues, who were still getting used to a more consciously planned approach to discipline transactions, said, 'I used to feel worse and more often when I tried to control my students. I used to get angry when students didn't do what I asked. I realise I often *demanded* respect – rather than behaving in a way that was likely to receive respect.' In short – as one colleague said – 'I'm more consciously aware of what's happening in discipline transactions now – and don't get sucked in to these typical "secondary behaviours" – I'm more aware but less stressed! Still annoyed at times – but not angry – well, not about these sorts of behaviour anyway ...' The issue of anger and anger management is addressed later in Chapter 6.

Beliefs, emotion and our behaviour

Bernard and Joyce (1984) and Bernard (1990) describe the typical teacher assumptions and beliefs that can significantly affect a teacher's frustration and anger in discipline contexts. I have adapted these in Rogers (2011a) and here.

Children *must* not question or disagree with their teachers or superiors

If it wasn't so ludicrous in its irrationality, it would be laughable to hold such an attitude at this *level* of insistence. I still meet teachers who believe this, and whose behaviour (and stress level/s) reflect such a belief. Students do question and disagree with their teachers. At times such disagreement is actually necessary to their *thinking*, to their reasoning as a student. This is to be distinguished from when they are overly and *overtly* distracting, disagreeable and defiant in their response to their teachers. Even then, there are approaches and skills that can mitigate the trading of verbal blows and contestable behaviour between teacher and student(s).

When my colleagues and I challenge such a belief (in our peer support groups page 15) we point out the obvious reality check – students do question, challenge, disagree ... *that's* the reality. If we demand what reality often won't give we'll be not only unnecessarily stressed but also less able to lead – or behave – constructively as a teacher–leader.

Children *should respect* their teacher

I've seen some school principals shout at children who stand before them with an 'attitude of disrespect' (hands in pockets, not giving 'proper eye contact' or 'lounging') – it's as if they *just shouldn't do that*! Some students do. For some, such body posture is attentional behaviour, for some it's even 'habit' (they may not even be aware). For some students it's clearly a power display – 'I'll stand like this to show you I don't really care; you can't *make* me respect you!'

Less stressed – but still effective – teachers have learned not to overfocus on such 'secondary behaviours' in the immediate emotional moment (particularly in front of a peer audience). They have learned that:

- They cannot actually demand respect from their students (or colleagues!). They can earn it by the kind of teacher–leader they seek to be.
- They cannot actually *make* a student do anything – they can remind, direct, enable fair choices, assert, even command – but they cannot *actually make* ...

● Students have no inherent magic to *make* us angry by the sorts of typical 'secondary posturing' noted earlier (see page 45). The emotional reasoning that says *he made me angry* is a common one. Clearly not all teachers are 'made' angry by the same kinds of student behaviours – something else is at work as well. When we import a characteristic *demand* into our beliefs, our reasoning and evaluations – *a good teacher must be in control at all times* – then it is easy to see why some teachers will feel not only more frustrated, but also angry by behaviour as shown by Travis (page 44). Such 'emotional reasoning' significantly contributes to the teacher behaving in a more angry, confrontational way.

There is a time to get angry – on issues that matter (racism, sexism and bullying). Even then, however, we can learn to communicate our anger in a way that avoids irrational and destructive outbursts (page 78).

Anger is a powerful emotion – we cannot simply stop it when we feel it. Often our anger is a signal about something happening to us (or someone we are responsible for) that is unfair or unjust. While we should never deny, or stifle, this emotion, we do need to learn how to understand our anger and communicate our anger (as teacher–leaders) in assertive but not destructive ways (Chapter 6).

Good teachers *must be in control* at all times (of their classes …)

While it is obviously crucial that a teacher is able to lead, guide and manage the teaching, learning and behaviour *contexts* in their classrooms, they – obviously – cannot control all behaviours at all times. Yet I've heard this statement (and its variants) made many times by teachers. The case examples given earlier of secondary behaviours (students' reactive sighing, whining, tut-tutting, eyes raised to the ceiling, overt frowning, averted eye contact …) are a significant cause for stress in some teachers. They want to control these aspects of behaviour – as it were – because the children *shouldn't* 'frown', 'pout', 'sulk' like that!

In such discipline exchanges, such a belief will stifle the teacher's ability to utilise appropriate tactical ignoring, selective attention, directed choices, take-up time, etc. (Chapter 7). The demanding belief directly affects emotional arousal, reaction and reasoning. To lead, guide, clarify consequences, to assert, is different from holding oneself responsible for controlling others, and to be *able* to control others. Some teachers easily resort to self-blame if they 'lose control' of a situation (or a class, pages 9, 10). Some teachers will blame the students (or even parents) for behaving in ways resistant to 'teacher control'. It is often only in a calmer, more supportively collegial reflection that such an insistent belief is seen for what it is – unrealistic, self-defeating and inherently stressful.

The reason my colleagues and I spend so much time on reflecting on the importance of a discipline plan (Chapter 7) is that such planning enables a more realistic understanding of how we can lead so as to enable students' self-control – instead of taking unrealistic responsibility to control 'all' elements of behaviour at all times in a class.

Emotional habits

What my colleagues and I have learned is to recognise the often 'involuntary' nature of frustration and anger in discipline transactions.

- We discussed imagining the typical situations in which we got frustrated (and, at times, angry); those behaviour issues (and even particular students) that lowered our tolerance to frustration.

- We even tried to write out how we interpreted such situations – what we typically 'said to ourselves' – where we could remember (!) Often colleagues said – it was after the event – that the demanding thinking about what *'should'* and *'shouldn't be'* often came out.

- We then tried to re-imagine the same situations with a *different thinking pattern* – less demanding, more preferential and realistic. Is my demanding thinking – in these contexts – affecting, even stifling what I actually do when I seek to manage difficult behaviours? (well yes, often). I enjoy respect; respect is worth having. That's reasonable, realistic – but it's pointless to *demand* respect (or plead for it!). Respect has to be earned by the kind of teacher–leader we choose to be. For *mutual* respect to occur with our students (and even our colleagues) we need to model it, to live it. Our respectful leadership, our ability to engage students in thoughtful and positive learning experiences, our consistency and fairness in our management and discipline will all enable that *mutual* respect.

  The characteristic explanatory style of '*I must* be in control at all times' was the early one we disputed (page 49). Once exposed, we began to realise it's unrealistic, and it's impossible self-demand. (Bernard and Joyce, 1984, Seligman, 1991, Rogers, 2002 and 2011).

- We then explored the sorts of teacher leadership behaviours, even specific language cues, we could use. This planning and 're-imagining' was an important part of shared professional reflection and skill development (Chapter 7).

As one colleague said, 'Do you know it's kind of easier to say the first thing that comes into your guts!' We were all learning to bring some voluntary, some conscious, focus back to *the links between emotion* (how we felt in given discipline contexts) and what we were *characteristically* doing in those contexts (our approach, our language, *how we progressed such transactions* and so on as in the case of Julie) (page 46).

What we found time and time again was that when we learned to *interpret* discipline situations differently (particularly how we perceived 'secondary behaviours') and learned to reframe our discipline language (almost a cognitive scripting at first) – then we felt better in those same discipline settings (Chapter 7). We not only felt better – less stressed – we also felt more 'in control' – as it were. It was not an issue of being *in control of the students* but *in control of how we progressed the typical discipline transactions we were facing.* In that sense it was about our own self-control in relationship to others.

We also challenged some of our characteristic thinking habits such as ' ... students shouldn't answer back ... or defy us ...' Well, maybe students shouldn't answer back, argue or defy, and maybe they wouldn't – in an ideal world – if they had better social skills, a more supportive home life; if they didn't need to use attentional and power-seeking behaviours to cope with insecurity and gain a sense of 'social place' – *but many students do behave this way.* This is the reality we have to address and manage, and work within as teachers.

If I *demand* students that respect me (when they don't); if I *demand* obedience (when I don't get it); if I believe *I must control them* (when there are clearly many elements and factors in a lesson I can't *directly* control, and I certainly cannot, directly, control students) then I'll only be more stressed. My leadership behaviour will be adversely affected because I am making demands that my social reality will not accede to. *I* make the very demands that contribute to *my* stress – it is not the social reality alone that is always the 'stressful culprit'. The *way* we think, too, can be habitual for good or for ill.

Ovid (the Roman poet) gave us a psychological axiom: 'Habits change into characters.'[1] That includes 'thinking habits'.

Our explanatory style[2]

We all use internal dialogue (self-talk). Sometimes it's active and conscious – even formatively helpful. At other times it seems to dart about all over the place taking us nowhere helpful. In one of Satre's novels the main character, Mathieu, describes his thought as 'timorous – darting into his mind (like) the furtive vivacity of a fish.'[3]

Inner speech is a critical feature in self-awareness, motivation and sense of self (and self-esteem). Inner speech also has an 'instrumental and self-guiding function'. (Bernard and Joyce, 1984 page 23). Inner speech is also an essential feature of interpretive coping in stressful contexts. Self-talk (like any talk) will better serve *our sense of self* if it's realistic.

How do you characteristically – typically – explain particularly stressful events to yourself?

NB Throughout this book I often use the adverb *characteristically*:

- To indicate the clear difference between what we say to ourselves (or others) on our better-than-average days and what we say on our 'bad days'. Hopefully we don't *always* use stupid, unrealistic, *over*rated, overblown, illogical – even irrational – self-talk.

- The bad-day syndrome – these are days when we manage ourselves and others ineffectively, poorly – perhaps badly. That's – most often – when we're tired, overburdened, at the end of our tether. On these days we may be using unhelpful, unrealistic, illogical, even demanding self-talk. That's our 'bad days'. These 'bad days' are hopefully not *characteristic* to how we explain our stressful realities.

What I'm advocating in this chapter – indeed the whole book – is that of developing a *characteristic* 'explanatory style' that is realistic with regard to how we cope with our social and psychological reality, and of developing a *characteristic* behaviour leadership practice based on a conscious sense of positive practices and skills. These skills include *learning to think more realistically* (with appropriate optimism) when we are under stress.

Martin Seligman's groundbreaking research into 'learned helplessness'(1970, 1975) indicates that the *characteristic* way we explain stressful events has significant implications for our mental, psychological and even physical health. Seligman's research has pursued how our explanatory style affects our emotional well-being and our coping ability. He initially coined the now well-known pattern of behaviour called 'learned helplessness'. *Learned* helplessness arises when one characteristically believes, evaluates and explains stressful events in dimensions such as permanence, pervasiveness and personalisation: 'It's *just me* ... (or it's *just them* ...)'; 'I *never* get it right ...'. 'I *always* fail ...', 'It will *last forever* ...', 'It will *affect everything* I do ...'.

Seligman (1991) has noted that when scanning the contours and contexts of one's stressful experiences, some people latch on to the most permanent and pervasive explanations for their stress – it's *me*, it will last *forever*, it will *affect everything* I do.

Seligman argues that we need to learn to catch ourselves thinking; to be aware of, and to learn, what it is we characteristically say during (and more commonly after) stressful episodes. Are the sorts of things I say actually helping me to realistically and reasonably cope with (my) stressful reality?

What is the likely outcome, the consequence of *this type of thinking* I currently and characteristically hold?

- 'I *always* muck up ...'
- '*All* the students here are awful ...'

- 'Children *should* respect me'
- '*No one* cares in this place'
- 'I'll *never* be able to manage that class … '
- 'I *should* be in control at all times …'

Reality – of course – is much more ambiguous than such 'explanations' as those noted above. Such an explanatory style (*'always …', 'last forever …','never be able …', 'affect everything …'*) overrates the effects of stressful and bad events. The excessive demands (*should, mustn't*) will easily exacerbate how I respond (or more commonly react) when they are not as I demand they should (or shouldn't) be. Seligman has argued that when a person *tends* to explain bad and stressful things/events this way, they are actually at risk of depression when bad events occur.

If – for example – you face a breakdown in a relationship, there may be a variety of reasons. If it is explained as something stable and internal ('I *always* muck up, *always* end up like …') then it is likely that the individual will expect it to happen again – showing signs of helplessness in future relationships ('learned'). It is not *only* a matter of poor 'choices', but also *how we choose to think* when bad and stressful events happen. If we then explain the stressful and bad event as *global* (rather than as a specific) – 'I'm *incapable* of doing anything right …' – then we're likely to expect bad outcomes in many areas of our life and we'll feel even more helpless. If we explain it as internal (only) – 'It was *all* my fault …' – then there is likely to be a lowered self-esteem and a lowered ability to cope.

Seligman's *optimistic explanatory style* acknowledges situational (and specific) annoyance, frustration, failure and pain as a feature of normal human reality but challenges global, *overly* internal, lasting and abiding explanations for stressful and bad events in our daily living and work.

> *Failure makes everyone momentarily helpless, it's like a punch in the stomach. It hurts but the hurt goes away – for some people almost instantly … for others the hurt lasts, it seethes, it roils, it congeals into a grudge … they remain helpless for days or perhaps months, even after small setbacks. After major defeats they may never come back.*

(1991: page 45)

Psychological junk mail

After a particularly difficult class, David sat and mused, 'I know I should be better prepared (!) I know I *shouldn't* scream at them – I've given up trying to be reasonable. Why should I get a rotten and awful Year 8 like these! I'll *never* be able to manage them … It's terrible!'

David's frustration is natural – so are his musings. Part of the problem with his musings is their relationship to his sense of isolation and comparison – almost always comparing himself to other more 'successful' teachers – 'I'll *never* be as good as ...'.

Talking with David, I frequently heard *loaded statements* such as 'I'll *never* ...', 'I *always* ...', 'I *should* be able to ...', 'I *can't* ...', 'I *shouldn't* get angry ...', 'Others will think *I'm a failure* ...', '*No one* cares ...'.

● We agreed it was a challenging class – I know, I'd taught them. David agreed that it was really only a small percentage of students who were particularly difficult and, at times, challenging. He began to realise he was rating the whole class by the behaviour of this small percentage of students. As Seligman (1991) argues, 'It doesn't make sense to base my worth as a teacher on a small percentage of students' (page 279).

● We agreed that it would take time, effort *and colleague support* to *refocus our* effort, planning and leadership of the class.

● It was also important to work through his *characteristic explanatory style*; to gently dispute the assumptions behind his thinking and encourage a more realistic, and hopeful, 'explanatory style' about his teaching reality.

● We also needed to work on his leadership approach in his classes – this included language skills, particularly in discipline contexts (Chapter 7).

We can't always change external realities (one's class, one's teaching requirements, etc.) – we can, however, do something about *the way we think about that reality* and (then), with colleague support, more optimistically address and *reframe* that reality.

● 'OK – yes I haven't planned as well as I could – what can I do, what do I need to do to improve things?'

● 'Yes, they're a very noisy class and I've shouted a lot *and* got angry – yes, *sometimes* I have got it wrong. So what can I do to change the way I begin each lesson and focus the class and the more challenging individuals?'. The reframing of our characteristic thinking also enables and motivates what we then do to bring about change in our practice.

● 'It's annoying – yes, at times it's stressful – to have those four periods a week with 8D ... however, other teachers teach them too. It's difficult, it is stressful – *it's not actually terrible*. What can I learn in discussion with them?' What support can I reasonably expect from my colleagues? (See David's letter that follows.)

This disputing of *global, abiding, loaded* and, at times, *demanding* patterns of thinking was a significant factor in David's ongoing leadership of that very challenging class in particular and of his teacher leadership in general.

When we learn to rephrase our self-talk we are beginning to re-map our reality – not deny it or pretend it's not stressful (when it clearly is). If we do nothing about our *characteristic explanatory style*, our working beliefs – we may only half do the job.

David became much more consciously aware of how he explained and evaluated his teaching reality and coupled with colleague support – over several months – saw a change in attitude and behaviour, even to the point where students noticed – and commented (positively) on how things were going with their teacher. I know, I was there.

This is an excerpt from David's letter.

I've had some problems with quite inappropriate emotions and classroom discipline. I was experiencing excessive frustration, anxiety and even anger at various times.

Thankfully my classes are no longer places where heated confrontations are common. I've learned a number of things in this last twelve months that have changed my thinking, my teaching and discipline.

- My 'beliefs' were causing my stress. I used to say 'I was hopeless' – rating myself. I used to demand obedience from my students ('you should obey me'). I used to insist on 'winning' ('I must win in my discipline'). I've since adopted more reasonable 'beliefs' that have helped me to engage student cooperation rather than obedience.

- I've also begun to understand the goals of some children's disruptive behaviour – why children seek attention and power. This has helped me to see it's not all personal (against me) and it's helped me to plan my discipline so that it's more effective. I no longer see myself as the 'victim'. The students can't simply *make* me upset – I too have a contribution to make.

- In my discipline I've moved from a more *control/punishment* perspective to try to develop self-control and respect for rights in my students. I now think about my actions in discipline situations, and *plan for when I have to discipline*. In this I am able to respond rather than react. My students also grow by making choices about both their behaviour and its consequences.

- I've set clear, fair rules and consequences with my students and I have less conflict – the rights of both teacher and student are now protected by these rules, stated clearly and positively. The rules derive from commonly accepted values such as human worth, cooperation, communication and self-direction.

- Lastly, peer support has really helped. I have listened to my colleagues, their ideas and advice; they have especially helped when I've had to use time-out procedures.*

In summary, my stress level is more under control because I have adopted new beliefs and new practices. I have been able to reassess my teaching skills by

> using a peer-support approach and learning to take a middle path – one of being assertive, actively resolving conflict with thoughtful planning, not swinging 'wildly' from one extreme to the other (from passively giving in to students to actively confronting them).

*David's need to use time-out significantly reduced over the ensuing months.

Positive disputation

One of the skills David developed (as he notes) was to challenge and dispute those 'beliefs' that enabled a more positive behaviour leadership in his teaching practice.

Disputational thinking is a skill we develop that enables us to:

- *Stop rating ourselves* – 'I must be thoroughly competent in order to be worthwhile … I must be able to control my classes … (page 49). If I'm not I'll feel awful and I won't be able to stand it.' A perfectionist stance is often expressed like this – it is not merely unrealistic *and very stressful,* it's also unreasonable. Yet I've heard it many, many times from colleagues.

  Our self-worth is not dependent *only* on our competence. This is – in part – the problem of rating and comparing ourselves to those we perceive as being more successful and better than us. Competence is a necessary aspect of our professionalism – it does not, however, define our worth as a person. To say we 'can't stand it' (when we *can*) is also directly feeding into the normative stress. We are 'standing it' – maybe poorly, badly, unhelpfully – but we're 'standing it'. How can we 'stand it' more effectively?

- *Learn to live with inevitable irritations and frustrations* – 'the slings and arrows …' (page xii). This doesn't mean we accede to the 'inevitable', it means we learn to live with it and change it where we can and avoid letting what is inevitable (in daily and normative stress) overwhelm us. It also means we accept our humanity and our fallibility (and others) without merely acquiescing to it!

- Resist the stupid *demands* we make on reality when we say things '*must be …*' – when they clearly are not. We cannot merely make social reality conform to our demands – 'children *must* respect me because I'm a teacher …', 'I *enjoy* respect, and I'll seek to lead my students in a way that is likely to engage and invite respect' is a more realistic and achievable belief. We also need to be aware of the sorts of practices and skills likely to engender respect and cooperation in our teacher leadership and our relationship with our students (see the case studies on pages 10, 32, 44, 46 and Chapter 7).

- Describe and evaluate normally stressful events as just that – *normally stressful*, difficult, annoying, inconvenient and frustrating – rather than 'terrible' and 'catastrophic'.

To talk about cognitive *disputation* and *reframing* is not mere clever psychological labelling. Talking, even self-talking, is an action, and actions have effects. Inaccurate, inflexible, overly and *characteristically* global – and negative – self-talk may become a habit. If not addressed, it may become so characteristic that it is no longer a conscious activity. And while it is in the past, over time, that experience (and habit) have interred such self-talk, it is in the *present* that we are using it and it is in the present that we need to consciously readdress, dispute and reframe our self-talk.

Mentally kicking oneself

In one of my classes, I'd arrived late. It's only the second time this year I've been late as a specialist teacher (grade 4). The class was already 'hyped-up' (they always are after Phys. Ed. – then I have to teach music!). To top it off I'd forgotten the worksheets so that made me more flustered and – blast it! – the deputy principal came in (had he been watching?). He could see I was hassled – surely! All he was interested in was asking if I'd finished my reports! And the look he gave me when he left …

If this teacher then adds to this experience the self-talk of 'I'm an idiot – I wrecked that lesson and he'll think I'm stupid – a failure. It's *awful*.' He takes the *perceived* failure (and the *feelings* of failure) and *turns them into residual self-judgement*.

Edwards (1977) calls this 'mentally kicking oneself' – my colleagues and I call it 'psychological junk mail'.

Learning to fail meaningfully means that we acknowledge where and how we failed – and, yes, it is *unpleasant* (page 53). If, however, we add to our mistakes and failures a *residual* litany of negative self-talk – 'I *shouldn't* have …, I *never* get it right …, I'm a *failure* …' – this has the effect of strengthening the very unpleasant feeling of failure. This has several outcomes:

- We feel worse than we need to feel – *naturally* we'll feel down and put out; we don't need to compound such feelings with 'psychological junk mail'.
- We'll find it harder to cope with the *specific* failure now and will be less energised to improve in areas where we may be struggling. We fail – we all do. When we fail it doesn't mean we *are* a failure, as if our essential 'being-ness' is failure.
- It is important, also, not to pretend that the unpleasant thing (or experience) didn't happen. It did – and it was *very* uncomfortable, unpleasant or worse.

We need to acknowledge the unpleasantness of the emotion, *and the failure*, without the self-downing.

● We need to challenge and dispute 'with ourselves' when we recognise the association of negative emotions and any *recurrent* negative self-talk when things don't go as we'd hoped or planned. The basis for our self-disputation is the dose of reality we bring to our perceptions, compared with the overgeneralisations and demands in our thinking.

We're likely to be using such negative self-talk when we're experiencing negative, upsetting emotions towards someone (even ourselves) or about some situation.

Try 'tuning-in the cognitive dial' as it were. Maybe we can't always tune into the first few negative thoughts but we can learn to take control of an *emergent* 'pattern' of thinking (Rogers, 2006).

This is a skill; the skill of 'catching' the thoughts –as it were – and stopping and checking what we're saying to ourselves.

Catch – stop – check – dispute – rephrase – refocus

This is what Albert Ellis and his colleagues called the 'ABC model of thinking', where the activity of disturbance or stress (A) has its emotional consequence (C) *affected* by (B) our 'rational' and 'irrational' beliefs that *intervene between* the (A) and the emotional consequence (C).

The B element – in such a framework of thought patterning – refers not only to thoughts we're thinking at a given moment but also to those thoughts we may not be immediately aware of 'as well as more abstract beliefs the individual may hold in general' (Bernard and Joyce, 1984, page 49). I recall hearing Albert Ellis speaking (back in the mid-1980s) describing this model of rational emotive therapy 'as simple as ABC' but that 'unfortunately *simple doesn't mean easy*!' We all know how to 'diet', to exercise (etc.) but it doesn't mean we will do it. What *we are able to do* is not the same as *whether* we can, or will, do it.

Ellis then went on to address the D and E (of his model) – the 'D' being the reasonable and realistic *disputation* we bring to the 'B' (the B beliefs we hold about the activating events A). It is the unrealistic and demanding nature of some beliefs that directly, and significantly, contribute to one's emotionally stressful consequences (C). Ellis argues that the skill of challenging faulty assumptions (he used the term 'irrational' beliefs) is the skill of learning to dispute their faulty *basis* (his D). When we do this, he argued, we will be less stressed and have more realistic and *enabling* consequences and behaviours. He called this *the effect* (E) arising from *disputation and reframing*. The 'effect' being a more reasonable, realistic way of thinking and addressing the activating events (or stressors) (A). For me (as an educator), this has an elegant simplicity. Life, of course, is not as simple as ABC even with the 'D' and 'E' added in! Ellis has, however, developed a practical, sensible framework of understanding about *how* we think that can enable us to cope with stressful reality more effectively. (See Bernard and Joyce, 1984; and Bernard, 1990.)

I am an educator – a teacher. I firstly see these thinking habits as skills that need to be understood – their meaning, their sense and application to our reality. We then need to learn how to apply those skills in our own daily reality. I know that one's private speech has a self-guiding and self-regulatory function as well as a maladaptive capacity to affect the degree of stress we experience. My colleagues and I have sought to bring these skills to our teaching reality to inform and enable our coping.

Contrast these phrasings:

- 'I *never* ...' with 'I *sometimes* ...' – so, what can I learn to do differently or more effectively and who can help?' 'I *always* fail ...' with 'I *sometimes* fail ... What can I learn from this?'

- '*Everybody* in this class is a ...' with '*Some* students are difficult and annoying *how can I better work with them* ... what will I need to do ...? *Most* of my students are reasonably cooperative and respond well to my leadership (well – most of the time!) What colleague assistance will help me to re-engage the less cooperative students?

- '*I've got a hopeless* class' with '*Most* of my class *are* cooperative and responsive'.

- 'This will *never* get better ...' with 'Things *can and will* get better *when* I ...'

- 'A good teacher *shouldn't* get angry ...' with 'A good teacher isn't perfect – I do get angry *sometimes* – it doesn't make me a bad teacher. What can I do in these situations where I get frustrated? What is it (in these situations) that lowers my tolerance to frustration? How can I communicate my frustration and anger in more effective ways? (page 77). How can I – then – address the issues of conflict when I'm calmer and more focused?

Reflection

Imagine your characteristic self-talk as a *realistic friend* (RF) or as a *personal and private critic* (PC).

PC: Loser! Can't you *ever* get it right! It *shouldn't* have happened this way! You *never* get it right! (generalised self-blame).

RF: Yes – I didn't get it right *this time*. I may well get it wrong from *time to time*. There *are* times I've got it right, many times. I did fail – *in this instance*. *It doesn't make me a failure*. I do feel uncomfortable; that's normal. Unpleasant but normal! If I haven't done the reasonable best I can do (or should have done) in this situation *what can I do to fix it*? (Is *that* possible, even in part?) *What can I do to improve things or make things better*? Is there anyone I can call on to help me? *Is there someone I need to apologise to – seek forgiveness from?* (Difficult as such a course is – it will always help.)

What can I learn from this?

PC: This *shouldn't* have happened to me. It's *not* fair! I *can't* stand it!

RF: OK; I *don't like* what happened. It *did* happen – *that's* the unpleasant reality. It's not a matter of whether I deserve it or not. It's happened *now*, so saying it 'shouldn't have' will only make it worse. It's *very uncomfortable* – but *it happened.* I can get over this; *uncomfortable* as I feel right now.

PC: You *should* be in control. You *should* have been able to do it! Good teachers *must be in control* ...!

RF: There are many things I can't control – *that's reality.* I do *sometimes* get angry. I doesn't make me a bad teacher. **Again** – what can I learn from this to enable me to move on ...?

That inner voice may often be unfairly critical – and unrealistic; but it can also be supportive and encouraging. It can also be self-deluding. In mentoring relationships we can learn to hear *realistic and non-judgemental feedback* from our colleagues (page 172). We can learn – from this – to be more honest, more fair and more helpful in how we see and interpret our reality to ourselves and about our professional leadership as a teacher–leader.

In my work as a colleague mentor these thinking skills form an integral part of behaviour leadership practices and skills.

The main reason for raising awareness about negative self-talk is that when we learn to catch ourselves thinking erroneously, globally or self-defeatingly *we can do something about that*. We simply can't control everything around us – we've all met the 'overcontrolling' personality; it's stressful just being around such a person. We can, however, learn to control that self-talk domain (upstairs) in our thinking – once we're more aware of how we *characteristically* think about stressful events. So, after your next lousy day, catch the *overly* negative thought (how you feel will often trigger such thoughts) and dispute them, reframe them and you won't feel *as* bad, *as* often for *as* long.

What we can/cannot control in our thinking: that first, and second and third thought

That first thought, that first negative thought: 'You idiot! *Why* did you do *that*?! Say that?!', 'Can't you *ever* get it right!?'

That *first* negative thought just seems to 'come' into 'our head'. Those *subsequent* thoughts – though – do not have to *repeat* those first incessantly negative thoughts. We can learn to check the progress of those first thoughts – to scan for reality and reasonableness. We can learn to check the *global, demanding, unrealistic* tenor and focus of those first thoughts.

What makes this a challenge is that when we are saying such things (as above) we're also *feeling* 'bad' about those things (i.e. because we failed). The negative demanding and, at times, unrealistic thinking and feeling seem *inextricably* connected, proving each other right.

When we're in a stressful situation (and *after* a stressful situation) and because of the degree of stress and tension, the recurrent thoughts of, 'I *can't stand* this!', 'It will *never* change …', 'It will *always* be like this!', 'I *should* be able to …!' make us doubly stressed.

It is possible, though, to challenge the first and second thoughts so that the explanation of failure or defeat doesn't end up in a self-defeating cognitive loop– 'I *always* …'. I don't 'always', I *sometimes* … perhaps even *often* but not *always*. What can I do to break the old pattern of thinking and behaviour and effect new patterns of thinking and behaviour? What are the skills I need to learn? Who can help me? When we easily, and repeatedly, say to ourselves, '*No one* can help …' '*Nothing* will help …' we increase the already negative spiral of hurt feelings. Further we are demotivated by both *how we think* (how we 'explain' our reality) and how we feel. There is always someone who can help and something that can be done to help and improve things. 'It's *impossible* …' – it's not impossible, it's difficult.

We tend to 'move' in the direction of our current thought – the more negatively insistent that thought (and its attendant self-talk) the more likely that our cognition, emotion *and behaviour* will reflect that self-talk.

Martin Luther (the sixteenth-century German reformer) is reputed to have said, 'Temptation is like a bird flying over your head. You can't stop it flying over your head. You can stop it *making* a nest in your hair.' I've emphasised the two main verbs to accentuate the point.

Pablo Casals is reputed to have said, 'It's impossible; let's take the first step.'[4]

When we self-assess: that inner voice

When we talk about monitoring that second and third thought, we are actually doing something constructive. If, for example, we've upset someone (said the wrong thing) we've failed. When we apologise and seek to repair and rebuild, we've done something – perhaps the best we can (assuming we've been honest and genuine).

We might then say, 'Well – I have done all I can.' That's probably true. If, however, we *keep* blaming ourselves by saying (to ourselves), 'Well – I *shouldn't have* said that – or done that …' (when we did actually do, or say that …), those recurrent thoughts are also within our domain. We, too, have to help ourselves repair/ rebuild. When we find ourselves blaming ourselves by saying, 'I *shouldn't* have!', we need to confront that second and third recurrent thought and say, 'Well, I did apologise, I did make amends – as much as I could … I have acknowledged I did the silly … the wrong thing … Yes I *did* fail … *however* I can now move on …'.

The *however* is our breaking of that cognitive cybernetic loop of 'I *shouldn't* have …', '*I'm* stupid …', '*I'm a failure*'.

Having grown up with others' approval of us – in all sorts of ways – from parents, friends, teachers, bosses, colleagues, etc., we may, perhaps, have got used to the critical voice (page 59). Hopefully, too, we have had positive, honest and useful voices to enable our growth.

Our internal voice can – so easily – reflect those less helpful, at times strident, carping and unreasonably critical voices. Having sat with many, many teachers in informal and formal mentoring contexts, that self-critical voice is not an uncommon feature of their stress – that easy self-judgement when they compare themselves to more 'expert' colleagues.

> ### If only … (!)
>
> Harvard psychology professor Ellen Langer (2000) notes, 'People who are waiting to live [*sic*] put off today in exchange for tomorrow. As soon as the children are grown I'll …' (page 86). When we evaluate *the present* it is, itself, a state of mind – it can obviously be broadly positive or broadly negative. 'That doesn't mean the consequences are not real. It means that the consequences for any action depend on the view we take of them. Actions and events do not come with evaluations – we impose them on our experience and, in doing so, create our experiences of the event.' (ibid)

Learned optimism

I have a mistrust of the *overoptimistic* – the bright, breezy, everything-will-be-alright disposition. The perpetual smile.

Many aspects of our life, and our profession, are inherently stressful – denial and playing them down, 'Well it doesn't matter – it will get better', can appear tactless, even heartless. As is the 'bright' and 'breezy' optimist who says 'all we need to do is have the right attitude!' (page xvii). Seligman (1991) argues that becoming a realistic optimist consists not of learning to be more selfish and self-assertive … overbearing … but of learning a set of skills about how to talk to yourself when you suffer a personal defeat (page 207).

Reflection: Habits of thinking

In Aristotle's *Ethics* he makes the point that 'it is difficult to change a habit ... for the reason that habit is a second nature.' He then quotes Evenus, 'Habit, my friend, is practice long pursued that at last becomes the man himself.' (Book 7, Chapter 10).

Can you remember *learning* to tie your shoelaces? (left over right or ?); putting on a tie (for those of us who still wear one); combing your hair in front of a mirror, buttoning up (or down) a shirt or blouse?

We probably can't actually remember the *learning to do* part because now it's habit. So too with our thinking habits and their role in managing our stress. It starts with understanding how we *characteristically* think when we're under pressure and how we *characteristically* think before and after stressful situations. What do we actually say to ourselves? How aware are we of the way we typically *perceive* and *rate* the contours of stress in our life?

Summary

Thinking about our stressful reality is also part of managing our stressful reality. We do this more effectively when we:

● *Learn* to live with the inevitable irritations, privations and stressors in life and work – 'the thousand natural shocks that flesh is heir to ...' (page xii).

● Acknowledge and accept the reality that the work we do – as teachers – will incur stress. This is natural, normal. Learn to distinguish between a normative and a more extreme stressful experience and how to address, respond and deal with it more effectively.

● Stop rating ourselves unrealistically, unfairly, too harshly ('*I'm* hopeless ...', '*I'll* never...')

● Accept fallibility in self and others, without merely acquiescing to that fallibility, and being willing to work for improvement.

● Resist the stupid demands that things *must be* as I say they must be, when they are clearly not.

● *Evaluate* the difficult and *normally* stressful events *as* difficult, annoying, inconvenient and frustrating, rather than terrible and catastrophic.

● Fail meaningfully – see the mistake and failure for what it is: *a* failure, *a* mistake, *a* temporary setback. Avoid letting thinking patterns go into *negative replay*, and 'psychological junk mailing' ('I *always* fail ...'). We need to track out of that negative thinking spiral – and reframe – so we can learn from those things that occasion our stress, our setback, failure and struggle ... (page 57).

- *Challenge and reframe* the demanding and 'catastrophic' thinking patterns when they make insistent and unrealistic inroads into your thinking. Disputational thinking (page 56) makes it possible to use the energy and emotion occasioned by stress to constructively refocus the problem and work on ways to cope more effectively.

- Accept that we cannot always address our stress (and the conditions that occasion our stress) by ourselves, alone. Colleague support is essential.

Notes

1. This is an axiom attributed to the Roman poet Ovid (438 BC to AD 17).

2. This is a term coined by the American psychologist Professor Martin Seligman. See *Learned Optimism* (1991).

3. In Sartre, J.P. (1945) *L'Age de Raison (The Age of Reason)* Penguin Books (page 13).

4. I heard this on a *Late Night Live* broadcast (on the Radio National programme: Australian Broadcasting Commission) from the radio commentator and author Phillip Adams.

Anxiety and worry

What this chapter will explore and develop:

- The nature of anxiety and worry, and anxiety and panic
- The difference between worry and concern – how to better use our concern when under stress
- Reframing our thinking around the nature of normal worries
- The physiology of anxiety and its learned associations
- How we can manage our natural anxiety in the classroom

Anxiety and worry

When sorrows come, they come not in single spies, but in battalions.

Hamlet (IV: 5: 78)

There is a normal, and natural aspect to anxiety in our human experience. Anxiety is a perfectly normal response to stressful situations (particularly those outside the range of our regular experience). When there is significant stress and danger, our anxiety alerts us and motivates the 'fight-or-flight' response – our ancient, hereditary, biological drive (page 20). That emotive state doesn't tell us, however, what to do with that 'alerting' drive. Our experience, skill, maturation, opportunity and necessity *and* what we say to ourselves when we're alerted will determine how effectively we address our anxiety.

'*What if I can't* manage that awful class *again*? *I'll never* be able to get through to them! Other teachers cope, *why can't I*? I've got them four periods a week and it's only term one! Should I say anything? What will my colleagues think of me? *I don't know if I can stand it …*'

Worry and anxiety are 'psychological bedfellows'. Our mind churns away – like above. The thoughts, at nanosecond speed, seem to race and chase each other. At other times our thoughts are like a cybernetic loop – and they go nowhere! It often gets to the point where we start to worry about (our) *worry itself.*

When you think about it worry has very little to do with the actual *present* (except to make it more stressful and miserable). Worry (as an emotional/cognitive activity) often focuses on the past (immediate, or even remote, past) or the future (the next class, next week …). Worry *dwells* and *churns over* past situations, past mistakes – what was done or said, or not done …; what was done to us; how we were treated. *All those stress hormones again.* As noted earlier the 'stress hormones' start 'overworking' (page 22) – but please don't worry about this!

The worry cycle

The cycle of worry often exacerbates the initial problem or concern – this, in turn, creating secondary problems. These problems can range from difficulty with, or even inability to do, constructive work through to health-related problems.

The 'emotional drives' within the worry episode – evoking the anxiety – often move us away from meaningful and helpful action on the issue, concerns or problem. Instead the emotion of worry is, itself, enervating and physically draining. Worry allows (*unthinkingly*) the problem to take on *disproportionate* dimensions. Even before the stressful occasion occurs we are investing time and emotional energy on 'what *might* be', '*could* be …', '*probably will be*!'. 'I *won't* be able to cope …', 'I'll *just be the same* …', 'It'll *never* change …'

> NB This kind of worry is more than 'stage fright'; and we're not actors by the way.
>
> I sometimes hear university lecturers (and consultants) say, 'to be a good teacher you need to be a good actor'.

We're not actors (unless you're in a drama production *per se*). An 'actor' is someone playing a part/role that is, normally, not themselves. We do need to project ourselves into a teaching/learning dynamic when we teach and lead our students. In that sense our use of voice, manner, and how we present and motivate are all features of our craft. That's not acting – it is using, and developing, our skills as a teacher to connect, engage, motivate and encourage our students.

Concern

Unlike *concern*, worry is wasted emotional energy. The German word for worry (*würgen*) means 'to strangle' or 'throttle' – all the energy (of worry) is churning the emotions, 'whirling' our thoughts. Little or no energy is directing the body (or mind) to do something constructive. And even if we cannot directly do something to change things, we can *learn to think about the issue* differently. Thinking is doing; thinking is also an *action*. *It matters, though, how we think when we feel worried and anxious.* As I write this, I am immediately aware of how difficult this is at times. Often we're not aware of how unfocused we are when we worry – that inert and anxious wasting of energy.

Concern, however, is active and constructive. Take the example of worry and the future – we worry about our finances, the bills, our health, our work, our relationships. We worry about our work as teachers. We worry about what could, should, didn't do, or what might happen tomorrow or next week. Have you ever said after a particularly stressful episode or event, 'Why did I ever worry about *that*?' We can actually do nothing directly about the future. It's not here yet! Yes, of course, we need to plan reasonably for the future (including that next lesson). The future, however, is the future and, however tautological that sounds, worrying about it won't help. Concerned planning and application of necessary action *now* can positively affect the future, like a decent exercise walk *today* (and reasonably regular ongoing walks) can affect our future health. Thoughtful lesson planning and behaviour plans (Chapter 7), and basic organisation of our lesson plans (within a unit of work) can positively affect our future teaching. Our best planning – supported planning – will always help; that's concern at work *now*. Worry is trying to *overimagine* and even 'control' the future – an overinvestment of emotional energy in what *might* happen. None of us can control the future; we can, however, bring reasonable control over our choices *now*. *This also includes what we choose to think when worry starts.*

Life often has enough problems for today – for now. As Jesus said, 'Don't worry about tomorrow. Tomorrow can take care of itself. One day's trouble is enough for one day.' This is more than stoic reality. Jesus is not saying don't be concerned about, or plan for, tomorrow. He's saying, 'Don't *worry* about (it) ...'[1]

- There are often enough problems for one day – particularly as a teacher. Make a list at the end of the day – it's often surprising how we cope so well with so much that we may have *over*worried about.

- We obviously don't *have* yesterday, we certainly don't *have* tomorrow but we *do have today.* Today is the only place, space and reality where we can actually *live*. Investing fruitless worry into (or over) the past *or* the future will lessen the necessary effort and energy we need for now – *today*.

- The more we *worry* about tomorrow or yesterday, the more we invest unhelpful (and unproductive) energy in a non-existent timeframe.

- The focus and energy of worry is, essentially, impractical. If we have behaved poorly – even wronged someone – this is in part remediable (at least on our part). If we have done – regarding the past – all we could, or should, have done then we can do no more except to move on (page 60). Perhaps we may have learned from past mistakes and behaviour – that is to be hoped.

- Worry often stifles action. Remember when you sat all those exams? Contrast the sitting and worrying about the looming exams *and* how it not only made us feel worse; we actually didn't study – *we worried* instead. There is a sense in which we can't actually study *and* worry at the same time. When we studied we, at least, applied our concern to what was needed; that was productive (and I hoped it helped when the exams came!)

Something can always be done – even if that something involves *how we think about the situation.* Our attitude, mindset and characteristic self-talk can enable a different, more realistically positive, more hopeful response *in* the situation. We have a choice not to think about the issue negatively and self-destructively. This is not a normal thinking habit for most of us – *it can be learned.*

OK – so how do I stop being concerned?
Well, we can't – we can't turn off concern or the feelings associated with concern. We can distract or divert the concern to essential action (depending on the degree of seriousness of the issue). What triggers concern is, generally, a valid human emotion and need. Concern focuses that energy necessary to address the need.

The fundamental difference between worry and concern is the direction or – more appropriately – the *redirection* of our psychological and physical energies. In that sense we can't be both worried and concerned – when we're concerned.

Describe, define, the shape of the issue
While it's pointless worrying about several things at once, it can help to focus by starting with a manageable issue or concern. Sitting down with a trusted, supportive colleague can help the refocusing process. It can help to articulate, define and delineate the shape and boundaries of the things we've been worrying about. We then need to take necessary, reasonable and possible action. Even if we cannot always *directly* change the situation and circumstance, *we can change how we think about it.* That kind of thinking is also enabling. A significant factor in reducing and managing anxiety is to develop a realistic plan for that which we easily get anxious about.

A good deal of my work involves working alongside colleagues whose anxieties, even fears, are affected by issues of management and discipline. In Chapter 7 the issue of developing a discipline plan is discussed at some length and in Chapter 9 the hard-to-manage class is discussed within collegially supportive approaches. Significant features of these plans are practices and skills we can develop to increase our confidence and ability in stressful situations.

Worry may become such a *habit* with some people – a habit that stifles reasonable and helpful action. Worry may, perhaps, even be self-pity masquerading as concern. Again, talking things through with a trusted colleague will always help.

Anxiety and worry: realistic, reframing thinking

- 'When I face these difficult issues, problems and people – and face them I must (it is self-defeating to just retreat or 'run away') then I at least also need to prepare for that facing of the issue ... I can get support for that, from colleagues *who have been there* ...' 'Even if I can't change these stressful situations, if I'm well enough (and with support) I can work on ways to address the hard class, the difficult student, the work schedule ...' (Chapter 7 and Chapter 9).

- 'There are many things, in our profession, that we can't directly control or directly change – I can learn to change the way I *think about* and *respond to* those things' (page 63).

- 'I can't directly change the past, though I need to address those issues, circumstances and actions that have hurt others and myself. I can do that – I can do that now. It's difficult, but with support I can take the necessary steps. *The way I think* about the past, and even the present, is under my control. The way I think *now*, and regularly, can enable me to feel more positively in control of how I manage myself and others – *now*.'

- 'I cannot make every student (or colleague) like me or respect me. While it's pleasant and enjoyable to be liked and respected, *that's something that is earned over time*. While I'm thankful for respect, liking and approval, there will be times when some students, parents and colleagues do not show such. That's disappointing – it doesn't mean I'm not a person of worth. My self-worth does not depend on others' approval' (page 25).

It's more than a deep breath when you're anxious and tense

When we are anxious, or angry, our breathing pattern will often speed up. There is a comfortable and an uncomfortable way to breathe when this happens. The uncomfortable way is rapid, shallow breathing, which only uses the upper part of the lungs and results in the inhalation of too much oxygen. Rapid and shallow breathing is a natural (unlearned) response to exertion and to stress. (Kennerly, 2009, pages 86–88).

You may have been told that you need to breathe deeply when you feel anxious and tense – however, you end up 'overbreathing'. It's better to breathe *calmly*, with a *conscious* muscle relaxing – almost a dropping of the shoulders. It also helps to sit up straight on a chair. As you breathe in through the nose – hold (for a count of three) then breathe out (through the mouth) to a count of three; *consciously* concentrating on normal – small – breaths. Some practitioners suggest we do this 'exercise' several times a day (obviously not in the middle of a lesson unless it's a skill you also want to teach your students).[2]

This is no 'new-age' practice; it is a conscious way of physiologically raising one's sense of bodily calmness. One of the books I've found particularly helpful in this area is *The Calm Technique* (Paul Wilson, 1985).

I have taught this approach to classroom groups, and – beyond initial giggles – it has always been well received. We breathe with the eyes closed and several times (count of three) – it seems easier with the eyes closed.

Another variation to this breathing 'exercise' is to add some tensing and releasing of the hands, and then lean forward in the seat to drop the arms by your side – relaxedly – and then sit back up again. Then we stand up and shake our hands (as if shaking off water droplets), shake the legs, stand relaxedly and breathe three or four breaths (to a count of three) – and *then* back to work.

These simple exercises are a way of *refocusing* tension (both cognitive and physical). See also Appendix 2.

You may also want to consider some relaxing classical music. Don Campbell (author of *The Mozart Effect)* notes that some forms of classical music can have a positive calming effect on both our perception and our physiology. My daughter (a primary teacher) would often play Mozart, Hayden, Bach pieces to her early years classes. They called it their 'thinking and relaxing' music.

Self-awareness of 'how we come across to others'

When we're very anxious (not merely nervous) our breathing can affect our voice so that it may become shrill, pitched high and paced too fast. The frustrating reality is that the more tense (and anxious) we are, the more tense and anxious we become.

Practising skills of voice projection and usage as well as the sort of postural relaxation that can signal our confidence (in front of others) will go a long way to reducing anxiety association about that central feature of our profession – the ability to teach and lead others.

These skills can be practised in safe settings with trusted colleagues. In those practice settings (see page 178) we can learn to be more consciously aware of how we breathe when we speak – even the pitch and variance in our voice, the pauses, our bodily posture. We can learn the difference between over (and under) projection of our voice, how we 'scan' the room (page 95), how we use our hands and bodily presence in the teacher–student context.

A good deal of our behaviour is 'communicated' subconsciously (as self) and others (students and colleagues) will pick it up clearly. They can read anxiety, indifference, respect, concern, trust, confidence, arrogance, care, etc. quickly (not always accurately – but quickly).

How we come across to others is an essential feature of our professional life, and while we're obviously not actors (page 66) we do need to pay attention to those characteristic aspects of non-verbal and verbal behaviours that can enhance and enable our leadership role. Every case study and case example in this book highlights these behaviours and how they operate in a dynamic way (rather than as isolated 'skills'). See also page 109 and Chapter 10.

Professional self-awareness in this area may be difficult on your own. Working with trusted colleagues in peer-support groups (page 15), in a mentoring setting (Chapter 10) even in role-play (page 178) can significantly help to build self-awareness, confidence and skill. I would particularly recommend Graham Welch's chapter on voice management in *the Teachers' Survival Guide* (not the most apt title!), Thody et al. (2000).

The physiology of stress: learned associations regarding anxiety

Anxiety can occur before we even walk into the classroom. The recent memories of stressful episodes in leading, teaching and managing the class rush back – we already feel the stress *even though we're not actually in the classroom at that point.*

There is a physiological and a psychological association at work here – and it is not always a 'conscious' association.

When I've sat with colleagues who are *naturally* anxious about having to face a difficult class, I can sense their perception of the looming challenge of facing *that* class again. I've felt that myself with challenging classes – I remember. The problem occurs when such feelings become debilitating, stifling our ability to think and manage the stressful context.

- *Already* they are feeling anxious, or even frightened.
- *Already* they are focusing on the perceived threat to their ability to lead, manage and cope.

- *Already* they are overestimating how bad, how stressful, it will be – 'Something bad is *bound* to happen … It *always* does.' Even when genuine support is offered they *under*estimate a colleague's ability to actually help; to actually enable them to see things and do things differently.

- *Already* their muscles are tensing – and remaining tense. They are 'locked' into an anxious frown and the more rapid breathing starts.

As Wehrenberg and Prinz (2007) note, 'The amygdala (that part of our brain associated with control of, particularly, impulse behaviour and survival) "learns" what is dangerous.[3] It learns from experience if sensory inputs are threatening or non-threatening. It very quickly forms associations between specific situations and pain, danger and negative outcome' (page 28).

So, the context and place where, and when, we believed we coped (or couldn't cope) with 8D – the noise, the faces, the physical space, the kinaesthetic tension – all associate such places and role demands as *very* stressful in our memory. However, that learning is not a permanently fixed learning. Those associations – originally occasioned by stressful episodes – can be unlearned and more positive and helpful associations relearned. That combination of challenging the frequent negative ruminations we have (when we think about *that* class, *that* student) and a willingness to pursue supportive colleague mentoring and skill development can enable a change in psychological and physiological associations (Chapter 10). The challenge is to take the professional risk of actively seeking colleague support to enable that process. This is worth it if we really want to continue in the profession of teaching.

Of course, if those stressful associations are chronic and in *any* sense debilitating, it is wise to take some leave before considering further options in your career as a teacher. After appropriate leave time, it can help to then plan out how best to re-enter your current school or, perhaps, seek an alternative teaching placement (pages 28, 29).

Anxiety and panic: 'I can't stand it!'

At its worst, this type of thinking occurs where the stress we experience arises from a feeling of powerlessness – we can't control the event, situation or circumstances.

It's a horrible feeling. It's the feeling that whatever we do, we won't be able to control the events creating the anxiety – or even control oneself in the stressful situation. This is particularly distressing in very challenging classroom situations where the class seems to be 'falling apart' and you are 'on your own' (as the only adult).

When anything like this does occur, it is crucial that the teacher seeks *immediate* colleague support. There needs to be in every school (not just the 'challenging schools') the collegial option of a staged time-out policy (page 124). Such options will even consider time-out for the teacher. This is addressed in Chapter 9 (pages 150–154).

Where the degree of anxiety – and even panic – is a frequent experience for a teacher, it is crucial that those who are aware of this extend not just sympathy and empathy to their colleague, but also link that colleague to structured colleague support options (page 141). Within the privacy of trusted collegial counsel, this may also occasion a recommendation for medical and professional counselling support (pages 28, 29).

Panic attacks[4]

These represent a physiological state – an episodic state – where one feels an overwhelming 'flight' response. The physiological feelings associated with panic attacks include a rapid heart rate, palpitations, rapid and shallow breathing, blood rushing to the extremities, and so on. I've talked with colleagues who felt that they were close to actually having a heart attack. In a 'normative' fight–flight response this would aid the *flight* from the stressful context, or taking the *fight* to the stressful context. It is not helpful to 'fight' or 'flight' though when one is required to lead a class; to conduct a morning assembly; when driving to school thinking about teaching and leading your class(es); follow up with challenging students; that difficult staff meeting or parent interview …

Panic attacks may be related to social anxiety disorder – the fear that one will be overwhelmed any minute or that others will evaluate us negatively and we will not be able to get over it.

If these symptoms and experiences are even reasonably frequent, it is crucial to get a medical assessment and support[5]. There may well be no medical reason for the above *symptoms* but even that assurance is crucial to one's ongoing sense of well-being.

While there is well-established medication support for panic/anxiety attacks, it is also crucial to have encouraging colleague support to explore any associated concerns or issues related to the context or relationships within which such attacks occur.

If a colleague breaks down …

It happens – I've seen colleagues walk out of a classroom in tears, in panic or in anger. It is essential we:

● Demonstrate our care and concern. We don't fudge, because we don't know why – *at that point* – *they left the classroom.*

- Encourage your colleague to go to a place of privacy where they can calm down and settle. Allow time for composure, tea and coffee.

- Reassure, asking, 'How can I help?' before you ask 'What happened?' I would advise that a female colleague be present if a female teacher is in distress.

Obviously after immediate support and follow-up we need to *then* work through the underlying issues to work on a longer-term plan to support the colleague. (See particularly Chapter 11)

Notes

1. Matthew's gospel, Chapter 6 (The New Testament).

2. See Jenny Rikards' excellent book – *Relaxation for Children* (ACER Press).

3. The amygdala (from Latin for 'almond') is located within the base of the *temporal lobe* in the brain. It is part of the *limbic* system. The role of the amygdala is significant in brain functioning and in discrimination about basic survival.

4. An interesting aside about the word 'panic'. In the major Greek myth 'The Clash of the Titans', Pan (the foster brother of Zeus) was a key figure in the final outcome. When the Titans were being pelted by rocks from the Three-Hundred Handed ones, Pan gave a sudden, and terrifying, shout that put them to flight.

   'This shout, which terrified the Titans, has become proverbial and has given the word "panic" to the English language.' (Graves (1955) page 50).

   One of Pan's noted characteristics (in Greek mythology) was his 'love of riot'. He would take revenge on those who disturbed him with a sudden shout 'which made the hairs bristle on their heads' (op. cit. page 102).

5. Extreme anxiety within – say – panic attacks lies on a continuum from the normal anxiety we all feel on occasion (the dentist – ouch!, the more serious doctor's appointment, an exam, a forthcoming operation …) through to those experiences of anxiety where our biology and psychology significantly impair and affect our ability to live our life and do our work. Those disorders that lie at the extreme end of the spectrum of chronic anxiety expression are often treatable with both medication and (often) cognitive-behaviour therapy.

Chapter

6

Anger: beyond frustration

What this chapter will explore and develop:

- The nature of frustration and anger
- What we can and can't control in an anger episode
- How we manage our own anger – particularly in relation to challenging classroom contexts
- How we communicate legitimate and just anger
- The stress of dealing with an angry parent – some key practices
- Anger and self-esteem

Anger and frustration

In teaching there are often occasions when we will be significantly frustrated – even angry. Anger is the most powerful of human emotions, and has the potential to be the most destructive. We've all felt that build-up of frustration, leading to an angry outburst where we say something we will later regret. Significant frustration can build up so that we may not even be aware of what we say and do in that immediate emotional moment when frustration becomes anger. I've seen some teachers get so angry that they lash out at students – yelling, threatening, even swearing.

I've stopped a few extreme cases myself – over the years – including teachers who want to chase students to simply 'get them'. Their anger is so intense that any emotional self-control has gone. On those occasions (when we've debriefed) they eventually agreed that even if they'd caught the little _____ they don't know what they would have done! Fortunately these cases are rare. Now and then the media gets hold of the 'worst cases'. But we can all remember times when we've felt the same basic feelings of wanting to 'lash out' (at least verbally) at some of our students.

Anger – as an emotion – lies on a continuum from irritation to annoyance, frustration, significant frustration through to anger itself. The continuum is one of *degree* of arousal, *intensity* of arousal and degree of perceived injustice in the situation.

When we experience anger, we feel a tenseness in our body – that rapid broiling of thoughts in the mind, the intense feeling we want to *do* something to address the source of the anger. With anger it's more common that we feel we want to 'fight' the source of our anger, but how can one 'fight' a traffic jam? ('why are these drivers so damned slow?!') – we can't fight an annoying, patronising, supercilious head teacher and we certainly can't 'fight' a really annoying parent or student – though we might be tempted to lash out with 'fighting words' (page 86).

What we cannot stop in our anger (the important distinction)

Aristotle, in the *Nicomachean Ethics*[1], makes the very useful observation that we can't stop *feelings* of frustration and anger 'coming' to us. In this sense – he says – we are bound to 'get angry' and this will happen in many areas of our life. An annoying, rude, arrogant, disruptive student; a rude, arrogant, insensitive parent or colleague will – naturally – occasion our frustration, and even our anger at times.

Aristotle argues that we need to learn to recognise those situations, circumstances and contexts that lower our tolerance to frustration and learn to communicate our frustration, or anger, in ways that are not destructive. This is a crucial distinction, and one that Aristotle comes back to a number of times in his *Ethics*. It is *the particular way* in which we get angry that is the 'learned' part of our anger – even if the original association between our feelings when we get angry and our more typical response to anger-arousing situations have been forgotten.

> ... *feeling angry (or frightened) is something we can't help, but our virtues are in a manner expressions of our will – at any rate there is an element of will in their formation.*
>
> (Book 2, Chapter 5)

The psychiatrist M. Scott Peck (1990) makes the point that 'without our anger' (as an evolved emotion) 'we would indeed be continually be stepped on' (page 66). In this sense the 'drive' of anger can be enabling to basic survival. He goes on to say that as human beings we must, however,

> *posses the capacity to express our anger in different ways. At times, for instance, it is necessary to express it only after much deliberation and self-evaluation. At other times it is more to our benefit to express it immediately and spontaneously. Sometimes it is best to express it coldly and calmly, at other times loudly and hotly. We therefore not only need to know how to deal with our anger in different ways at different times but also to match the right time with the right style of expression.*
>
> (Page 67, ibid.)

When I first read this, as well as releasing a long sigh of 'I agree ... but ... how ...?' I recalled Aristotle's teaching in the *Nicomachean Ethics* (Thompson, trans., 1969) in 310 BC:

> *Anger may be produced by a variety of causes, but, however that may be, it is the man who is angry on the right occasions and with the right people who wins our commendation.*
>
> (Book 4, Chapter 5)

Any 'rightness', 'virtue' or 'justice' in the way we communicate anger is learned in the social context – it doesn't come naturally.

Aristotle is saying that in any 'virtue' we exercise, when we express our emotions (in this case anger), there is an element of conscious will – 'One must 'will' their action for its own sake' (Book 2, Chapter 4, ibid.). It is in this sense that what we do, *when* we're angry, can have a relative 'goodness' or 'badness' as well a more or less effective outcome in contexts or relationships where we experience frustration and anger. It can have a more positive outcome only when we learn to be more aware of what we think and do in situations that easily occasion frustration and anger.

When we get angry

Frustration and anger are on the same emotional continuum. We feel the build-up of frustration (at times *very* quickly): our heart rate increases, blood pumps rapidly to the extremities, our muscles tighten, we frown and we may have an impulse to 'strike out'. The arousal is natural; we're mobilised – for what though? When the emotion of anger is prevented from its 'expression', it will take its toll. The emotive energy driving what we call 'anger' has to 'do' or 'go' somewhere or express itself in some way – this is true of all significant emotions (such as worry, anxiety, frustration anger and rage).

What we do *when* we feel this way will depend on how we've learned to *think* about anger-arousing situations, and how we've learnt to think *in* – and respond to – what happens in the immediate emotional context of the anger episodes. Obviously it is difficult to think clearly when one is very frustrated or angry (some people find it impossible to *think* at all when they're very frustrated). As well as the physiological arousal, there is often a sense that a perceived injustice is at stake – for us, or someone we care about. There are many occasions in teaching where we perceive such injustice and the stress occasioned by behaviours such as bullying, lying, cheating, stealing, and so on. Physiology and perception are powerful allies at this point – they don't, however, tell us what to do.

The question is not merely what *can* we do in typical anger-arousing situations as a teacher, but what *should* we do; what *will* we do? Utility needs temperance and guidance, from value-driven will. Left to our unmanaged will, anger will often take the most reactive route! Our behaviour *when* we're angry is not merely incidental or accidental – it is 'learned' (as Aristotle contends in his *Ethics*).

Anger, itself, is neither good nor bad

We wouldn't say to a child they are 'bad' for being angry – we might say that what they *did* when they were angry was inappropriate or wrong. So too with ourselves, we need to be understanding of this emotion, forgiving of ourselves when we are less 'controlled' in our expressions of anger.

Managing our anger and the anger of others

The point has been made several times in this book (in different ways) that it is not only events that *cause* how we feel, but also our perceptions and beliefs that we bring to bear on those events. The intensity of *how* we feel – when we're frustrated and angry – may well be related to beliefs that are also insistent, demanding and unrealistic about the issue occasioning our anger.

I have actually seen teachers chase rude, arrogant, defiant students down corridors and across playgrounds when they are angry, in order to 'catch' the student. And then – what? Hammer them? Most teachers – thankfully – do not hit out at children physically (these days), but some will lash out verbally. There may be a temporary assuaging of frustration or even satisfaction at getting them (!) – but at what cost? While an anger-fuelled tirade *appears* to temporarily assuage the pent-up feelings of frustration that 'fuel' the anger, such actions (these days) are often likely to result in a solicitor's letter on the head teacher's desk, irate phone calls from threatening parents, messy union/school involvement and, perhaps, newspapers and a TV crew!

Also, if I *remain* very angry after a stressful event, that *degree of anger – again – may well be related* to what I'm saying to myself about the incident or person, for example *nursing* grudges and resentment. 'They *shouldn't* have spoken to me like that!' (they did – that's the unpleasant reality). 'How *dare* they …!!' (they did). Again it is unpleasant reality – but it is reality nonetheless. Recurrent self-talk – like this – only feeds and sustains resentment and it won't change the stressful reality; it will only make it worse. It will also make any workable resolution very difficult, if not impossible.

Some teachers will get angry very quickly over 'small issues' (like lateness, uniform concerns, homework not done or calling out, students chatting while they are teaching). There is a difference in *degree* of arousal between concern, irritation, annoyance and anger. *Anger* ought to lie at the high end of the emotion spectrum, in contrast to – say – annoyance and irritation. If we easily get *angry* about small issues (such as those above), where will student's perceive our sense of 'moral weight' in (say) contrast to racist, sexist and bullying behaviours?

Communicating our anger

The justice of anger: asserting

At times it is right not just to 'get' angry about what is unfair and unjust, but also to let others know what it is we're angry *about*. The just response to racist, sexist and abusive behaviours directed at us (or the welfare of students we have responsibility for) is to express our anger clearly, decisively and assertively. Some teachers are able to do this more 'naturally' – and effectively – than others; the rest of us will need to learn the skills of assertion.

When we *assert,* we are communicating our feelings, needs or concerns to another (a student or an adult, at times to a group). We are seeking to make our *rights and needs* clear in a firm and non-aggressive way. Our assertion may also need to be expressed in order to protect others' rights or needs – as when we assertively confront a student who is putting another student down or is engaged in bullying behaviour.

There are teachers who – when frustrated or angry – respond in hostile, even verbally aggressive, ways to those who are the source of their frustration. This creates stress for all involved. When it occurs in front of an audience of students, it also creates ill will in those cooperative students whose support we need when managing the more disruptive and challenging students.

The more demanding teacher – for example – will often overrate the threat posed by challenging students, and that demanding belief is then expressed in a hostile, or even an aggressive, tone of speech and body language (page 37).

The *skills* of assertion are essential in our profession (page 104).

Reflect for a moment

I lost my temper! Where?

I have sat with many students who have got disturbingly angry and caused a major ruckus, or behaved aggressively and had to be directed to time-out (page 124). When we're talking (in that calmer moment) they'll often say 'I lost my temper ...!' They sometimes add '... I couldn't help it.' I've heard adults use that phrase too – many times.

In effect they didn't *lose* 'their temper', they found it. If they did 'lose' it from time to time it might do us all a favour! It's an interesting choice of words, illustrating – no doubt – how easy it is to *lose control* of one's behaviour when we're angry.

There are other teachers who are overly concerned with 'losing their temper' when addressing challenging students (or parents). They still *feel* the significant frustration or anger when students are rude and confronting, but allow others to effectively abuse their rights or fail to protect students whose rights are being abused. The fear of losing control in anger-arousal situations is made worse by a belief that 'a good teacher *shouldn't* get angry ...' Why ever not? Some situations will *naturally* occasion our frustration – argumentative and challenging behaviours, others taking advantage of us, lying, cheating, bullying. On these occasions justice will demand expression of our *assertive* anger, to confront and address the cause.

Some teachers will feel guilty when they finally yell, even scream, at students when their self-restraint fails them (as they perceive it). This is why it is important to learn to 'read' our emotions and be – rightfully – able to express our frustration and anger in an assertive way, rather than simply giving free rein to how we feel.

It is not uncommon when we lose our temper to become angry with ourselves. We're angry that we got angry! Or, more correctly, were angry about the way we *behaved* when we were angry (shouting or yelling; the easy blame or overblaming of others); the miscued blame when we blame the wrong person; the nagging, the holding of grudges; the continued sulking ...

It's easy to perpetuate such 'self-anger' as, for example, when we call ourselves 'stupid', 'idiotic', 'you never learn, do you?!', 'you *shouldn't* have got angry …' 'Why *shouldn't* we have got angry?'

Maybe we shouldn't have said or done what *we did* when we were angry – we have to decide what is justifiable about our anger. It is unrealistic, though, to then *perpetuate* feelings of self-blame and self-downing *because* we got angry (page 57). If what we did, and said, *when* we got angry was unfair, intemperate, mistargeted, unjustified and wrong then we should apologise and seek appropriate restitution. That, at least, is the right thing to do – the difficult thing but the right thing. Restitution and forgiveness – at the very least – acknowledges our fallibility, our humanity. To work with that in others also does likewise.

> Chronic remorse, as all moralists are agreed, is a most undesirable sentiment. If you have behaved badly, repent, make what amends you can and address yourself to the task of behaving better next time. On no account brood over your wrongdoing.
>
> Rolling in the muck is not the best way of getting clean.
>
> Aldous Huxley *Brave New World* (1932) Foreword page 7.

Developing the skills of assertion

Assertion and merely 'ventilating' our anger are not the same. *Assertion* is the way we express our strong feeling about something to an individual or group. That may be motivated by the justice in our anger or the necessity in the situation. Assertion is a way of communicating our anger as judiciously as possible – using the physiological signals we experience *alerting us* to *address what we're angry about*. It is a learned behaviour and a necessary skill in our profession.

- When we assert, we need to present a confident body language to others – an assertive message will be misconstrued if we gesticulate or point, or wag the finger or clench the fists. An open hand, or – at times – a blocking hand if the student (or adult) keeps trying to butt in, can still communicate an assertive stance.

- Conversely we don't speak in a timid, hesitant, pleading voice, tone and manner … We speak clearly, *firmly* and 'calmly'. This may sound contradictory. By calmly I mean our voice sounds as if we are in control of ourself (we can't directly control the other person's behaviour). That *calmness* is crucial when we're asserting; it enables the likelihood of what we say actually being heard – not just by the difficult student but also by the audience of peers. An extended, open, (or a blocking) hand combined with a clear and decisive 'I' statement – 'I don't swear (yell, scream, threaten, use abusive language, etc.) at you Craig, I don't expect you to swear at me.'

'I don't make comments about your body (or clothing, or sexuality or ...) I don't expect you to make them to me' – this to a student who has made a sexist comment to the teacher.

If the student says 'It's just a joke! – can't you take a joke or something?' (a common – feigned – sulky retort from some male students) we'll respond with a firm, clear, decisive, calm tone and manner. 'It's *not* a joke to me – it stops now.' If the student continues to be hostile, arrogantly rude or aggressive – in any way – we'll also need to employ appropriate time-out procedures (page 124). It will be essential to also follow up with that student – later – (one-to-one) with the supportive advocacy of a senior colleague.

- It can help to discuss with colleagues the sorts of things we can say when we are dealing with hostile, arrogantly rude, verbally aggressive or challenging students (or parents). It can also help to practise the sorts of things one can say within the typical occasions when we need to assert. It's not as 'easy' as it sometimes looks on paper.

- We avoid arguing when we assert – we're making a *necessary*, just point about the other person's behaviour. If they start raising their voice, *our* calmness – and necessary assertion – will go a long way towards helping them to regain some relative control over the situation. If the student starts to raise their voice again, we find that 'break in their verbal traffic' (as it were) and then say (e.g.) 'I'm not shouting at you ... I'll listen to you when you stop shouting ... (here be specific) ...' If they are too emotionally unsettled (or worse) we will need to utilise time-out procedures (page 124). Sometimes with older students (and adults) it can help them to verbally 'run out of steam' – vent their spleen – before we reassert. We would only do this if there are no safety concerns at stake. Where one's physical safety is compromised or threatened we should immediately seek for senior teacher support. (Schools – normally – have clear protocols in place for that rare occurrence). Again it's worth discussing these sorts of contexts with colleagues.

Case example

When Ibrahim was stabbing his worksheet with his scissors (grade 1) and causing the other students a lot of anxiety, I walked over to his table group, 'Ibrahim ... (I had to repeat his name several times to get minimal eye contact) give me the scissors *now*.' It's an assertive (but calm) command. No 'please' – it's not a request. He said – loudly – 'I'll be ALRIGHT NOW!! PLEASE Mr Rogers.' 'Give me the scissors *now*.' Firm, *calm*, clear (not fast speech or loud speech – that will only increase emotional arousal).

He slammed the scissors on to the table. I picked them up and – then – directed him away from his table group to 'cool-off time' in the corner of the classroom (a desk and chair – slightly screened off from the rest of the class group). Again he started loudly whining 'I'll be alright now!! MR ROGERS, I don't want to go …!'. 'Ibrahim – come with me – cool-off time.' I walked away to indicate I expected him to come. He followed, stamping his feet and loudly saying, 'I DON'T LIKE YOU!!' I *tactically* ignored this and walked with him to the time-out area. When he was seated I said – quietly – 'I want you to think about how to use the scissors safely.' 'When you've stopped being really upset, and you're feeling better (I pointed to my heart to convey "feelings inside" …) then you can come back to your table group …' I then left him in 'time-out' for five minutes or so and then went over to escort him back to his table group. Later, I followed up with him, one-to-one, to have a chat about his behaviour (page 119). The fair certainty of the consequence (here) is important. Some teachers will accept a student's 'plea-bargaining' ('I'll be alright!'); this sends a confusing and mixed message not only to the student needing time-out but also to the other students as well.

Principles of anger management

We need to distinguish – in our thinking –between our own anger (about others, or about what has happened *to us*) and *how we express it*. We also need to think about how we deal with *others'* anger. As teachers we will often have to address frustrated or angry students (even – at times – angry parents or colleagues!). There are some key principles that relate to both areas of anger management.

● *Anger cannot tell us what to do* – we need to learn to recognise, and be aware of, the situations, contexts and people that lower our tolerance to frustration (the M25, OFSTED, *that* student, *that* class, *that* parent, *those* meetings.) We also need to learn how to respond *when* we're angry and the *important follow-through when we (and the other person/s) have calmed down.*

● Our more *characteristic* expressions of frustration and anger (what we do and say *when* we're angry) are learned behaviours – they are not merely the result of our social biology or mere reactions to stressful situations. Even if we've forgotten the genesis of that learning, we need to take control of our *current* anger behaviour (and thinking) as a teacher. We can learn to differentiate between what we feel, and how best (and when) to address the source of our frustration and anger. Of particular importance here is learning *how to communicate our frustration* and anger – particularly in discipline contexts (page 104).

● *Learn to 'get angry' about issues that matter* – some teachers will get frustratingly upset, even angry, about issues such as lateness to class, homework not done, uniform 'misdemeanours', students without equipment. These behaviours merit – at the most – irritation or annoyance (homework not done or uncompleted assignments need our *concern* as well). If we frequently get angry about such small issues, students will not appreciate the scale of concern or 'moral weight' about issues or situations we rate as significant enough to express our anger about.

The 'moral weight' of our anger is relative – and we should get angry (for example) about racism, sexism, injustice and harassment . We should also (of course) learn how better to convey that anger – even forcefully – so that our passion addressed is likely to have a constructive outcome as it addresses the issues or causes. In the immediate emotional moment of expressed anger (hopefully assertively expressed) we cannot directly address the cause in any meaningful way. We need to make the assertive point – at that moment – and then, later (when the other person/s, and ourselves, are calmer) we work on the precipitating issue(s), cause(s) or behaviours.

- *When we communicate our frustration, or anger, we address the issue, the behaviour, the concern rather than 'attacking' the person* – this isn't easy; there will be times we feel like unleashing the floodgates of our frustration. I was discussing with a colleague who – still upset about a very arrogant Year 10 student – said, 'Bill, would you agree with me that Rachel's got a slappable face!'. I said, 'Yes'. I understood how my colleague had felt as she 'let off steam' to this arrogant young woman. It's not easy being professional. It's also important to debrief with a colleague after a particularly stressful anger episode.

- When we've said 'our piece'; when we have asserted – where necessary – we need to allow de-escalation of the tension occasioned by the emotional moment. This may mean that we direct a student to take some cool-off time (or, even, formal time-out). On other occasions if we are the one who is significantly angry – perhaps even too angry to address the issue – it is more politic for us to take some time-out. It is unhelpful (at times destructive) to *keep on speaking* when we're really angry. It is better to say *what* we're angry about briefly, clearly and assertively (as best we can) and leave it at that *for now.*

  Later, when we are feeling calmer, we can speak with the other party at more length when we and (hopefully) they are calmer. It may be helpful to say – in the immediate emotional moment – 'I am too angry to speak any more about this right *now.* I'll talk with you later.' Avoid being pushed into arguments if you (or the other party) are really frustrated. Better to make the assertive point and then allow (or direct) time-out.

- If we've said something hurtful when, or while, we're angry it will be crucial to apologise later. As St Paul said, 'Don't let the Sun go down on your anger.'[2] Even that day – if possible – apologise and reassure. Take time to go back to the individual or the class group (or colleague) and repair and rebuild. If a student has expressed their anger poorly, it's often the teacher who has to make the first move to assist the student in restitution.

- Be aware that a demanding explanatory style – when we are angry – will exacerbate hostility and blame. If we believe we *must* always do well; *must* always be calm and focused and 'in control' – if we firmly believe, we *cannot stand* to fail or make mistakes. If we believe that students *must not* answer back, be rude, challenge, and so on then these sorts of demanding beliefs are as much a driving 'force' behind one's expression and degree of anger as the precipitating event or circumstance (Chapter 4).

We're back to an explanatory style that says, 'It's unrealistic to demand perfection of self or others ... I need to be aware that there *are* many demands on my time, and many *pressures with those demands*. There's no reason why I should be *perfect*. There's no reason why I should always be calm and focused and in control at all times. *Yes I need to control myself in a stressful and demanding situation* and, at times, that will mean I need to express my anger clearly, firmly, decisively and assertively. At other times I'll need to express my anger after some calm reflection.'

'If I fail or make mistakes *I am human* (!) I need to admit I will not be able to do everything – in my work – well, or at *all* times (!) Others will not *always* relate to me as I'd like or want. I'll do my best to enable mutual regard to others *and that's possible.*'

- If and when the other person is angry, and we – as teacher–leader – or colleague have to help them to remember:

  - the first person to calm is ourselves. We can't actually 'calm' another person – merely telling them 'to calm down' rarely helps. This is essential if the student (or parent) is threatening or verbally aggressive.

  - avoid getting too close to the angry person or physically reaching out directly to 'calm' them (particularly with children diagnosed with autism spectrum disorder)[3].

  - tune into how they may be feeling (without saying 'You must be angry'). It can help to say, *calmly*, 'I can see you're upset, or angry.' Reassure by asking if (and how) you can help. 'I want to help ... how can I help ...?' Hopefully a reassuring, calm manner will help them regain a sense of emotional security *at this point*. That is why we do not use a loud, fast voice – or sudden, rapid movements.

  - If there is a safety aspect at stake, we need to make sure the other students feel safe and that they sense their teacher knows what they're doing. Again, our firm and clear assertion where necessary and calm manner will always help. It is also essential to have school-wide protocols for getting adult assistance in a crisis (page 150) and for the constructive use of time-out (page 124).

Anger – easily and quickly 'unleashed' – can turn into (a) rage. It is in this expression of anger that the emotion of anger is the most destructive. Some of our students go home to such environments every day.

At least in school (we would hope) they find a place, a space and adults that enable safety, sanity and security even when angry.

The stress of dealing with a very angry parent

My colleagues and I have had the experience of an angry parent storm into our office (even a classroom at times) – shouting, sometimes screaming and even yelling threats and incantations!

Most parents when they present the school with a concern – even when frustrated – will normally moderate their frustration, even their anger *if* we (as the teacher) make the effort to listen first, show we care and seek to enable a supportive response to the concern/s.

There are those few parents, however, who (like some students) lose all social restraint – their emotion outruns their self-control (we can, at least, understand that from our own experiences).

If we know that a very difficult parent is coming for a 'meeting', it will help to let colleagues know, who can be available to help. Also make sure you've got the facts about the issue (at stake) clear and written down, *beforehand wherever possible*. There are times, though, when some parents are so angry they ignore any normative social protocols in communicating with teachers. No warning, no prior phone call – they just 'storm in'. Even before they barge into the office you can hear them ... 'This f___ing school, nothing but a bunch of f___ing a___holes! You've never give a sh _t about us.' When confronted by such behaviour, we find it professionally apposite to:

- Let the parent 'run out of steam' as it were. Whenever confronted by angry adults (or children) in the course of our professional work, it is crucial to remember that our calmness will – normally – enable their calmness. If the parent is ranting at us, by 'letting them vent' (as it were) they will often expend their built-up frustration (however ill-founded or miscued it may be).

- Once you can sense a break – in the psychological traffic of their anger – it will help to briefly tune into their frustration. 'Mrs Whingingsod (please use her correct name, even if you feel like appending a different name!)[4] I can see you're really upset about your son being temporarily suspended from school ...' Often, before we finish they'll add, 'too f___ing right I'm upset ...!'

As with all *very* frustrated, or angry, people, we can't directly control them. We can, however, control our responses to them. The essential protocol here is that we speak and act calmly (no sudden movements) and focus their concerns and needs *before* we give the school's response to what they are angry about. Communicating calmness does not mean an anodyne, monotonic, 'nice' blandness. Calmness and appropriate firmness can work together. Our ability to read the situation will enable, and determine, how firm we'll need to be within that 'calmness'.

- Seek to focus their need and concern. Invite them to sit down (it decreases their pent-up, whole-body energy!). Let them know you care – this is not easy, it takes moral effort! 'I know you care about Travis. You wouldn't be here if you didn't care. We care too ...' ('not much' you might be tempted to add!). If the parent is calm enough, but still punctuating their list of grievances with swearing, you may want to add, 'I know you care; however, I'm not swearing at you and I don't expect you to swear at me. Let's work together to see how we can support your son – that's why we're both here.'

- When we discuss their concerns (about the school, a particular teacher, other students – whatever) it is important not to compromise the school's code of rights and responsibilities (for example, with regard to bullying, violence stealing, drugs etc.). It is also important not to make promises or 'bargains' that deny a student's accountability for their behaviour.

- It will help, too, if we can cue a senior colleague to be around – available if we need them. No doubt the parent will have noisily heralded their presence anyway so there will be a colleague (or two) available to come in and support or (on rare occasions) contact the police. With a distraught – and angry – mother (or female care-giver) it will help to have a female colleague with you in the room if you are a male teacher – not the least for ethical probity on your part. Be sure you are able to get to the door *if* the parent is very threatening (I'm not joking). Hopefully *your calmness*, your demonstrated willingness to listen will have helped defuse the intensity of their anger.

- If the parent refuses to settle and continues to threaten, you will need to make clear that if they continue to threaten we will have to contact the police. Again – thankfully – this is rare. Know the emergency procedures in advance.

- *Always* debrief with colleague/s later – some hot, sweet tea will help. Avoid self-recrimination and self-blame. *Some* parents can be devastatingly insensitive, even cruel in their comments about teachers and students (other than their child!). (See Rogers 2009, Chapter 7).

Teacher morale and self-esteem

Morale and our self-esteem are intertwined. It is clear from our experience that when we feel confident about ourselves – when our work with students and colleagues is valued – we feel better about ourselves.

While others clearly affect our sense of self, it is important to also remember that self-esteem (as an adult) is just that, *self*-esteem. We may have worked in schools where colleague acknowledgment is poor, factional, bound in cliques. It can be dispiriting to work in such schools. It is a hard lesson to learn – in life generally, and in our professional life in particular –that our essential value of ourself is what we give it; *valuing ourselves as a person*. Learning to accept ourselves – at present – with our strengths and weaknesses and seeking to honestly address them where we are – at present – in our life journey. It is easy to blame others, or 'the system', or overly blame ourselves for how we feel about ourselves.

Yes, it is ideal, helpful and enjoyable when others affirm, acknowledge and value us as individuals – in our shared humanity – and in our work as teachers. I will argue, later, that this should be a characteristic of a collegially supportive school. However, if you're in a 'soddish' school – at the moment – this will probably not be the case. One of the indicators of a healthy self-esteem is our ability to 'separate', in terms of our self-worth, what happens to us from what essentially we value in ourselves. If I spend a lot of my psychological energy, effort and thought seeking (or worse, demanding) approval from others, I'll feel worse when it doesn't come. Assuming you're not a lazy, indifferent, uncaring teacher who might make it 'easier' for others not to 'respect' or value you, then you can learn to *accept yourself* without demanding others' approval.

Notes

1. Aristotle's last book (effectively the substance of the lectures he delivered at the Lyceum). I have quoted from J.A.K. Thompson's translation (Penguin Classics).

2. *Letter to the Ephesians*: Chapter 4, verse 26. (The New Testament).

3. Children diagnosed with ASD get very anxious, even frightened, when adults speak very loudly or very fast – or communicate with rapid, or 'hostile', body language.

4. Most parents (in such cases) are women. In this I am being descriptive – it is often the mothers who pick up (or are left with) the demands of raising their children and dealing with their, sometimes, complicated and disturbing lives at school.

A behaviour management and discipline plan at the classroom level

What this chapter will explore and develop:

- Thinking ahead to the first meeting with a new class
- The essential elements of a management and discipline plan
- Essential core routines for classroom behaviour and learning
- Addressing distracting and disruptive behaviours – key practices and skills (these are explored in a case study format). These practices and skills are foundational to the mentoring model addressed in Chapter 10
- The skill of communicating calmness as well as necessary assertion

- How we develop discipline skills under pressure – the difference between skill and personality
- The importance of a whole-school approach

This is the longest chapter in this book. It addresses a 'lynchpin concept' in our daily practice – how we see to realistically plan for the typical distractions and disruptions of students in day-to-day teaching. There are two parts to this chapter – part A addresses the key elements, practices and skills of such a plan; part B addresses the out-working of that plan in the development of those practices and skills.

A behaviour management and discipline plan is an essential feature of a teacher's leadership of a class. It is also integral to a whole-school approach to behaviour management and discipline (Rogers, 2006). It is an aspect of whole-school planning and practice that can significantly – and effectively – moderate the natural stress occasioned by our role in behaviour leadership (Rogers, 2011).

The classroom is the fundamental teaching and learning space – and social space – in the life of a school. A lot of time is spent there *for teacher and students alike*. It is the quality of classroom life that determines the quality of a school as a local learning community; such a plan enables respectful relationships within that community.

Natural frictions will arise in any classroom with disparate personalities, varying learning needs and varying levels of social skill in the students. A discipline plan – within our overall teacher leadership – is our best attempt to thoughtfully and comprehensively think through the *typical*, and even likely, behaviour issues that arise in classroom groups. Nowhere is this more crucial than in the first meetings with our classes in the establishment phase of the year.

Such a plan can also decrease natural anxieties about discipline and management because we have thought through – collegially – the sorts of things we need to say and do in discipline contexts. The practices and skills within such a plan also enable *a shared sense of purpose and approach* about the range of behaviour and discipline issues that are likely to occur.

PART A
Key elements, practices and skills

Thinking ahead: the first meeting with a new class

Most teachers know well the kinds of distracting and disruptive behaviours that might occur in their classes (even if they don't know their students as 'individuals' yet). They also know the crucial phases of a lesson and the 'trigger points' for attentional and off-task behaviours (pages 9, 10, 32). A discipline plan seeks to think through the better, more positive, more effective management practices and interventions to address such behaviours. The immediacy of the 'emotional moment', the creative tension that can occur when we have to intervene in distractions and disruptions is the last place to be thinking, 'What *can* I / what *should* I do and say *now*?'

A thoughtful discipline plan consciously addresses *the language of discipline*:

What can I *do/say* ... when, for example:

- several students call out during whole-class teaching time?
- several students are chatting when I'm trying to teach?
- a student walks in five minutes late 'showing off'? (page 37)
- several students are fiddling (loudly) with pencil cases, water bottles, key rings ...?
- students are task-avoiding, wandering, calling out ... during the on-task phase of the lesson?

We cannot plan for every contingency – we can plan for the typical distractions and disruptions within a least-to-most intrusive degree of intervention (as is necessary). We can also plan for those episodic occasions when students are argumentative, challenging, swearing, hostile, resistant or aggressive (pages 45, 129).

Further – we know that our students are psychologically and developmentally ready in those critical first meetings (in the establishment phase of the year) for us to clarify – and teach – the rules and responsibilities and essential routines that enable learning and cooperative behaviour in classrooms. This understanding is crucial to our discipline plan. Effective teachers plan their behaviour management, and discipline, as thoughtfully and carefully as they do individual lessons and units of work (Rogers, 2011).

In developing a discipline plan it is important to work with colleagues on a common framework so that, as much as possible, our professional behaviour leadership reflects school-wide preferred practices and skills. A summary of the cores skills of such a plan is detailed in the case studies that follow.

The key elements of a behaviour management and discipline plan

- The **essential core routines** that involve the reasonably smooth running of a classroom (see below).

- The **classroom rules** (they reflect school-wide rules) – these will seek to protect the core rights *to feel safe at school* (including psychological safety), *to learn* (without undue distraction or disruption) and *the right to fair treatment and respect*.

- How we will address distracting and disruptive behaviour in the *key phases* of the lesson from entry to settling, through the whole-class teaching phase to the on-task learning phase through to lesson closure, exit and follow-up of any particularly disruptive students (pages 119–121).

- We are enabled (in the above) by having a framework of intervention from least-to-more intrusive (page 105). A key feature of such a framework is a conscious awareness of how we use discipline language.

- The framework of behaviour consequences for use *in the classroom* and for follow-up with students one-to-one *beyond the classroom*. It is advisable to think through the typical behaviour consequences we use from after class chats (page 191), to behaviour interviews, to subject-teacher detentions and year-level detentions. We will also need to have clear referral procedures for more *repeatedly* disruptive students. Even here, though, we (the classroom teacher) will need to be willing to follow up, follow through and seek to repair and re-build with students we have referred on to senior colleagues.

- Time-out support procedures for when we need to remove from the classroom a student who is *repeatedly* disruptive or potentially dangerous. On such occasions a teacher needs to be assured they will get immediate support and backup. Clear cues and procedures need to be established, maintained and monitored on a whole-school basis. (This is discussed in Chapter 8.)

The essential core routines

A good, and fair, routine enables what is *routine* in classroom learning and behaviour expectations to be achieved – I know that's tautological but that's the point. When we think about core classroom routines, we are thinking about procedures, ways of doing things (in the small space of a classroom) that enable the day-to-day smooth running and 'routine' of teaching and learning. Ways of doing things that will enable the students – with their teacher – to get on with the purpose of why we are together every hour of a teaching and learning day *in this place*. The routines also *enable* more positive relational dynamics by thinking through, easing and moderating normative social, spatial and relational tensions in that small space.

A good, and sensible, routine will enable reasonable consistency of behaviour by clarifying and reinforcing and *habituating* fair expectations.

We need to discuss and develop such routines with our colleagues *prior* to our first meetings with our new class(es). Some routines will be school-wide (such as bell times, entry and exit from classrooms, leaving-the-room procedures); some routines will need to be fine-tuned to particular subjects such as 'movement around the room'; distribution, use and pack-up of materials; 'how to get teacher assistance during on-task learning time' (the difference, say, between a typical maths class and a food technology or drama class).

Explain, establish and habituate

It is crucial to establish these routines in those first critical meetings with a new class – particularly with more restive and attentionally fractious groups. Even if we know the students well (from other classes or years) we will still need some discursive establishment time with them in our first meetings. I labour this point a little because it is my experience in countless mentoring sessions (over the last 15 years) that inadequate, poorly expressed and poorly *maintained* classroom routines are a significant stress point in a class that has become increasingly difficult to manage and lead (page 140).

In our first meetings with a new class, we need to explain and even teach these core routines – we do not need to 'defend' them. If a routine is necessary, fair and sensible (in its form and purpose) then we don't need to defend it each time we remind our students about how we enter the classroom and settle; the necessary seating arrangements; cues for whole-class discussion (hands up *without calling out or clicking fingers;* wait your turn; wait for the teacher to call on you; if you disagree with a fellow student do so respectfully); noise levels during on-task learning time; movement around the room; how to get teacher assistance (during on-task learning time); packing up, settling and a considerate exit from the classroom.

The core routines involve:

● *'Lining-up' and considerate entry to the classroom*. Many schools still have a 'line-up' policy (particularly at primary level). This can enable a sense of calming and physical settling *between* 'social time' (outside of classrooms) and entry into 'classroom learning space and time'. However, even if there is no actual line-up practice, it will still be important to verbally cue the class group as they enter the classroom – particularly the more kinaesthetically restless students. We do this to cue all the students that we are here – in this place and space – for a purpose. Our movement patterns, our noise levels and how we communicate all need to change when we come inside this place and space. When boys are 'playfully' testosteronically bonding (the 'punch', the 'strangle', the 'push' and 'shove' …), we'll need to confidently remind them, 'Fellas (…)' (eyeball them), 'Come on – playtime's over – remember where we're going.' We'll also need to remind the students with hats and sunglasses to take them off. If we suspect iPods are still on or students are fiddling with phones, we will need to remind them, 'Before we go into our classroom hats, sunglasses, iPods and phones away. Thanks. And, chewy in the bin on the way in. Ta.'

The reason my colleagues and I focus, briefly, on 'hats off' (or beanies or 'hoodies' off) is to draw a conscious distinction between students' 'social time' and 'classroom learning time'. We convey – by our positive tone, manner and expectation – to our students that we are *now* going into a different place and space. And we need to consider certain behaviours that enable us to enter, settle, relax, relate to – and even enjoy – this learning environment we call our classroom. We need to lead this student consciousness – it doesn't happen by osmosis (Rogers, 2011).

I've seen students effectively push their way into the classroom – almost pushing past the teacher (even ignoring their teacher), *still* speaking loudly, *still* kinaesthetically restless. Such an entry (into a classroom) makes it much more difficult to focus the class *and enable that calmness* that is essential for whole-class teaching.

It is always worth discussing how other colleagues in one's grade team/ faculty positively cue their students in that transition from 'outside' to 'inside'. It is always worth discussing actual language cues for this (and for all) core routine/s.

- *Settling into one's seat (or on the carpet area with early years children)*. It is important not to initiate or get drawn into long, individual conversations with students at the classroom door. For example, I've seen secondary teachers trying to deal with several querulous students at the door, while the rest of the class is (often noisily) trying to get past to their seats. We need to positively greet all our students *as they enter* the classroom and head towards their seats.

It is worth discussing with grade/faculty colleagues the most appropriate seating plan for age/subject. If you suspect (or know!) you have a more fractious classroom group, it is wiser to avoid friendship groupings (in seating arrangements) until you've got to know your class dynamics. It is also worth considering the physical layout of seating (as well as who sits with whom). A more 'formal' seating plan is preferable in the establishment phase. Later, when we've got to know our students as individuals – and the particular dynamics of our class – then we can alter the seating arrangements. We should not merely leave seating/student grouping to chance, or just hope the students will behave cooperatively if we let them sit where they want and with whom!

● *Initiating and sustaining whole-class attention and focus.* This critical phase of a lesson involves that initial several minutes of classroom entry, settling into seats, and, then, cueing the whole group. This is crucial to all we do from then on in *that* lesson. I have seen countless teachers (over the years) begin to 'lose' the class in the first 5 to 10 minutes of a lesson. It will be important to 'anchor' the students' expectation of *their* focus and attention by standing at the front centre of the classroom. We stand relaxed, scanning the faces of all our students – a brief and positive transitional eye contact will help 'connect' and engage our students. A *brief* waiting for any residual noise to settle. If there is residual chatter, fiddling with objects (at desk/table) or calling out continues (during this initial phase), *we will need to cue for considerate behaviour.*

Avoid pointless questions such as 'Are you still talking?' or 'Do you have to call out ...?', or 'Excuse me, why are you fiddling with that pencil case? How can I teach when you're making that noise?!' 'Can't you see I'm trying to teach – do you have to call out like that?!'

Avoid simple negatives – 'Don't talk when I'm teaching, thank you!', 'Don't fiddle with the window blinds', 'Don't call out ...'. A mere 'don't ...' cue only tells the individuals or the group what you don't want them to do (page 97).

My colleagues and I have found it helpful to *describe* and *direct*; or *describe* and *remind* – e.g. 'A number of students are chatting ...' (the *description* part of the cue to the class, as a group); this raises the 'behaviour awareness' of those chatting. 'You need to be looking this way and listening (...). Thank you.' Allow a brief tactical pause for cognitive take-up (...) (page 35). This is the *directional* part of the cue.

If several students are calling out at the beginning of the lesson, we can briefly *describe* their behaviour (to raise awareness) – 'A number of students are calling out' and add a rule reminder, 'Remember *our* rule for asking questions, thanks.' This assumes, of course, that we have established such a rule.

At this stage of the lesson (the first few minutes) we are briefly, positively, expectantly cueing the group or the individuals – 'Shannon (...) that water bottle is really distracting.' The descriptive cue may be enough. If the student doesn't stop we will need to add the direction or cue – 'Leave the water bottle – thanks. Eyes and ears this way. Ta.'

We actually haven't said 'Good morning' *to the group* as yet (see later). We're waiting for that reasonable settling, attention and focus of all the class. If a few students are still chatting, we will need to cue them – by name – and describe and direct. 'Melissa (…), Lola (…) you're chatting. You need to be looking this way and listening, thanks' (the *directional* part of the cue). At this point some students will sigh, raise their eyes to the ceiling, fold their arms, frown … These 'secondary behaviours' may be intentional or unintentional (habituated). At *this point* we tactically ignore such behaviour (page 45).

- *Cueing the whole class.* Whenever we cue the whole class to settle we'll give a *general cue,* and the sorts of brief cues (to individual students) I have mentioned above.

'Settling down, everyone (…)' This may need to be said a little louder (but not an *overly* loud voice and NOT SHOUTING!) A brief, tactical pause (…) as we scan the faces of our students. We'll add cueing such as 'Eyes and ears this way, thanks (…) and listening.' Another *brief,* tactical, pause to allow for 'cognitive take-up'.

This doesn't take long – a few minutes at most. I have spelled out the process – and even the language – that my colleagues and I use because this routine, and the language cues, are foundational to a positive and relaxed class beginning.

When the class is settled, listening (hopefully relaxed) we'll thank them – 'Thank you; you're much more relaxed now. Good morning everyone.'

If we say 'good morning' while the class is *still* overly restless – settling noisily or chatting or calling out – then we cue a positive greeting at an inappropriate (noisy) time. The greeting is – effectively – lost in the restlessness.

When giving a general cue to all the students avoid saying things like, 'WILL YOU PLEASE BE QUIET AND LISTEN?' It is not a request – we don't need to ask their 'permission'. We also avoid talking *over* their noise or competing with it (!) This only reinforces that its 'OK' for students to 'compete' with our need for their attention by their ambient chatter and calling out. We also avoid saying, 'I'M WAITING! I-AM-WAITING-PLEASE!'

Some basic points to remember when initiating and sustaining whole-class attention:

- Anchor your position at the front of the room, standing relaxed, 'open' body language, a *brief* calm waiting for the group settling.
- Scan the faces of your class – *briefly* connect with each student.
- Positively cue the whole class 'Settling … looking … listening.'
- Positively cue the more restless students by name, even. Avoid the overpraise one sometimes hears, 'Oh!! Look at Sean and Travis! Aren't they sitting so LOVELY!?' A brief and positive acknowledgement is enough. Thank those who are settling (this is helpful even in middle school years).

- Use descriptive, reminding cues when engaged in discipline – avoid easy use of 'don't' and 'why'.

  When engaged in any correction (in whole-class settings), we seek to be brief, to focus on the actual behaviour and – where possible – use positive corrective language, e.g. brief *description* (of behaviour), or *direction* to required behaviour; or a *rule reminder*. There are times, of course, we will need to use a clear desist such as 'Stop that now'. With any such desist as well as a direction to stop ... always add what you do want (or expect) the student to do instead ('You need to be ...').

- Smile (not an overwrought 'entertainment smile' – how is it they have so many teeth and so white?!)

- When the class is settled – looking and listening – then give a whole-class greeting at *every lesson*.

- Communicate calmness and expectation (page 103).

It's not the use of 'don't ...', 'can't ...', 'mustn't ...', 'shouldn't ...', stop ...' that's at issue in our discipline language – it's the overuse. Clearly there are occasions when we need to use such imperatives, as when we need to give a decisive unilateral command (behaving unsafely, fighting, even play-fighting).

I have been in many classes, however, where the teacher's normal reminding and correcting language is phrased in negatives – 'Don't call out ...', 'Don't fiddle with your pencil cases when I'm trying to speak.', 'Stop talking ...', 'Can't you listen?!', 'You shouldn't be talking when I'm trying to teach ...'.

It is the frequent and characteristic use of such language that creates an unnecessarily negative tone to daily classroom life. Such usage also minimises the potency of such language when it is context-appropriate.

When you see a confident teacher–leader doing this, it looks simple. It isn't – it is the result of a conscious awareness and skill. Those skills create the kind of climate and relationship that enable students to respond positively to such a teacher–leader and enable a positive teaching and learning dynamic.

- *Sustaining whole-class attention, focus and interest.* Once the class is settled and reasonably focused, we now have to sustain that focus and attention, and engage their motivation and interest. I recall an old teaching maxim, 'A good lesson is a good teacher.' That's half true – our ability to engage and motivate interest is crucial to any effective teaching *and learning*. We also need to be able to address any distracting or disruptive behaviours *during* the whole-class teaching phase of the lesson so that we can keep the whole class as focused and engaged as possible.

This is where our behaviour management and discipline plan will enable us to address such behaviours briefly and, we hope, positively. There are times when our first response may need to be assertive. (This is addressed later on page 104. See also pages 79, 81).

If students are leaning back 'heavily' in their seats (for example), it may be enough to address them, by name, and then give a non-verbal cue to indicate 'four on the floor' (we indicate with our thumb and three fingers extending downwards). The first time we use such non-verbal cues we also need to associate the non-verbal cue with the verbal reminder e.g.: 'Jayson (...) four on the floor, thanks.' We find the word 'thanks' (at the end of the reminder or direction) is more 'expectational' than the word 'please' (Rogers, 2011a). When a student is calling out, it may be enough to verbally cue by name, 'Shannon (...)' and indicate with a hand raised that we are reminding her to put her hand up. If she puts her hand up and calls out, or clicks her fingers, we will need to verbally cue, 'Shannon (...) remember our rule for asking questions thanks' (or for 'group discussion'). If she whingeingly procrastinates, 'I've got my hand up' then a brief, specific direction is enough, 'In our class it's hands up without finger clicking or calling out (...), thanks.' We'll then *resume the flow of the lesson* and tactically ignore any residual sulking. The rest of the students (who are not behaving distractingly) need to see and hear our confidence when we cue those who are distracting or disruptive.

It can help to have a rule poster at the front of the room from day one – large enough to be seen by students at the back of the classroom, and in a clear font.

We've all got a right to learn

To learn well here we remember to:

- Get to class on time
- Have our necessary materials
- In class discussion hands up (...) FGFA
- Partner voices in work time
- If you need teacher assistance – check first with your classmate, then hands up for your teacher.

NB In the poster above, the brackets (...) indicate that in our class we put our hands up without calling out, without finger clicking and one at a time so we get FGFA – *fair go for all*.

It's helpful to remind the class (in the first few lessons) that when a student is asking a question or sharing a viewpoint '*that* student's contribution is not just for me (the teacher) *it's for all of us*. Just as when *you* share *you* want others to listen, so it is when your classmate shares ...'.

- *Keeping the whole-class focus.* If several students are chatting during whole-class teaching time, it will help to *briefly target those students* before we regroup, and sustain, whole-class focus. *Briefly* cue the whole class – 'Excuse me class (...)' (they, after all, have to cope with the 'chatterers' ...). This brief cue effectively says, 'I know it's annoying everyone – I'll be brief'. We then cue the chatting students – 'Chantelle (...) Krystal (...) you're chatting (...); it's whole-class teaching time.' If they do not respond to this brief (and positive) *descriptive comment* we will need to give a clear, simple, brief direction, 'Looking this way and listening thanks,' we might also add, 'without chatting'.

  It is also important to then *regain the flow of whole-class teaching*. For example, if a student walks in late without knocking, we will stop and cue the whole class, 'Excuse me, class', welcome the latecomer by name, and direct them to a seat (see case example page 37) and then resume the flow of the lesson. Problems occur in classroom leadership when a teacher starts to overfocus on distracting or disruptive behaviour by getting caught up in 'discussion' or argument or overfocusing on 'secondary' behaviours (page 45).

- *Transition between whole-class teaching time and on-task learning time.* In our first meetings with the class, we will need to make clear the expected behaviours and routines that enable the transition between the end of whole-class teaching time and individual, paired or group classwork.

  I've been in many classes – as a mentor-teacher – when the class teacher has directed the students to 'get to work' (or words to that effect) and I have little idea what the teacher actually wants them to do regarding the classwork in the next 15 to 20 minutes. If I don't know (and I was listening in the team-teaching phase at the front of the room *with* the teacher), I'm sure many students will also be unclear. *Task clarity* is essential in any lesson or activity. We need to make clear what the learning task or activity involves – even a brief written step-wise plan on the board, or a 'mind map' will help (particularly for visual learners).

  Behaviour clarity involves discussing with the class the expectations about – noise *volume* during classwork (*partner* voices as distinct from 'playground' voices); how to reasonably, and fairly, obtain teacher assistance; students without equipment (page 145); *appropriate* movement around the classroom; leaving the room procedures during class time (to, say, go to the toilet); early finishers (and what options when a student finishes a task early). With expectations such as reasonable noise levels, it can help to model, even role-play, these with younger students at primary level. I've also used modelling of voice levels at lower secondary (in good fun) to indicate the difference between 'partner' voice levels and corridor and playground voices – 'We all have to work, share, chat, discuss ... in this small space. That's why we need to use a "partner" voice (or "inside" voice, "study" voice, or "working voices")'. Students can learn (over several lessons) to develop the habit of voice-volume moderation through our clear expectation and that balance of reminders and encouragement during on-task learning time.

It is important that these expectations and routines are clearly established in the first meeting with a new class. Never assume, or merely hope, that the students will remember such routines from last year (though many will). Even writing them on a chart can help, even in middle school (see the earlier example poster page 98).

- *Lesson closure and considerate exit from the classroom.* I've seen classes race out of the classroom, *very* noisily as soon as the bell goes, ignoring their teacher's last few words. Boys re-engaging in their 'playful punching' and barging into other students from other classes in a busy corridor. Then there are students who try to 'beat the bell'. Furniture is left in disarray with bits of litter on the floor.

It is important to plan for lesson closure and considerate exit. Point out to the whole class (day one, and every day until it's *habit*) that 'We do the next class a favour, thanks. We straighten the furniture (at the end of the day we put chairs *on* the table – we do the cleaner a favour). We pick up any residual litter (even if we didn't actually produce it!) We leave row by row' (at the teacher's direction). We exercise this basic lesson closure, pack-up and exit routine at least up to Year 10. We do so from day one. In time – when their behaviour is cooperatively habitual – we can drop the reminders.

As with any core routine, we need to explain the *reason* why we do 'these things' and then maintain and 'habituate' that routine with a positive expectation, necessary reminders and goodwill – lesson after lesson in that critical first few weeks of the establishment phase.

Always give a 'goodbye' to the class, and a brief personal greeting as each row (or table group) leaves the classroom.

There is a sense in which a sensible and fair routine has an appropriate element of 'training' in the critical first lessons, particularly at primary age level. With goodwill, encouragement and reasonable consistency these routines will become *reasonable habit*.

Summary: Part A

A discipline plan needs to consciously address the key stages of a lesson/activity (in any context):

- Entry to, and settling in, the classroom/area at the outset of the lesson/activity. In some schools or contexts this will still include some form of 'lining up'.
- Transition from whole-class teaching time to on-task learning.
- How we address the on-task learning time itself (noise volumes, time on-task, giving teacher assistance).
- Lesson closure and exit from the classroom.

At each 'stage' of a lesson/activity, there is the potential for distracting and disruptive behaviour – obviously – but the degree and extent will vary significantly from teacher to teacher and between subjects/contexts. A discipline plan has several crucial elements that enable, direct and support a teacher's daily behaviour leadership:

- *Core behaviour leadership practices* – ideally these practices should have a general school-wide consensus . See, for example, the least-to-most intrusive practice (page 105) and Appendix 3.
- *A core 'skills set'* (Rogers, 2011) – whenever we have to discipline we have to do/say certain things. There is wide, ample – school-based – research that highlights the need for a conscious level of skill, particularly in *what we say* when we discipline. As noted earlier, the least helpful time – and place – to 'decide' what to say (in a stressful discipline context) *is in the emotional moment*! While we obviously can't plan for every contingency, there are core skills – widely recognised in the teacher literature – that enable positive and appropriately assertive approaches to discipline language. These language skills are illustrated in the case studies used throughout this text.
- *The necessary expectations and core routines for behaviour and learning in day-to-day classroom life* – these routines address basic issues (deceptively basic issues) such as classroom entry, settling procedures, seating plans, working noise levels, how to get teacher assistance, etc. through to lesson closure.
- *School-wide procedures for addressing time-out contingency* – time-out can range from in-class cool-off time to a supervised removal from the classroom of hostile or aggressive students. This is addressed in Chapter 8.
- *School-wide follow-up procedures* – involve one-to-one meetings with students, whether an after-class chat, *any* form of detention, an informal (or formal) behaviour interview or any form of mediation session. These procedures are also addressed in Chapter 8.

These are the essential elements of a personal discipline plan. It is important that a 'personal' discipline plan reflects school-wide aims, values and practices about behaviour leadership (see below). When this happens we can say – with meaning – that we have a whole-school approach. The days are long gone when teachers could teach, and discipline, and apply behaviour consequences from personal bias, whim or emotional reaction to events as they occur.

PART B
Balancing practices and skills

Communicating calmness in behaviour leadership

I have consistently noticed – over the years – that a teacher's *general calmness* is a significant factor in how responsive, and cooperative, students are to a teacher's leadership. By 'calmness' I do not mean we are unemotional or quiescently passive but rather that the teacher is 'in control' of themselves in relation to how they conduct themselves – particularly when it comes to behaviour management and discipline. The teacher conveys a sense of confidence in how they communicate, even when conveying necessary frustration and anger (page 81). This is an assertive calmness (not cockiness or arrogance) – it is based on a conscious awareness of how we can utilise language in discipline contexts and also how we enable workable relationships with students, colleagues and parents.

For example, there are teachers who have a *characteristically* louder (than average) voice and have an 'edgier', 'nit-picky', petty tone when addressing distracting and disruptive behaviour. Their bearing and movement convey an overly kinaesthetic, motoric presence in a small place like a classroom. These teachers, by *their* behaviours, create an ambient tension that can significantly affect student restlessness, inattention and learning, as well as student self-esteem, goodwill and general cooperation (Rogers, 2011).

I've frequently seen teachers pace up and down at the front of the classroom *while* seeking to engage whole-class attention and focus at the beginning of the lesson. When I've team-taught in such classes I've also noticed that the more restless students will overly track the teacher's kinaesthetic wandering, and vigorous hand-gesturing, and *not actually be listening to what the teacher is saying*. The teacher's overt 'kinaesthesia' is telegraphing restlessness – 'triggering' a corresponding restlessness in such students. Calmer, more relaxing hand gestures – without pacing – can increase student attention and produce a more sustained focus (Rogers, 2011). This assumes, too, that the teacher can also engage the class and sustain that engagement by what (and how) they teach. Of course, there are times, and contexts, when a teacher's voice and sense of drama need to vary to suit the teaching context – to engage, enthuse and focus student attention. That's an essential aspect of teaching itself. What I'm talking about here is the 'calmness' we convey in situations where natural student tension is raised when we need to engage and focus in student management contexts.

Our *characteristic* tone of voice can also engage reciprocal calmness (or tension) in our students, depending on how positive our tone and manner is – how fast-paced, jerky, passive, expressive and confident we are when we speak to (and with) our students. Conscious awareness of *how we come across* to our students is an essential feature of our overall behaviour leadership.

If our *general* facial expressiveness is overly tense (or anxious), if we frequently frown or overuse 'the glare', if we have clenched hands and jerky body language then we look as if we are not in control of ourselves. Students tune in quickly and respond to how they sense 'we are' as confident teacher–leaders in our relationship to them. For example, when engaged in least-intrusive discipline exchanges, a brief frown and raised eyebrows is naturally appropriate – we then relax the facial muscles as we *continue* to speak. We indicate by our facial expression and corresponding confident tone of voice that we expect the student's cooperation. When we address distracting behaviour with positive corrective language (wherever possible), in a way that indicates we are not 'threatened', it *conveys* a confident (not a 'cocky') calmness. It conveys a sense of appropriate authority in one's role (Robertson, 1998; Rogers, 2006 and 2011).

Assertion

Assertive language and cueing is particularly important when we address challenging student behaviour, particularly noxious put-downs, threatening use of language, swearing (*at* the teacher), bullying behaviors, and so on (see also pages 79, 81, 130). Firm assertion in such contexts is not inconsistent with calmness. There are times when we need to clearly, firmly and unambiguously assert what is unacceptable or wrong in a student's behaviour. A firm, *raised*, voice is clearly necessary, at times, to 'break into' a situation where there is potential safety at stake. We do this to stop the fractious punching or overdone play-fighting that goes on from time to time (even in some classrooms). A *sharper,* raised tone of voice is sometimes necessary – we then drop the voice level once we have their 'attention'. It is helpful, then, to use a calmer, slower voice to enhance a sense of security in the student audience observing a high-arousal incident. Assertion is not about winning either – it is about leading in a decisive, and respectful, manner. Pyrrhic victories based on petty meanness create a reactive, uncooperative, climate even in generally cooperative students.

Calmness is enhanced – always enhanced and strengthened – by thoughtful planning in classroom organisation, lesson organisation and development of a personal 'discipline plan' (page 92). Such a plan will include a framework of least-to-most intrusive interventions we *characteristically* use to address distracting and disruptive behaviours. A crucial feature of such 'interventions' will be our use of planned positive corrective language balanced by regular encouragement and feedback.

Reflecting on practice

A point to reflect

As Aristotle has taught us (*Nicomachean Ethics* – Thompson, trans., 1969) 'We learn how to do things by *doing* the things we are learning to do ...'[1] It sounds deceptively basic – it isn't. Skill development takes time (page 109). This is in part a conscious exercise of *self*-awareness, a perspective taking of others' needs (our students) and our preparedness as a leader. We communicate calmness by thinking through how best to communicate under pressure. We then need to develop those actual language and communication skills – they rarely happen 'naturally'. Reflection, planning and developing and using those skilled approaches enables calmness in our leadership.

There are, of course – 'bad days' – our own tiredness, the weather, our health, the 'last straw' ... whatever. On those days we sometimes 'snap' at our students, say things we regret later. On such days it is crucial that we seek to repair and rebuild with the individual and the group. This will convey our essential humanity and normative fallibility. *Characteristic* and reasonable 'calmness' is not inconsistent with 'bad-day' syndrome.

Children need to know, and be aware, that we like them – that there is a fundamental humanness in our characteristic relationship as teacher to student(s). On our 'bad-days' our students are still secure in that relationship because they know what we are normally like. Our *general* calmness, (bad day notwithstanding) will enable that quality of relationship between teacher and students that is at the heart of any effective teaching and learning.

The least-to-most intrusive principle in behaviour management

The principle of least-to-most intrusive in behaviour management emphasises that we have *a wide language repertoire* for management and discipline. The language skills noted throughout this book enable a teacher to:

- Keep the degree of necessary teacher intrusiveness 'low' wherever possible.

- Keep a *positive language focus* when engaged in discipline transactions wherever possible (see the case examples that follow in this chapter). There are times we need to communicate assertively and to express appropriate anger. There are practices and skills that can enable us to utilise such assertion (pages 79, 81).

- A *least-intrusive principle* also enables, and invites, a sense of 'behaviour awareness' in student/s wherever possible rather than simply *telling* them what to do (eg. pages 95, 106).

- This approach also maximises appropriate use of 'behavioural choice' (within known rights, rules and responsibilities) – see the examples below.

For example, if a teacher is being distracted by two lads fiddling with the window blinds (while the teacher is engaged in whole-class teaching), it is often enough to use brief *descriptive cueing*, 'Damien (…) Troy (…) you're fiddling with the window blinds. It's really distracting.' Said positively and confidently (without sarcasm) this 'form' of words raises the students' 'behaviour awareness'. After all they *may* be unaware their behaviour is actually distracting. If they are doing it for attention, they may well continue with such behaviour. In this case the teacher will give a *simple direction* – 'Damien (…) Troy (…) leave the blinds – thanks – and facing this way and listening.' The tone of voice is pleasant and confident – with that brief tactical pausing, and *take-up time,* as the teacher re-engages the whole-class teaching focus. If the students sigh, lean back in their seats and mutter, 'OK, OK' (more residual attentional behaviour), the teacher will *tactically* ignore this. This least-intrusive principle is also likely to create a more cooperative behaviour management climate among the class group generally. The teacher may – of course – have a quiet *after-class* chat with these two students to further clarify fair, and considerate, behaviour in class time (page 119).

The other students in the class observing their teacher take note – they clearly sense their teacher is confidently in charge of the teaching and learning dynamic. If the teacher were to be unnecessarily intrusive over 'small' distractions/ disruptions (like those above), he would soon lose the goodwill of the majority of cooperative students.

Contrast, for example, a teacher responding to such behaviour by simply saying, 'Don't fiddle with the window blinds' or even less helpful, 'Why are you fiddling with the window blinds?' 'Are you supposed to be doing that?' (Such questions are unhelpful to say the least, and likely to overengage the attentional students).

With younger students (lower primary) we would probably leave out the descriptive cue and use positive behaviour directions or rule reminders. For example, several students are eagerly calling out (with their hands up) during whole-class teaching time. If the teacher has communicated the rules and routines (through class discussion), she will need to use reminders and directional cues to establish and 'habituate' fair group discussion.

Often this involves general group reminders as well as individuals who are more attentionally persistent. The teacher scans the faces of her class, pauses and says, 'Remember our rule for asking questions (or group sharing).' Sometimes we'll need to add the additional cue, 'Hands up without calling out thanks.' The emphasis is the positive cue 'Hands up …' (rather than 'Don't call out' or merely the overuse of 'Shhh!'). With individuals who continue to call out several times, it can help to tactically ignore such students *until* they put their hand up without calling out or clicking fingers. With some students we'll need to verbally cue – 'Michael (…) Dean (…) remember (…) hands up without calling out'. At this point the teacher will focus on students who have got their hands up and briefly thank them and cue them in turn. She'll also tactically ignore Michael and Dean's sulking (they frown and fold their arms as if to say it isn't fair). Even in this 10 minutes of class discussion with seven-year-olds, the teacher has an impressive array of skills operating together – positive eye-scanning; a calm, confident and expectant manner; a positive (and confident) use of voice and actual language when reminding and correcting; use of take-up time; *tactical* ignoring and selective attention. If they make a habit of calling-out behaviours (in the first week or so), she'll follow up with them one-to-one (page 119). She may even need to develop an individual behaviour support plan with them. Within such plans the teacher will teach the student (in non-class time) 'how to put their hand up without calling out / eyes and ears facing the front / wait for your teacher to call on you in turn.' These behaviours will be modelled by the teacher one-to-one with the student. She will also practise these behaviours *with* the students so they are clear about 'their plan' when back in classroom time (see Rogers and McPherson, 2008).

Clarifying consequences

If students persist in distracting or disruptive behaviour(s), the teacher will clarify the consequence.

If a teacher has, for example, given a student (high school) a directed choice about putting an iPod or phone away (' ... on my desk or in your bag, thanks' – see case study page 46), the teacher will give the student take-up time by moving away to convey the expectation (and confidence) that she expects the student to put the item away. Most students do, with some grumbling. It is helpful (at this point) if the teacher *tactically* ignores sibilant muttering, sighs, raised eyes and whingeing of, 'It's not fair other teachers let us ...' (page 45).

As she does the rounds of the class during on-task learning time she notices the student hasn't put the item away and has re-engaged their iPod. She doesn't argue ('Why haven't you ...!') nor does she threaten ('If you don't put it away you'll be on detention'). She clarifies the consequence – 'Jayson I've asked you to put the iPod away. If you choose not to I'll have to follow this up with you after.' She does this quietly, clearly and calmly. She will not brook any discussion (or argument) at this point. She will leave the student to 'own the consequence'. She'll also *tactically* ignore further whinges. If the student says, 'I don't care!' (I've had that many times over the years), it is enough to say 'I care' and leave it at that *for now*. If they choose not to work within the fair school rule we will need to follow up with the student later, *as we said we would do*. It is the *fair certainty* of the consequence (later) that is more powerful than arguments or threats at this point.

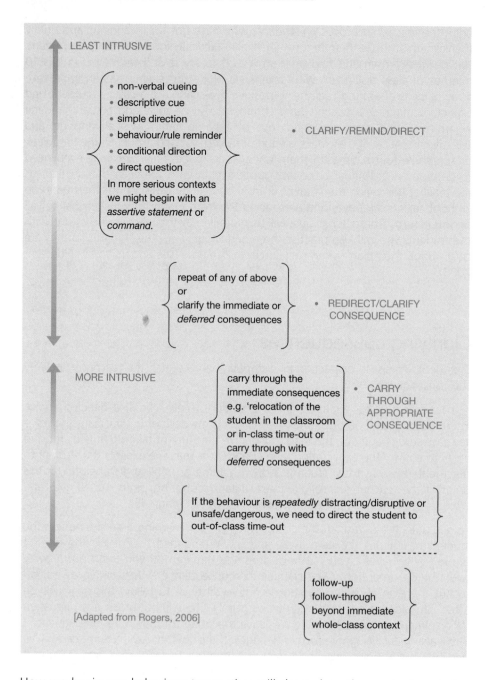

LEAST INTRUSIVE

- non-verbal cueing
- descriptive cue
- simple direction
- behaviour/rule reminder
- conditional direction
- direct question

In more serious contexts we might begin with an *assertive statement* or *command*.

• CLARIFY/REMIND/DIRECT

repeat of any of above
or
clarify the immediate or *deferred* consequences

• REDIRECT/CLARIFY CONSEQUENCE

MORE INTRUSIVE

carry through the immediate consequences e.g. 'relocation of the student in the classroom or in-class time-out or carry through with *deferred* consequences

• CARRY THROUGH APPROPRIATE CONSEQUENCE

If the behaviour is *repeatedly* distracting/disruptive or unsafe/dangerous, we need to direct the student to out-of-class time-out

follow-up
follow-through
beyond immediate
whole-class context

[Adapted from Rogers, 2006]

How we begin any behaviour transaction will depend on the *context* – whole-class teaching time; on-task learning time; non-classroom contexts (corridor, lunch supervision, playground). For example, we wouldn't normally use direct questions 'What are you doing ...?', 'What should you be doing?' (page 110) during whole-class teaching time or, say, an assembly. In whole-class contexts we tend to use non-verbal cueing, descriptive comment, simple direction, rule reminder (where necessary) or a conditional direction.

Skills under pressure

We need skills of behaviour management – particularly when we're under pressure. As noted already, the last point *in time* when we need to be 'thinking' about what to say and do (in any discipline context) is when we're under pressure – in the stress of the immediate emotional moment, when students are distracting or disruptive.

A conscious framework of practices and skills is fundamental to any discipline plan. While we obviously can't plan for every contingency, we can prepare for what we are likely to face as we lead young people day after day. This is critical in our first meetings with a new class. We can plan for *what to do and say* when faced with the normative stress occasioned by distracting and disruptive behaviour. Such planning heightens appropriate confidence through shared professional assurance that such practices and skills are more likely to enable the aims of discipline (page 113).

The practices and skills noted throughout the case studies in this book operate *dynamically* – not as some kind of formulaic, stepwise, response to disruptive behaviour. No skill operates in isolation. For example, the difficult skill of *tactical* ignoring relies on our ability to sense when it's appropriate to *tactically* ignore a student's sighing, pouting, eyes-to-the-ceiling, tut-tutting, and so on (page 45). Our ability to convey and communicate calmness is also fundamental when tactically ignoring 'secondary' behaviours and selectively attending and encouraging our students when they are engaged in cooperative, supportive behaviours.

Case study

A challenging Year 7 class – it's on-task learning time in social studies. Several students are out of their seats (for no good reason I could see). My colleague (who I was team-teaching with) had struggled for some time with several task-avoiding students. I suggested we go up to each student and – quietly – enable them to refocus. I went up to each student (in turn) and quietly and clearly redirected them back to their seats and to the learning activity. When I went up to Travis, even on receipt of me asking his name he sighed and frowned, 'What?'. It is this aspect of the student's overall behaviour (the sigh and frown) that I chose to *tactically* ignore *at that point* in this brief transaction. We keep the management focus directed to the →

student's primary aspect of behaviour by raising his awareness (about his behaviour) and *directing that awareness*. I asked him for his name again – quietly. He let out an overdrawn sigh, 'Travis'.

'Travis (…) you're out of your seat' (a brief descriptive cue). He replied, quickly, with, 'I was just getting a ruler from Adam', (more sighing and eyes-to-the-ceiling). I reminded him he could use the rulers (or pens, pencils, etc.) in the 'materials box' (page 145). This class, like many I get to work with, had developed poor *habits* of classroom behaviour commonly in areas like task-avoidance, loud social chattering, inappropriate wandering and calling out to get teacher assistance (without making any personal effort to read through and comprehend the learning task).

I asked Travis, 'What are you supposed to be doing now?' (the tone and manner – of course – need to be positive, not accusatory). 'My work' (more sighing). 'I'll see you a bit later, *at your desk* Travis, to see how you're going. Thanks.' I gave him some take-up time as I walked off to the next student. Travis trotted off – sighing again – to get a ruler and a pen from the materials box. He walked across to his seat, slumped down and sulked. I heard some sibilant muttering as he no doubt regaled his classmate about this annoying new teacher …

It took my colleague and I several minutes to refocus each wandering student. This included returning to their desk area, later, to give selective attention *and encouragement* when they were attempting to 'work'. By this time each student – and the class generally – had become more settled. It was tiring but necessary. We were slowly re-engaging the class by encouraging positive learning and behaviour habits (page 92).

A direct question ('What …?', 'Where …?', 'When …?', 'How …?' is more likely to focus a student's behaviour awareness than a 'Why?' question. It would be really unhelpful to ask the student why he's out of his seat or, the equally unhelpful question, 'Are you out of your seat?' (Of course he's out of his seat!). It is more helpful to describe and then use a focused question – for example, 'What are you supposed to be doing now?'

Sometimes we will get the ' … don't know', or even ' … don't care!' We avoid pointless arguments and direct the student to what they need to be doing now. It can often help – at this point – to reassure the student you'll be over to help soon (as we give them take-up time to re-engage their work).

Yes, there is social intelligence at work here as we lead, guide and encourage our students – as we 'read' their body language and assess what to focus on in the immediate emotional moment, and when – and what – to *tactically* ignore; what degree of assertion we exercise (in tone and manner); when to give take-up-time and when to go back to the student to encourage and reinforce. Some teachers argue that 'all this' is down to personality. Yes, there is personality present, but there is also a degree of *conscious skill* that enables one's social intelligence and leadership behaviour.

Experience and skill – more than *just* experience and personality

Edward de Bono (1986) makes an interesting point about experience and skill. He notes that it is a fatal mistake to assume that experience is the same as skill, or that if a 'skill' is used it must somehow be 'right', because of the years of experience in its use. He gives the example of a two-finger typist (say a journalist) who goes through life with a two-finger repertoire – serviceably but inefficiently (at least for words per minute). Such a typist is contrasted with one who has spent, say, six months learning efficient skills and practising them. Such a typist can, with some ease, out-distance a two-finger typist with 15 years' experience.

De Bono compares this example with that of participants in 'conflict situations' whose years of inefficient conflict-resolution behaviours may only have served to handle conflict poorly – the 'years of experience' count for little. Skills and experience are clearly not the same thing; *skill at what?*

I have seen this analogy of contrast frequently in our profession where a teacher will – for years – manage students in a certain way that is ineffective (in the light of the sorts of aims and practices expected in classrooms these days). They will even continue with such practice despite the stress it creates for themselves, their students and, even, their colleagues. The suggestion of reflecting on one's practice *and skill* is sometimes seen, therefore, as a sore point – a criticism of their 'experience'. 'Been there', 'Done that', 'Doesn't work' and 'You can't teach an old dog new tricks!'.

More than personality?

I often hear teachers raise the issue of personality when exploring the issue of positive and effective classroom management and discipline – 'Oh, it's just their personality – that's why those teachers can get through to those kids!' The other one I hear is, 'Oh, they're *lucky* (the more effective teachers), they can connect with their kids ...' The other comment I hear (from *some* older teachers) is, 'You can't teach an old dog new tricks'. As an older teacher, my standard reply is 'You're not a dog – you're a human being who's chosen to teach.' I say this with goodwill and some intentional attempt at a humorous retort. I don't know if 'old dogs' can learn new tricks – teachers can always reflect on, reassess and develop their teaching practice. Further, what we're working on in skill development is not 'tricks', or even techniques. There is an old saying, 'Don't learn the tricks of the trade – learn the trade.' If we choose to teach and want to teach, there are practices and skills that enable more positive – and effective – teaching and behaviour leadership. These practices and skills are well established in the literature.

In the peer support groups I mentioned earlier (page 15) the 'personality'/'luck'/'old dog' and the sighing 'Well, it's just me' responses are often raised. Our response – beyond natural whingeing – is:

- Is getting to class on time and *being prepared* more than personality? Being prepared should be so, even for a single lesson (or unit of work) we've taught many times before. While we can 'wing it' from time to time (and students know the difference), we should never simply rely on 'Oh, it'll be alright on the day!'
- Is a whole-class calm-settling and a positive greeting to the class down to mere personality? (pages 95, 31)
- Is conscious use of positive behaviour leadership language (particularly discipline language) merely down to personality? (page 46)
- Is the willingness to plan well (within our faculty and grade teams) for mixed differentiation due only to personality?
- Is the ability to positively motivate and thoughtfully encourage *all* our students the result of personality or a 'bag of tricks' ...?

Well – I think you get the picture. What I'm saying here is that there are transferable practices and skills *that do not stem from personality alone*. Our personality and temperament clearly affect the way we approach anything we do. What makes the difference is our willingness to *be aware of what it is in our temperament and personality that affects our ability to develop positive practice as a teacher–leader.*

A whole-school approach to behaviour management and discipline

In the 1990s the Department of Education (in each state of Australia) started to consciously address, and encourage, what was termed 'a whole-school approach to discipline and behaviour management'. While this 'whole-school' approach took many forms, and had varying degrees of take-up and success, it certainly marked a decisive shift in the way schools were encouraged to think about student behaviour. We began to reassess and usefully reflect on concepts and seemingly familiar understandings about discipline in light of new understandings about child development and theories of behaviour and the links between learning and behaviour. We began to understand, and struggle with, the challenges (and justice) of inclusion in mainstream schools (of students with learning and behaviour disorders); the concept of rights and responsibilities as applying to all members of the school community; and an increasing emphasis on teachers working collaboratively – and supportively – in these areas.

The Elton Report (1989) in Britain reported and recommended similar whole-school emphases.

Corporal punishment was abolished in Australia (and the UK) in the mid-1980s – the whole-school emphasis on the way we should address behaviour issues was, in part, a response to that decisive and essential shift in school discipline. Not all schools, or teachers, took up these emphases with the intent and purpose with which they were heralded. This is still the case – schools vary in their degree of consciousness and professional goodwill about whole-school emphases on issues of behaviour and discipline. Individual teachers vary in their presuppositions and values about discipline and in their conceptions about, and practical expressions of, leadership, control and power. In my day (when I first started teaching) there were still many teachers who believed that the power of teachers was essentially our power *over* our students – corporal punishment was an obvious corollary to that view.

When we develop shared practice (within a whole-school approach) we are aware of using our power (as teacher/leaders) *for* and *with* our students – not merely *over* them in the sense of mere force and control. This understanding has practical implications for the way we discipline and manage. It is a central premise behind our practices and skills – it shapes and directs our skills.

A whole-school approach to *anything*, let alone the crucial area of behaviour, requires a genuine effort by the school management to work with *all* teaching staff, as well as the students and (to some extent) with the parents in clarifying understanding and encouraging a shared purpose (and values) about *how* we lead, teach and manage young people. In the research on teacher stress there is a consistent finding about the correlation between a supportive, and whole-school, approach to behaviour management and discipline and reduced levels of teacher stress. There is also a clear and positive correlation between the degree of colleague support and genuine development of whole-school approaches in schools (Rogers, 2002).

The essential aspects of a whole-school approach

● *Shared aims* are based on common values about respect, mutual regard and core rights (such as the right to feel safe, the right to respect and fair treatment and the right to learn). These aims enable us to think about *why* we discipline children and young people – what do we seek to achieve and address when we have to correct, apply the rules *and* consequences? What is the difference between punishment and consequences? – between power and control?' between 'force' and directed choices? the fair certainty principle when carrying through with behaviour consequences (as contrasted with punitive intent)? How can we enable our students to be *aware of and take ownership of and accountability for their behaviour?* These are challenging aims and they require us to think about our behaviour leadership practice as it seeks to address those aims.

The central aims of discipline

Whenever we discipline a student (in classroom or non-classroom settings), we are seeking to enable the student to:

- *be aware of their behaviour and how it affects others*
- *to take ownership of their behaviour.*

The teacher will do this in such a way that it is likely that their discipline will:

- *focus on desired behaviour (wherever possible), as well as addressing distracting and disruptive behaviour*
- *keep the fundamental dignity and respect of the student intact (wherever possible).*
- *How aware are you of your characteristic discipline language – the way you remind? your use of questions? your use appropriate 'choices'? your assertive language?*
- *How does your discipline language relate to sorts of language described in the case studies?*
- *How aware are you of your characteristic – and general – tone and manner when you engage in typical day-to-day discipline and management?*
- *How does your own discipline plan relate to the concepts of least-to-most intrusive (page 105)?*
- *How does your characteristic behaviour leadership (what you do and say when you discipline) enable the aims noted above?*
- *Shared and preferred practices delineate the way we lead young people as teacher–leaders. These practices are based on those aims and values. These practices describe how we speak to, how we treat and how we manage, counsel and support young people to be aware of their rights and their responsibilities. What we believe about management and discipline is reflected in what we do – hopefully that link between beliefs and common practice is a conscious one (Appendix 3).*

→

- *Shared plans to address the day-to-day management of children and young people in school. These plans address three critical areas:*
  - *behaviour management and discipline at the classroom level (pages 91–111)*
  - *behaviour management and discipline at the duty-of-care level (in the corridor, in the playground, lunch supervision, wet-day supervision, excursion and out-of-school supervision).*
  - *behaviour leadership and support for students with learning disorders and diagnosed (or symptomatic) behaviour disorders. These students often need an individual behaviour plan and some degree of individual case supervision with adult mentorship to support both student and the classroom teachers.[2] (pages 121–122)*

Each of these areas of planning (above) need colleague collaboration and ongoing collegial review so that what we actually do within those shared aims *and* preferred practices reflects whole-school aims and objectives (bad day notwithstanding!)

When teachers have been given the professional opportunity *and* professional dignity of working collaboratively on these areas of common concern in their behaviour leadership, they feel valued *and* supported. There, in place, is a known school-wide policy *and plan* that acknowledges the normative challenges of behaviour management and discipline. That policy and plan demonstrates that we have thought through critical questions about *what to do and say* when we lead young people. We have developed reliable alliances – collegially – so that when we are addressing particularly challenging, and at-risk, students we have a supported and *collegial approach*.

Any school policy needs to reflect what we *characteristically* do – day after day after day. It is not merely a mission statement and 20 sheets of paper bound in a glossy folder.

Shared goals, shared expectations (realistic expectations), shared practices and *workable plans* create a strong sense of communal identity in a school and increase a *positive* sense of consistency in day-to-day behaviour management – we feel better (less stressed), we work better (more collegially) and our students benefit (the reason for why we exist as a school). (Rogers 2006, 2002).

A whole-school behaviour policy has to realistically answer fundamental questions such as:
- *Why should we do this? (our values)*
- *What are our aims when we engage in any form/expression of discipline and behaviour leadership?*

> ● *What should we do? (practical utility based on our values)*
> ● *How best can we do it? (the practical planning that enables and realises our values and our behaviour in a day-to-day sense)*
>
> *When we work collaboratively to address, and review, these questions, we are supporting one another and enabling the mission of making a difference in the lives of young people (we might even do 'well' on the OFSTED treadmill in the process!)*

Notes

1. *Nicomachean Ethics*: Book 2: Chapter 1. (Thompson, trans., 1969).
2. This book does not address this issue in any detail. Readers may wish to read Rogers (2004) or Rogers (2009). Both books address real case studies of teachers working directly with children who have diagnosed (or symptomatic) behaviour disorders.

Chapter

8

Difficult and challenging students: follow-up and support

What this chapter will explore and develop:

- The essential need to follow up one to one with distracting and disruptive students
- The core protocols, and skills, of one-to-one follow-up with a student (beyond classroom time)
- The nature and use of time-out
- The policy and practice of time-out
- The reasonable support of senior staff for (and during) time-out
- Swearing and stress

Following up with students one-to-one

Eddie had made his presence felt early on in the lesson (a particularly challenging Year 9 class). I'd been introduced to the class by their harried teacher in the first few minutes. My colleague finished the brief introduction and 'handed the class over ...'. It was my first team-teaching lesson with this class – I was cueing the class to settle (page 95). As I was reminding the class – for the third time – to 'settle and face this way ...', Eddie called out yet again, 'Hey Bill, I'm talking to you. Why you here? You going to be a new teacher?' (I need to briefly note, it was a school where students are allowed – encouraged – to address teachers by their first name). His voice was like a verbal neon sign. I managed – just – to find a break in his 'verbal traffic' as it were, and I interrupted his flow ... 'Eddie (...) Eddie (...)' Before I could go on, he leaned back in his seat, hitting the back of the classroom wall. 'What!?' I broke into his plaintive oration ... 'Eddie, you're calling out. If you want to ask a question it's hands up thanks. We all get a fair go then.' As I turned back resettling, and focusing the class again, he called out, 'Gees! Can't I even ask a question!?' I replied, *briefly*, 'Eddie (...) hands up and a fair go.' He leaned back – loudly – (hitting his chair on the back wall) folded his arms and said, 'Well, I won't say nothing then ...!' He sulked (loudly). I *tactically* ignored him at that point. While some of his mates laughed at his behaviour – surprisingly – the class seemed to sense that what I'd said was 'OK.' They settled down and we moved into the lesson proper.

I looked across – briefly – to Claire, my colleague who had asked me to work with her in this maths class with her as a mentor. A brief spasm of remembered, and familiar, annoyance showed on her face. I sensed (also) she was saying, 'Now you know what I have to put up with ...'

The lesson progressed reasonably well – many students even 'got some work done'. Towards the close of the lesson all I could think of was a coffee, but just before I dismissed the class I said to Eddie that I wanted a brief chat with him after class (before lunch recess). His immediate response was, 'What did I do?! C'mon; why do I have to stay back!?' 'A few minutes, Eddie (I replied) I want to see you after class.' He folded his arms and sulked loudly – he seemed good at sulking.

When the bell went I dismissed the class. Eddie stood by the classroom door arms folded, scowling. A few of his mates hung around outside the classroom. I directed them to 'leave and enjoy their break'. Before I could say anything Eddie immediately asked me why he had to stay back after class, 'What did I do?! C'mon – what did I do?' He was clearly annoyed and frustrated.

The one-to-one meeting

In *any* follow-up (one-to-one) with a student where we need to address our concerns about their behaviour, the student is often annoyed, frustrated or angry.

Sometimes they are anxious. They don't always see their behaviour in the same way we see it. They don't feel the stressful effect of their behaviour *at the time* it occurred during class. The teacher, too, is often annoyed . It is easy (perhaps even tempting!) to want to 'get our own back' in this one-to-one setting.

I've walked down many school corridors over the years and heard (some) teachers 'speaking' to a student after class along these lines: 'You could be outside now couldn't you!? No – you're always the big man in front of the class! You've done virtually no work this lesson have you? HAVE YOU?! I said that if you didn't get some work done and stop wasting everyone's time you would have to stay back – DIDN'T I SAY THAT?! And what did you say? – you said you didn't care – you're caring now aren't you?! ...' I could record pages of the typical things I hear from next-door class teachers, or as I walk past a class and see a teacher shouting and gesticulating to a student ... I'm sure you've seen it.

Of course it's stressful. The student was disruptive, insensitive, attentional, rude, disrespectful. Some teachers may even think they're making an important point when they speak to the student in such a way after class. Clearly such student behaviours are stressful, yet students will *obviously* turn off if we merely berate or harangue. Some will get even more annoyed or angry – some will just walk off with the teacher 'chasing'. Most will carry their resentment into the next class.

Fundamental protocols of follow-up

Back to Eddie – my colleagues and I find that, while it's important to follow up behaviour incidents one-to-one with the student, we can almost always reduce relational stress when we:

- Emphasise respectful *certainty* rather than intentional severity (the unnecessary – if tempting – harangue above). The message we're seeking to convey to the student is that this *period of time* (the brief after-class follow-up, the behaviour interview, the detention, etc.) is based on a fair consequential certainty that relates to their *behaviour* as it affects us (or other students). This 'certainty' principle (when carried through respectfully) is a much more powerful learning that any vilifying retort.

- Briefly tune into how the student is probably feeling *at that point*. We do this without being patronising or self-seeking – 'Eddie, you're probably feeling annoyed that I've asked you to stay back. Five minutes you're out of here ...' In such brief class 'chats' or brief lunch-time interviews (5–10 minutes) I'll always specify the likely time.

  Our calmness will also help focus and enable the student's 'calmness' at this point (page 103). Eddie immediately said, 'What did I do – I didn't do nothing?!' He was less annoyed now (I'd said 'five minutes' – I think that also helped).

- Focus the student's awareness on the behaviour, issue or task you've directed them to stay back for. In a five-minute chat – keep that focusing *brief* – 'Eddie when I was trying to teach the class you called out at least a dozen times.' 'What? – what do you mean calling out?' I asked him if I could show him what I meant. It can sometimes help to clarify to the student what we heard/saw regarding behaviour by showing them – briefly. My colleagues and I call this 'behaviour mirroring' (Rogers, 2004). This enables the student to be more 'behaviourally' aware. We *always* ask the student's permission if we can show them what it looked/sounded like when ... (here we refer *briefly* to the student's distracting behaviour). 'Eddie I want to show you what I saw and heard when you were calling out.' In Eddie's case I asked if I could give a quick demo. He sighed, 'Yes – I don't care ...' I went to the back of the classroom, actually sat in his seat, leaned back and called out, 'Bill! Bill! – C'mon I'm talking to you ...'

  I 'mirrored' his behaviour for – perhaps – 5 to 10 seconds. He laughed and smirked (this is normal/typical with boys). I walked back to the front of the classroom, 'That's what I mean, Eddie.' I pointed to the vacated psychological, kinaesthetic 'space' – he got the point.

NB With any such 'behaviour mirroring' with students, we only ever conduct such modelling one-to-one – *never in front of other students*:

- Ask if you can show them what it looks (or sounds) like when they ... (here be specific about the actual behaviour ...) 'Can I give you a demo ...?' (this to older students).
- Keep the 'mirroring' brief (5–10 seconds).
- Physically step away (as it were) from the place/space of mirroring and refer back to what you've just done ('*That's* what it looks like when you ...').
- *Only* use such 'mirroring' to raise a sense of kinaesthetic awareness in them.
- Do not use this approach if the student is overly hostile.

They often laugh (that's normal). If you are hesitant about using such an approach (for any reason) then focus on brief, descriptive language about their behaviour.

Caveat: we would not use this approach with students diagnosed with autism spectrum disorder.

- *Always give the student a right-of-reply* – in fact before I could say, 'Is there anything you want to say ...', Eddie said, 'I don't do that all the time!' (he was grinning). I replied, 'I don't know what you do all the time, Eddie – you called out like that, though, easy a dozen times while I was trying to teach the class today. Not just with me, with Claire too' (his regular teacher). 'Other kids call out too, not just me.' He said this more than a little defensively. I agreed (partially), 'Others do call out from time to time, Eddie. When I asked those students to remember our rule for class discussion – they did. And I'll ask other students to stay back when I think their behaviour is unreasonable or unfair. I just wanted this brief chat to remind you about our fair rule for class discussions. Is there anything else you want to say?' He asked, firstly, if I was going to teach his class again. I said I was. He frowned, then smiled and said 'Can I go now?' He was a lot calmer, but keen to get away (I, too, was keen to get my fast-diminishing tea break!).

- *Separate amicably* – this is a point that some teachers seem unaware of. They will finish a 'chat', a behaviour interview or a detention session and the last thing they'll say, before sending the student 'off', is something like, 'You do that again, you waste my time like that, you upset my lesson like that ... and you won't just be speaking to me, or the year adviser, or the principal! I'll ring your mother and I'll ...' The student then leaves with that last – primary – memory. They'll come back to class with that same memory.

  Having had countless such chats – and longer follow-up sessions with challenging students – I almost always find it improves relationships *next time we are together in class* if we separate amicably.

  Some teachers will complain that all this kind of follow-up is too time-consuming – they may want a senior teacher to 'fix' the student. While there are many factors that affect a student's behaviour (even on a given day), the student is still the student *in our class* and we will need to find some time to speak with them and seek to work through *our concerns with them as their teacher.*

- If we are particularly struggling to connect with the student, or if we are uncertain how best to develop any one-to-one meeting, it is always worth asking a senior colleague to sit in on such a meeting. We will need to plan ahead for such a meeting and if we conduct such meetings with goodwill, and a student right-of-reply, they are often surprisingly productive.

Ongoing patterns of distracting and disruptive behaviour

If the student continues (over the next lessons) being distracting and disruptive (in class time), we will need to:

- Check with the year adviser to see if there is a *similar pattern of behaviour* occurring in other classes. This is crucial. Students do sometimes vary in the kind of, and frequency of, distracting and disruptive behaviour across classes and across teachers. This does not necessarily mean one teacher is more adept, skilled or effective in their management with such students. We can, though, utilise the knowledge, awareness, understandings and skills of such teachers to support colleagues who may be struggling with the more challenging students.

- Organise a collegial review with all teachers who teach/work/support that student to see if we can develop a year-level approach to working with the student. Such a review will address the nature/context of the student's distracting and disruptive behaviours, along with the *frequency* and *duration* of such behaviour (how often in each lesson and is it more than bad-day syndrome?) This feedback is crucial to the development of any individual behaviour support plan for the student. Any such plan must have a whole-team, year-level commitment to enable any success.

Such a plan would – normally – be developed by a senior teacher working with the student one-to-one. The senior teacher would then communicate the aims and elements of such a plan to each teacher (and teaching assistant) who works with that student. Guidelines for how to manage the student, within his plan (during class time), are discussed with all colleagues who teach (and support) that student. Suggestions for how best to motivate and encourage the student are also shared.

At primary level such a plan is normally initiated and developed by the grade teacher. That plan is then communicated to all specialist and support colleagues. A behaviour plan at primary age level will often utilise 'social stories' and picture cues, as well as modelling, role-play and rehearsal by the student (one-to-one with their grade teacher).

Any individual behaviour support plan will aim to teach the academic and social skills the student needs to cope and manage his behaviour and learning at school (Rogers, 2004).

Any such year-level plan for the student will also involve a very clear, staged time-out approach. This will include what to say (and who to call on) if/ when the student becomes hostile, threatening, aggressive or (effectively) 'holds the class to ransom' by *repeatedly* disruptive, or dangerous, behaviour.

Time-out

Case study

A challenging Year 7 class, first term, second week. Rosie (my colleague) had warned me before we 'went in'. It took us a while to get the class settled and begin our English lesson. There were several students who were very attentional – personal chatting (seemingly ignoring their class teacher), frequent calling out, vigorous seat leaning ... One lad, Scott, was very persistent with his calling out and clowning comments. When I directed him to put his hand up (without calling out loudly) he would try to start an argument. We refused to argue with him and briefly continued to remind him of the fair rule. At one point he sulked – loudly – adding, 'You can't say nothing here!' Several times he muttered swear words to try to get attention from us and the rest of the class.

Later – in the on-task phase of the lesson – Scott took his chair into the middle of the classroom (Rosie had a U-shaped seating plan), banging past several students. One of the girls challenged him and he told her to 'shut it!' It all happened so quickly. It was a blatant expression of attentional posturing. He sat – centre of room – arms folded and started to sing. A number of students – obviously – started to laugh at Scott. This triggered a louder sing-song voice. I walked over to him (not too close) and said, 'Scott, you know you need to be back in your seat. When you're back there, I'll come and help you with your work.' He wouldn't return any eye contact. As I moved away, to give him take-up time, he began to sing, 'I'm not f---ing doing it, I'm not f---ing doing it ...' Rosie and I'd looked at each other across the classroom – I saw stress, concern, frustration and uncertainty. I suspected he would not leave the room for any *directed* time-out (he was – effectively – holding the learning of the class to ransom). I decided to quietly ask Rosie to take the whole class out, row by row. She did. To their credit, the rest of the class left reasonably quietly. I stayed by the door in case Scott might have 'done a runner' (even then I would not have restrained him – there was no actual danger; just *persistent* and very loud disruption). In most cases of time-out (of any sort) the aim is to direct a student away from their immediate peer audience so that a safe, learning classroom environment can continue *without significant, or persistent, disruptions or dangerous behaviours*. The aim then is to enable the student in question to calm, settle and refocus. The sort of time-out we used with Scott is the exception – not the rule.

As Rosie left, with the class, Scott continued swearing – loudly – and provocatively. Within a minute of the class leaving it was just Scott and I in the classroom. He ran to the back of the classroom and 'sat' under the computer table crying very angry tears. I left him for a while – *tactically* ignoring him as I sat on a chair by the classroom door. Eventually, as his crying lessened, I quietly said, 'Scott, when you're calmer I want you to come with me to the year co-ordinator. When you've calmed down – later – we'll talk about what happened.' More muttered swearing, but eventually he came with me. Rosie returned – with the class – about 10 minutes after we left.

It was messy and inelegant – but this form of time-out enabled the class to feel safe, to get the peer audience away, and – eventually – get Scott to a senior colleague.

Scott had been diagnosed with attention deficit hyperactive disorder and oppositional defiance disorder – he was on two major medications. There were also three other boys on medication in the classroom. It's a challenging school, yet one that is willing to work with very troubled and – at times – damaged young people like Scott.

This was Scott's first few weeks in this high school. Within the week, a 'case supervisor' was appointed to work with Scott on an *individual behaviour support plan*. This role was taken by a senior colleague skilled in working with students having a behaviour profile like Scott. That teacher was given dedicated time release to set up this plan with Scott. He met twice weekly with Scott (teaching behaviours one-to-one) and communicated regularly with all Year 7 colleagues. It was this whole-school commitment that began to see a difference not only in Scott's behaviour, but in staff consensus and shared purpose in supporting Scott *and each other*.

Time-out is a behaviour consequence

Time-out is a *necessary* consequence whenever a student's behaviour is *persistently* disruptive or dangerous. Students have the right to feel safe in a classroom and to learn without continued and persistent disruption from fellow students. Time-out sets up an appropriate 'if–then' understanding and a fair and necessary consequential reality. Teachers should not have to put up with the stress occasioned by students who, like Scott, effectively hold a class 'to ransom'. A well-planned time-out policy is no panacea – it is no substitute for a well-developed discipline plan (Chapter 7). It is, however, an essential part of a whole-school approach to behaviour management. Teachers need the assurance and professional (and established) security that when a student is as disruptive as Scott was then we can expect (and receive) senior colleague support, without blame or censure.

A whole-school approach

All staff need to be clear about what we mean by time-out *as a consequence – the forms of time-out* used in the school (in Scott's case we were using the most 'extreme' form); how we cue students (what we actually say to them when applying the time-out consequence); what we do if a student refuses to leave the classroom to go to a time-out place (i.e. a senior teacher); what happens to a student *during* time-out; *the role of the initiating teacher in follow-up and follow-through with the student they have directed to time-out* and what support they should expect from senior colleagues in *any* follow-up (beyond time-out itself).

The forms of time-out, within a whole-school approach – normally include:

- In-class cool-off time (at infant/middle primary level) – a student is directed to take five minutes cool-off time to calm/settle and think about their behaviour (see case example, pages 82, 83).

- Directing a student to go to a class *nearby* (colleague-assisted time-out) – the colleague (in that nearby class) will decide if (and when) to send the student back during that class period. There must be very clear guidelines about how we use this approach including, obviously, how we direct the student to the teacher next door (or across the corridor). With younger children we'll need to send them with a responsible student. It is important to use a calm, clear voice – no gesticulating. 'I've asked you to settle down. You haven't. I want you to go to Mrs Smith's class now.' The teacher walks a student to the classroom door and directs them to the appropriate classroom (this may be a class with older students).

> NB If you have decided that the student needs time-out, of *any* kind, and they start 'plea bargaining' – 'Miss I'll be all right!! I won't stab the furniture with the scissors ... I won't keep punching others ... I won't *keep* calling out, and running around the room, and jumping on tables ...! I promise Miss!' – do not accept their 'plea bargain'.
>
> It is the *certainty* – the fair certainty – that you will carry this consequence through (the 'if–then' ...) – that is far more effective than arguing, shouting or responding to their pleas and 'promises'. It also communicates your commitment to enabling the safety and ongoing learning of the other students.

- *Senior teacher assistance* – in some schools (larger schools) teachers are asked to send a very disruptive (or dangerous) student to a nominated senior teacher. Some schools provide a 'thinking room' or 'time-out room' – staffed by senior teachers (and other teachers willing to use their 'spare', non-contact periods to supervise the time-out room). Some schools send a responsible student with the timed-out student and a note is signed (and returned to the class teacher so that we know the student has 'arrived' and is being supervised).

- If a student refuses to leave to go to a nominated senior teacher, we need to be able to call on an allocated senior colleague by phone (or a nominated student 'runner'). The key is to keep the time-out *process* as calm as possible. The other students witnessing any time-out episode need our calm reassurance as the teacher–leader that we are in control of the situation.

Our calmness also minimises the peer audience to the disruptive student. The senior teacher will then escort the student from the classroom to a time-out 'place'.

Crisis time-out

We cannot *make* a student leave a classroom, and restraining them (unless they are a *significant* danger to themselves or others) is rarely appropriate. If a student (like Scott) is persistently, and *significantly*, disruptive and is likely to refuse, or – when directed – refuses to leave the classroom, it is better for the senior teacher to stay in the classroom with the disruptive student and for the class teacher to calmly – but decisively – escort the class away from the classroom. Normally, within 5 to 10 minutes, the timed-out student (now without a peer audience) will leave with the senior teacher.

Supervising a student during a time-out episode

Time-out is just that; time – *out* and *away* – from the other students (and the teacher) affected by significant disruptive, unsafe, dangerous or aggressive behaviour. It is not a counselling session. Students sometimes utilise disruptive episodes to get out of the classroom (and any attentional 'pressures' about 'work' and behaviour) in order to have a pleasant chat with a supportive adult. The problem is that while such chats are obviously helpful, they set up an unhelpful reinforcing association *at this point* in the behaviour cycle. We save counselling sessions for another time (even later that day) when the student is calmer and we, too, have the time to talk with them. Time-out is time for the student to sit, calm themselves and think about their behaviour.

It can be helpful to direct the student to fill in a pro forma with some guiding questions about their behaviour, or – for younger children – the teacher asks the questions and records their answers. They will only be asked to do this if and when they are calmed down – it is not a forced process. The initiating teacher (who has directed the student to time-out) then works through the responses (to the questions) with the student – later that day – as part of the follow-up. Sometimes such follow-up may need to be postponed till the following day (or two) – particularly at secondary level.

> **Key questions to ask the student during a time-out episode with a senior teacher**
>
> These questions can be directly asked of a student to raise awareness about their behaviour and its effect, and the teacher records the student's responses (particularly for younger students and those who we know struggle with

writing or presenting their thoughts in written form). Younger children can also draw pictorial responses to 'What happened?', 'What can I do to make things better?' and the class teacher can use this, later, to talk through issues with the child.

Many schools use such questions in a written pro forma (Rogers, 2006):

1. *What happened* ... (to cause you to be in time-out)?

2. *What rule* (or right – for older students) *was affected by your behaviour?*

3. *What can you do to fix things up – make things better? work things out* (with your teacher/other affected students)?

4. *How can your class* (or grade) *teacher help you* (to fix things up, make things better, work things out)?

It is also unhelpful to give the student a special task or 'job' when sent to a senior teacher for time-out – 'Would you like to do a job for me?' The student – again – sets up associations, 'I muck around ... I get sent to Mr. Smith ... he gives me interesting jobs to do ... I like that!'

Time-out – by itself – will not change a disturbing and dysfunctional pattern of student behaviour. It will set up a fair consequential outcome and (hopefully) a fair 'if–then' reasoning with the student. If a student has been in time-out (*any* time-out) several times in close succession, we will need to pursue an individual behaviour management plan for that student (pages 121, 122).

Some teachers, unfortunately, will move to time-out (as a discipline 'strategy') far too quickly in seeking to address disruptive behaviour. Time-out (as a behaviour consequence) must be seen as part of an overall, whole-school plan for behaviour management and discipline (Chapter 7).

You fix him!

Some teachers – pushed, no doubt, to the limit – will shout at students to leave the classroom. 'Get out! Go on – get out (!) If you can't learn to behave with some basic respect you can get out of my classroom!!' In the immediate emotional moment it is easy to see how a teacher would vent their spleen and start shouting at students like Scott (page 123).

Some teachers will send a student to a senior teacher with the expectation – even the demand – that the deputy head teacher 'fix this student!' It needs to be made clear, as a school-wide policy *and practice,* that the senior teacher's role in any given time-out practice is to support the teacher in the first instance, not to 'fix' the student. Later, the senior teacher can *support* the teacher in any 'secondary consequences', or in developing any individual behaviour agreements with the student concerned (pages 121, 122). It is not their job (in the time-out phase itself) to merely berate, 'fix' or even counsel the student.

It is the class teacher's responsibility (the teacher who initiated the time-out consequence) to do *any* follow-up and follow-through with the student concerned. In this, of course, they should expect senior colleague support (page 119).

Time-out – the role and *reasonable support* of senior staff

The new principal of a large primary school had said ' ... if you've got any problems with difficult students send them to me.' At least this is how many teachers heard it. Within a fortnight he had queues of students at his door and was trying to work out and fix up what was going on. Within the month he was very stressed. He had, unwittingly, made a rod for his own back.

It wasn't all the teachers sending students – I know, because together we started to sort out what was actually happening. Most of the teachers who had 'sent' students to the principal ranged from those who wanted him to 'fix the student', to a few who were genuinely struggling and were grasping at the 'offered straw'. What he was doing, in effect, was taking away the teacher's responsibility to work with their more distracting and more challenging students. He had done this with the best of motives – he genuinely wanted to support his colleagues.

Of course, we need to support colleagues with challenging students – this is a crucial matter in any whole-school approach. This does not mean that the senior team picks up every single incident of distracting and disruptive behaviour that occurs in classrooms.

When we explored further what was happening, it was clear that some teachers clearly had no 'staged' intervention within their classroom discipline (pages 105, 108). Many more were, also, not following up with the students they had *sent* to the principal (page 119). A few teachers clearly needed longer-term mentoring support (Chapter 10).

We discussed – within the grade teams – the need for a conscious. positive, discipline framework for the classroom. We also agreed on, and developed, a *staged* time-out plan that involved colleague-assisted time-out as a first response, only calling on senior colleagues when a student was clearly resistant (page 125). One of the unfortunate aspects of some teachers' practice was their 'shouting students down' as they told them to 'get out of the class!' While their frustration (easily heard in a long corridor) was understandable, we needed to work together on assertive but calm cueing of students whenever we chose to use staged time-out. More crucially, we started to develop some least-intrusive practice that would enable colleagues to address attentional and challenging behaviour more calmly in the first instance (page 104). In this we focused on our characteristic language in managing distracting and disruptive behaviours (Chapter 7).

We also developed *a school-wide preferred practice for follow-up of all students* that any teacher had directed to any level of the staged time-out support. This preferred practice for follow-up (beyond time-out) is explored in the case study on page 119. Colleagues realised that, while senior staff would *always* be supportive of a teacher in the time-out of very disruptive students, the primary responsibility for follow-up and follow-through has to reside with the initiating teacher. They, after all, were there in the context of the disruptive behaviour. We agreed – of course – that senior staff would support colleagues in any follow-up, particularly with the more challenging students.

All of this entailed professional development both in grade-teams and with the whole staff team.

We also began to develop a school-wide approach to the most at-risk students, realising that time-out (of itself) would not change patterns of disruptive behaviour (page 121). Time-out is an opportunity (an essential opportunity at times) for the student to calm down, to give the class teacher (and grade) temporary respite and act as an appropriate if–then consequence to the student in question.

It is never an end in itself.

Swearing and stress

It was an English lesson – Year 9. Towards the end of the lesson I'd noticed Craig tearing strips of paper from his workbook, chewing it and spitting it on the floor. It was the last five minutes of the lesson. He noticed me looking in his direction and stopped – he grinned. I tactically ignored him. Just before the bell – and just before I went through the tidy-up/pack-up routine – I said I wanted to see Craig after class. He hit the desk with some explosive force with his hand, 'F---! What did I do?!'

When the bell went, he walked out of the classroom. I called him back. 'Craig, I asked you to stay back …' Before I could finish he swore again. 'A couple of minutes that's all … If you leave now I'll have to involve the head of year …' He swore loudly under his breath and walked off.

I did follow up (later that week) with Craig and the year coordinator. We worked through the issue of the spit-balls, he did some civic duty 'cleaning' (in his own time).

It is important – at this point – to recognise that:

● I can't *make* him stay back

● his frustration swearing is not directed *at* me

● his swearing cannot – of itself – make me angry

- we need to emphasise the fair certainty of the consequence (needing to follow up the necessary clean-up of the spit-ball mess, and understanding about future behaviour in class) – even if that 'certainty' is 24/48 hours in some cases

Swearing: *why* does anyone swear?

Students swear for the same reasons as adults – normal frustration, low frustration tolerance, habit, attentional grandstanding among their peers. My colleagues and I distinguish between several 'forms' of swearing:

- Conversational – most commonly in the playground (or sometimes the classroom).
- Frustration (as Craig above – poor thing!).
- Sotto voce – under their breath. This is another form of frustration and – at times – is also 'directed' at the teacher (though not face to face).
- Directed *at* a teacher or *at* another student.

Not all swearing – then – is the same. I believe our response to swearing needs to reflect that reality.

Swearing and beliefs

I had been called to an upper primary classroom to 'exit' a student who had been disruptive and uncooperative. The school had a well-established procedure that enabled teachers to call for support when needed (page 125). Being new to this school, this was my first experience as an 'exit collegue' (senior teacher).

I entered the room where children were continuing with activities pretty well as usual. In one corner of the classroom, an eleven-year-old girl was talking loudly about what she wasn't going to do. I approached her quietly and asked her to come with me. As if waiting for an opportunity to vent greater anger, she spun around and said, 'You can go and get f-----. I don't have to do what you say!' These bitter words were spat out with real venom – her eyes sparked with anger, fists were clenched, body tense and ready to fight.

A few years ago, a string of abuse like this would have caused quite a dramatic emotional reaction in me. I would have felt a surge of blood to my face and my heart pumping harder, maybe a rush of anger. Thoughts going through my head would have been something like, 'What right has this brash, aggressive person got to abuse me? I've tried really hard for these kids and look what I get! This child *just should not be* talking like this.'

In such a situation, I now see a child who needs help to cope more effectively →

with a life problem. In seeing the child as having the problem, and my role as a mature adult to help her behave more appropriately and work out better ways of handling difficulties, I am able to cope with the verbal abuse in a very different way. *I don't take the abuse personally.* I am now able to act more rationally and calmly when confronted with such abuse – rather than becoming emotionally distressed and dysfunctional.

My response to the child who had just abused me? In a quiet, friendly voice: 'Tania, I can see that you are upset. There is a problem here and that needs to be sorted out. I don't want the teaching and learning in this classroom disrupted. Come with me now, please, and we can sort this problem out.' Tania came.

I am not saying that this scenario is the only possibility. There are situations where children like Tania may still refuse to cooperate. Other actions may need to be taken (page 126). However, the important point is that I was able to act in a rational, sensitive way; to be calm and reassuring, rather than overly emotional, in dealing with this situation.

Inappropriate or 'bad' language or swearing

Even teachers (teachers?) swear – in staffrooms, in the photocopy room (because of, or *at*, the photocopier!) or after a hostile parent has finally left. Whether we like it or not, swearing (or sometimes 'bad' language) – as it has been traditionally understood – is more common today than in times past; or is it? For some people swearing is even *passé*[1]. Certainly in many films, books and TV shows (and, it seems, for most comedians) it is 'normed' into descriptive dialogue as well as expressions of frustration and anger.

Thoughtful teachers will distinguish between a child who mutters, 'Sh-t' (*sotto voce*), even f___, out of frustration and a student who swears *at* a fellow student or teacher. Some swearing is also muttered (*ex parte*) as when the student walks past or away from the teacher ('wanker', 'a__hole', 'dick head', 'bastard'). Sometimes the student may be right in the muttered description (hopefully rarely).

Hostile swearing

Swearing *as hostile intent,* directed *at* another person (student or teacher), needs to be dealt with immediately by the teacher – firmly, without aggression (this only feeds the latent hostility or anger). For example, 'Michael (...)That language is unacceptable here. When you've calmed down we'll sort this issue out.' Or 'Michael (...) We don't swear at anyone here. Full stop.' 'If you're uptight with me – find another way of saying it.' Make your point briefly, clearly, decisively. 'Block' any argumentative appeals as to why they swore at so and so (or even why they swore *at you*). Avoid pointing, gesticulating, hand movements. An open – 'blocking' – hand movement helps to assert the firm voice without aggressive intent. Direct the student to take informal, or formal, 'cool-off time'. It is pointless asking (or demanding) from the student 'reasons' why they swore at you (the teacher) or at a fellow student *at this time*.

I have known teachers who 'appeal' to a swearing student, 'Why are you swearing at me, I'm not nasty to you, am I? What have I done to hurt you?' This non-assertive stance, expressed in a please-be-nice-to-me voice, is counter-productive and often feeds latent student attention and 'power'. It also sends mixed messages to the other students in the class.

In the immediate emotional moment – when hostile swearing is present – it is important to keep the assertive statement *brief* and focused on the issue or rule (about language or respect) (page 79). As noted above, it is probably helpful to direct the student to take some cool-off time and follow the issue up later with a third party (a senior colleague) for support. The senior teacher support (in that later follow-up session) clarifies the seriousness of the behaviour to the student and gives supportive advocacy to the teacher in question.

Younger children (primary age) will need a direct, immediate rule reminder: 'We don't say things like that in our class' or 'We don't use words like that in our class.' If the swearing is repetitive or aggressive, it is normal policy to follow through with *immediate* time-out. The kind of time-out will vary with the age of the child. The most common form of time-out for such swearing and attentional aggression is out-of-class time-out (page 124). Some schools have a unilateral consequence of swearing *at* a teacher (e.g. a day's suspension from school – or an 'internal' day's suspension from all classes at school).

It is also important – in the immediate emotional moment – to avoid long explanations about *why* such language is unacceptable and resist the moral lecture, 'Is that the kind of language you use at home?!' I've actually heard teachers say that – and I've heard students reply in the affirmative. We should never impugn a child's home background (even if that's the formative genesis of their swearing language).

Swearing, at infant level, may mean something different to a child's perception. One of my colleagues recalled the occasion when a student came up to him with a most serious look on her face and said, quietly, 'Sir ... Con said the f___ word.' 'Did he, Maria – really?' 'Yes, he did.' 'Are you sure?' 'Yes ... the f___ word.' The teacher thought he would check and very quietly asked, 'Maria ... what did he say?' Maria replied, with the utmost seriousness, in a frowning whisper, 'He said, he said ... **stewpid**!' and then covered her mouth as if to say 'sorry I had to tell you he used the f___ word' (which in her mind meant '**stewpid**').

Sotto voce swearing

If a student swears *sotto voce* – on the run as it were – such swearing can sometimes be tactically ignored in the immediate, emotional moment and *followed up later* when the student has calmed down. In depends, in part, on how *sotto* the *voce* actually was (did we really hear a frustrated, loud whispered 'wanker'?) and in part on the audience reaction. It is often enough to direct the student aside and to quietly say something like 'Paul, (always use the child's first name – it gains some attentional focus, it also 'personalises' the adult–child discipline role) … I heard what you said; I don't speak to you like that, I don't expect you to speak to me like that.' Then direct the child back to the task at hand, or to what he should be doing now, or to cool-off-time if necessary.

If we can direct the student aside for a *brief* chat, even better (similar language to above). If other students have heard the muttered swearing, they need to see us 'do something'.

We can sometimes add (in the one-to-one aside) 'David … I heard you swear at Paul earlier …' I've had students look puzzled here (because they don't always 'see' or 'hear' as 'swearing' what we take as 'swearing'.) I sometimes quietly include the swear word they used, or write it down. 'Look, I know you were uptight with Craig before (this briefly tunes in to how the student was probably feeling); you know we've got a class rule about respectful language …'

In a particularly challenging high school in the western suburbs of Melbourne I was teaching an English class. As I was moving around the room (in the on-task phase of the lesson) I overheard one of the more vocal (and time-wasting) lads call a girl near him a 'f---ing bitch', just above *sotto voce*. I knew they were friends but I could hear the frustration in his voice. I went over and said something like, 'Look Adam, I heard what you said to Belinda …' I handed him a piece of paper on which I had written down his swearing language. 'I didn't say that!' (he sounded annoyed). I added quietly, 'I heard you Adam …' He explained 'I tell you I didn't say that! I said f--- off you bitch. I didn't say f---ing bitch. Gees!' He was upset that I'd got the verb and participle misconstrued, *not* that he'd used such offensive language(!). The annoying thing was that when I called them both back later (after class), to engage in some brief mediation, Belinda seemed unfazed – she shrugged her shoulders and said, ' … it's just Adam … that's how he is …'

Part of the problem when addressing swearing with some students (adolescents most notably) is the 'no-big-dealness' of it all. It can often help to raise the issue of swearing and offensive language more widely with the whole-class group in a classroom meeting (Rogers, 2006). Ideally classroom, or tutor, teachers should have covered the issue of interpersonal communication, mutual respect and careless, thoughtless, disrespectful and abusive language within the framework of a *classroom agreement on rights, responsibilities and rules* (Rogers, 2011a). A classroom meeting can reaffirm the issue of 'our right to respect and to feel safe here'; the use of respectful language and reassess 'how we communicate with one another here'.

Beliefs and standards

As noted earlier (Chapter 4) some teachers have a particularly demanding mindset and explanatory style about swearing (at times *any* kind of swearing). 'Children *shouldn't swear* (!)' An *idée fixe*. Unless this mindset is challenged within the context of social reality, no amount of discussion about 'types' of swearing, or moderating our responses will help. The teacher's stress about swearing and their reactive response to it is directly correlated with such demanding beliefs and will significantly affect how stressed they feel in the presence of swearing (even conversational swearing).

The discussion (here) about swearing does not mean that we ignore, play down, delimit or acquiesce to swearing in our schools. It does mean that we take stock of social reality and develop strategies (whole-school) to both manage swearing (at source) and create a more reflective culture with our students about such language.

Conversational swearing

It is not uncommon – even in primary schools – to hear 'conversational swearing' – I also hear it (at times) in classrooms (and staffrooms): 'Did you see that fantastic f---ing game the other f---ing day. Sh-t! How was the f---ing score they got, eh? The other team; they're rat sh-t!'

Should we ignore this kind of 'swearing' in the playground? Should we relegate it to the argument of, ' ... that's the reality now. That's how it is today – it's just "street language" ...' (?) I have heard this argument many times now – principally from non-educators.

Ignoring such language when we hear it in non-classroom settings, or even in the classroom (as a *sotto voce* exchange), can easily send the message that we do not care how our students speak, or that such language is 'OK', or is even the 'norm' (as a conversational exchange).

Of course such language is 'street-language' – however, a school is not merely a 'street' and acceptance can easily excuse, even ratify, such language norming. The issue for educators is how can we encourage our students to converse without lazy recourse to 'effing and blinding ...'? And how can we do this without prudish moralising?

A group of students were discussing the latest 'f---ing film' they saw recently – some action-packed thriller with serious maim, gore and gratuitous ... (well, gratuitous anything, really). You could hear the descriptive qualifiers quite clearly, several yards away. It won't help if the teacher charges in, moralising 'Oi!! I could hear every word you said!! Is that the kind of language you use at home – is it? You disgusting creatures!!'

It may well be they use such language at home (even regularly) but simplistic, reactive judgement will get a hostile reaction (particularly in more challenging schools). Further, it won't help in any useful reflection on the student's part about their language.

The issue of 'conversational swearing' can be addressed by a quiet acknowledgment, followed by a rule reminder about use of language (assuming that the issue of 'thoughtful and respectful language' has been explored across the school). Sometimes a humourous question, or an aside, can also enable a bit of self-checking – the teacher walks over, casually, and greets the students, 'How's it going?' (the returned non-verbal body language suggests, 'Well, we were going OK till you walked over – really.' (Their *actual* reply is, 'OK') The teacher leans a little towards them (as if to suggest he doesn't want others to hear) and asks a question about the 'effing film' they had momentarily been discussing (without using the participle they used) – 'Seen any interesting films lately beginning with "f"?'

The students catch on with a weary, tolerant smile and sigh. The teacher can then have a brief chat about thoughtful language and walk off with a pleasant 'goodbye for now'. Relaxed vigilance.

If some students habitually, and loudly, converse with 'strong' attentionally conversational swearing, it is worth following up with these students – at a later stage – to discuss their behaviour and their responsibility for the way they communicate. Most 'conversational swearing' is an *unreflective habit* – some (of course) is peer-group – positional – strutting ...

If the issue of 'conversational' or 'banter' swearing is more typically frequent (particularly at upper primary and secondary level) it can help to run classroom meetings in tutor/form groups – to raise the issue, to define what is meant by 'bad' or 'inappropriate' or 'disrespectful' language and swearing and to discuss its effect. This meeting will enable discussion on how feelings are affected by 'what we say' and 'how we say it' and readdress core rights and responsibilities about respect and people's feelings. If you're not confident in conducting such a meeting, or if it is outside your experience, ask a colleague to conduct the meeting with you.

Whenever we address non-confrontational swearing, we work at getting a balance between language probity, thoughtful discipline and discussion with our students. Our own modelling, as teachers, will go a long way in demonstrating that one can communicate frustration – even anger – without resorting to the lowest common language denominator.

NB Most of my work is in more challenging schools. If a student swears *at* a teacher ('directly' or 'indirectly') we try to resolve that (later in the day) by mediation, apology by the student and acceptance of the student as we move on together beyond the incident.

As noted earlier (page 132) some schools have a mandatory sanction for such swearing – say, a day's suspension from the school. It is important to be aware of the school's policy on swearing but still be willing to engage in repairing and rebuilding with the student concerned when they return to school. This is crucial to any ongoing success in our relationship with more challenging students.

Note

1. In a newspaper article entitled *'90 per cent of Britons are not offended by swearing'* it is noted that the average Briton utters 14 expletives a day (where do they get so specific a number?) 'Men admitted to being the more foul-mouthed gender ...' The article goes on to add that over 80 per cent of women swore on a daily basis. The survey was not sourced (annoyingly) though it does indicate a more common national view – or perception – about swearing and 'offence'. (*Daily Mail*, 16/01/2009). What it didn't differentiate though is the 'types' of swearing I've tried to list in this book (page 130).

Hard-to-manage classes: a collegial response

What this chapter will explore and develop:

- The typical characteristics of a hard-to-manage class
- Why some classes are harder to manage or *become* harder to manage
- The unsettled, fractious and very restless class – how to respond
- The role of senior teachers in supporting teachers with known hard-to-manage classes
- How to address the 'out-of-control' class
- The bullying of teachers by (some) students
- Conducting an accountability conference with bullying students

The hard-to-manage class

'I can hear some of them before I even get to class. It's the noise – they're raucous! I'm thinking – already I'm feeling – how will I cope today? Will it be

the same? Students crowding at the door, pushing and shoving. It takes ages for them to settle – the calling-out; that chatting while I'm trying to teach; the students who constantly avoid tasks; students without equipment ... And the other day, when the deputy head walked past, what the hell must he be thinking ?..?'

I've sat with many colleagues who recount their ongoing stress of working with such a class. The 'hard class' is more than a bad-day experience – it is that *durable knowingness* of what one has to face – often 'alone' (the only adult); the feeling of apprehension and anxiety (page 71); the wondering if it will ever get any better. And – disconcertingly – comparing oneself to other, more successful, teachers. And, at times, worrying about how senior staff perceive and judge one's leadership ability as they walk past that noisy class in Room 15(!)

There are a number of reasons why classes become harder to manage (Rogers 2006):

- The *transitional* reasons such as timetable changes, weather, cover classes outside our comfort zone. This is, normally, 'bad-day syndrome'.

- The 'skewed' class – knowingly given to a newly graduated teacher or a teacher new to the school. A class that already has 'a reputation', or because it has a 'skewed distribution' of more challenging students or students with significant learning needs. Such classes have the potential to develop a reputation quickly!

  If you 'smell a rat' on this one – if you believe you've been shafted with a particularly challenging class in a particularly challenging timetable slot – it will be important to seek out your team leader and communicate your concern professionally *at the outset.*

  At times it seems as if the senior teachers who timetable these classes are unaware of how stressful such classes can be for newly qualified teachers. At other times it seems as if it's deliberate 'policy'. I've heard some senior teachers trot out that pathetic line, ' ... Well, it was done to us when *we* started teaching ...'. *Done* to us(!)?

  Approaching a senior colleague (particularly as a beginning teacher) about an issue like class allocation and timetabling is not easy. However, if you don't, the stressful reality will probably continue. Marshalling and framing your concern will not be easy. It can help if a trusted colleague supports you in exploring your concern (in writing) before any such meeting. It may be that the administration cannot (or won't) change the class allocation – however, you have a right to ask for realistic support, such as mentoring options (Chapter 10), a clear time-out plan and support for students with diagnosed (or symptomatic) behaviour disorders (page 121).

- Sometimes it's a subject perception held by the students. In some schools, for example, subjects like foreign languages, religious education, 'careers' and 'consumer education' are not perceived by some students as worthwhile or 'worth the effort'. Negative parental attitudes about such subjects (like foreign languages) don't help either. It is crucial that all staff validate such subject areas and support colleagues who struggle in them (if this is the case). I've heard staff – in front of their students – make patronising and disparaging comments about foreign languages and religious education.

- Sometimes it's the way that the class is *treated by the teacher*. There are still teachers who, for example, will punish a whole class for the disruptive behaviour of a few students. This is *always* counterproductive (if it ever worked). There are few occasions when we need to keep a *whole class* back for some kind of detention (say, something valuable has gone missing ...). In such cases we would almost always send for senior teacher support. This is to be distinguished from a 'whole-class detention'.

- Sometimes it's a general – and negative – perception of the class by the teacher. 'They're all animals!' As I walked with my colleague down to a Year 8 science class, he looked rattled – very rattled. He'd asked me to work with him in his class as a mentor (a little reluctantly on supportive advice from his head of department). 'All?' I asked (as we headed towards the science wing). 'What?' he asked. '*All* animals?' I asked with a wry smile. 'Well – you know what I mean!'

We got into the classroom and the students filed in noisily – a fair bit of silly play-punching from some of the boys, a lot of very loud talking and a number of students asking me (*en route* to their seats) why I was in the classroom. I greeted them and reminded them they needed to be in their seats. I added a brief, 'When you're all in and settled, I'll let you know why I'm here. Thanks.' My colleague eventually 'started' the lesson. He frequently told them to 'be quiet'; to 'stop calling out'; 'Stop talking when I'm speaking'. Eventually he explained why I was in the class, and stepped to one side. I began to team-teach. They were a fractious class but they did settle and shared with me what they had been 'doing in science ...' There was calling out, chatting while the teacher/s was teaching and loud working noise later in the lesson. This was addressed with descriptive reminders, take-up time and tactical ignoring of the posturally attentional students. By and large, though, we had a reasonable lesson. Better than I'd thought considering my colleague's discussion with me before we went into the class.

His perception of the class was clearly very negative – even over coffee later. 'Didn't I tell you – they *never* listen?' 'They're *always* being silly and stupid. I can *never* get any proper experimental work done!' He was still quite angry. However, I hadn't seen the class that way, 'Yes – I agreed, 'there were several students whose behaviour was – at times – silly, actively clowning around but, clearly, *not all*'. I mentioned some of the responsible students; some of the moments in the lesson when I'd felt it had gone well – when students (even most) *were listening; were applying themselves* and even some of the difficult students who had been clowning who did – eventually – 'come on board'. 'Yes, but they're *not normally* like that ...'

My colleague's *perceptions* ('never', 'always', 'only', 'they're *just* ...') had clearly affected – and influenced – his treatment of the class. Clearly he had become quite stressed over the weeks with this class. Those perceptions – above – affected his ability to extend goodwill to his students and build those crucial teacher–student relationships. As well as offering longer-term mentoring support to enable a 'fresh start' with his class (Chapter 10), we also talked through his perceptions about the individuals and groups (Chapter 4).

- An issue that frequently appears in stress statistics (but is hardly addressed in management texts) is that of teachers bullied by students. Harassment of teachers does occur in some schools. Psychological harassment from several students who – as a power clique – make teaching very stressful for several teachers, at times even impossible. This issue is addressed at some length later (page 155).

- The most common reason my colleagues and I have noted for a class becoming hard to manage is inadequate, or poorly managed, establishment (by the class teacher) of *the 4Rs* – rights, rules, routines and shared responsibilities. The establishment phase is a crucial time in the life of a classroom group, *as it is for their teacher* (page 93). The students expect their teacher to make clear *how things need to be in our class – and why* (even at early years level students have this 'perceptual awareness') (Rogers and McPherson, 2008).

It's often 'deceptive basics' such as how we explain, discuss and monitor routines such as the entry to class; the settling and calming (before whole-class teaching time); the appropriate seating arrangements; how to initiate whole-class attention and to focus and lead class teaching time and class discussions; an appropriate noise volume level during on-task learning time; how students can reasonably cue for teacher assistance (during on-task teaching time); movement patterns around the classroom – right through to lesson closure and an ordered exit from the classroom (page 92).

We need to be able to confidently, and convincingly, establish our positive leadership of a class within essential rights and responsibilities. If this does not happen, the attentionally demanding, or power-seeking, students will start to seek their sense of social belonging through their distracting, disruptive and challenging behaviours. This is a typical, frustrating and very stressful feature of the 'hard-class syndrome'. It is more likely to occur in schools where teachers are left to struggle on (with such a class) 'on their own' – where a teacher is hesitant to ask for early support lest they be perceived, even judged, as an ineffective teacher.

A fresh start

Where a teacher has begun to lose confidence in their leadership of the class group; where there is noisy and distracting behaviour in whole-class settling time; where there is frequent calling out and talking while the teacher is talking; where there is frequent task avoidance and student socialising and wandering (and loud chatting) during on-task learning time – it will be important for the teacher to seek support from a senior colleague. That support will be most effective when such support enables the class teacher to work directly with the class/es to develop a fresh start. The earlier such support is sought, the more effective the outcome.

Essentially, a 'fresh start' approach involves the grade/classroom teacher working with a senior colleague to reengage the class in a process where the class teacher (often with a colleague mentor) raises issues of common concern with their students (see key questions – page 142) in either an open-meeting forum, or through a class questionnaire. These questions enable the teacher to give the students a 'guided voice' about how they (as well as the teacher) perceive, and feel, the class 'is going' at this time. [Rogers, 2006 and 2009 (Chapter 4)].

Early intervention is essential before that habituation of distracting and disruptive behaviours become a term-two problem.

What is crucial in any kind of 'fresh start' approach is that the grade/class teacher is willing to seek, and work with, colleague support. This support will often necessitate the grade/class teacher pursuing a conscious and willing opportunity to reflect on their characteristic teaching practice – particularly in the area of behaviour leadership.

Avoid easy blame

Blame – of students *or teacher* – as to why the behaviour of students is so distracting and fractious is unhelpful. That kind of blame is simplistic and – clearly – counterproductive.

Teachers clearly have a responsibility for leadership of their class, but where they have taken on a very challenging class, that responsibility needs to be matched with adequate colleague support – moral support (not blame); professional support and structural support, such as common year level approaches to core routines; individual behaviour plans for students who have learning disorders and students with diagnosed or symptomatic behaviour disorders, along with clearly supported time-out plans and follow-up procedures (Chapter 8).

Working with the students

When working with a colleague with a very challenging class, it is important to work with the students to engage their response to the issues of concern and about behaviour and learning.

We engage their awareness, and support, through a classroom meeting that gives an appropriate voice to student (as well as teacher) concerns. It particularly gives a voice to the larger – often 'silent' – majority of the students. It re-engages the (often) latent goodwill of most of the students.

Focus questions for class discussion

The three key questions we ask the class (or in a written pro forma) are:

1. *What's working well in our class?*

   At the moment what are the things we do, in our studies – and the way we work together – that you believe work well for us *and why*? (Always start with the positive question).

2. *What's not working well and why?*

   What concerns do you have about the way we work together? What concerns do you have about the behaviour of members of our class? If you have any personal concerns about me – as your teacher – you can always put these to me in writing and I will respond.

3. *What suggestions do you have about what we can do to improve the way we work, learn, and behave in our class group?*

   Remember, we're all responsible for how we work together here.

   Remember, these questions are our opportunity – as a class group – to reflect on what's going on in our class and what we can all do to improve things.

   When such questions are asked through a pro forma we add the following:

   Your answers to these questions can be confidential – unless you want to share the issues further with me.

   Thanks – your teacher and I [here we put the name of the senior colleague assisting with the fresh-start approach with the class] will get back to you very soon to take these concerns and suggestions forward for a fresh start as a class.

Whenever my colleagues and I have conducted the '3W' exercise – above – they are often surprised at how supportive many of the comments of the students are. It reaffirms the common experience that there is often a 'silent majority' of students in the class who are thankful for the opportunity to share 'their voice' and are hopeful, too, that the class can (with supportive teacher leadership) work its way out of its current state. It also helps to reframe a colleague's overly negative impression of the class *as a group*.

The very unsettling, fractious, noisy class

It doesn't take much for a challenging class to slip into fractious, noisy, unfocused behaviour. Frequent calling out, 'Hey Miss, Miss ... ! Can you help me with this ...!?'; chatting distractedly; wandering around class for no good reason; time off-task and task avoidance.

In those critical first weeks with a new class, a significant aspect of our leadership will involve enabling cooperative student behaviours by being vigilant in how we lead and discipline – *relaxed* vigilance. Our discipline plan will enable, guide and support such 'vigilance' (Chapter 7). This is particularly important when several students are distracting or disruptive at the same time (see below).

If we have established positive routines for behaviour and learning (page 93); if we have a clear framework of rights and responsibilities; if we have a discipline plan that enables us to address distracting and disruptive behaviours thoughtfully and we follow up (one-to-one) with students who need that extra assurance that we care (page 119) then there's a good chance we'll have a reasonably cohesive class. On the days when the class is particularly restless, though, it will be important to *refocus the whole class*.

Case study

I was mentoring a colleague in a challenging Year 7 class (UK). During the class period in question we both were moving around the room during on-task learning time (maths). The lesson task activity was clear, but several students had started to wander around the room distractingly –at the same time.

Several more students were calling out to get the teacher's help. 'Miss! Miss! Can you come over ...?' The general noise level was very loud – restless and unfocused. I noticed (corner of my eye) one of the boys throw a pen on the floor and *en route* back to his seat hit the student in the next desk (playful testosteronic bonding). He, later, told me he was 'just mucking around', and 'we're good mates anyway.' He also admitted that his regular teacher had 'let him get away with it ...' (he meant, by this, that no action was taken – apart from the teacher frequently asking him why he did such things).

One of the boys, I noticed, had chewing gum protruding from his nose like a 'stalactitical protuberance'. He was rolling the rest of the chewing gum out on his book (no doubt for the next nostril!). All these behaviours – you understand – *were happening at one and the same time*.

My colleague had said this kind of thing might happen. She had said that she felt this class were 'slipping away from her'. She had tried detentions. She admitted to shouting at them many times – but they were wearing her down: *'it's like too many things happening at once – and it's every lesson!'*

When this level, and degree, of fractious behaviour is happening it is essential to *refocus the whole class; there and then.* Otherwise it's trying to put out too many little brush fires all at once! We need to go to the front of the classroom and *cue the whole class.* We'll need to *raise* our voice (not *shouting*). 'EVERYONE (...) stop what you're doing (...) *now* (...)'. A brief tactical pause (...). The class did attend, the noise level initially dropped ... I cued the main distracting students: 'Kristin (...), Rebecca (...), Cameron (...) back in your seats.' They protested ... I repeated the direction (verbally blocking their whingeing ...) 'back in your seats *now.*' They sulked as they clomped back to their own seats (my colleague and I *tactically* ignored the frowning, whingeing and the sulking (page 45). 'Andrew (...), Rory (...) leave the pen there.' This to Andrew, in particular, who had thrown his pen yet again. 'Callum (...) I'll be over with some tissues in a moment.' (This to the creator of the stalactites – the chewing gum).

By now the class was settled and reasonably subdued. The main attentional students (about five – with several followers) were visibly frowning or sulking. I addressed the class: 'That's better ...' I said as I scanned the faces of this new class. 'A few minutes ago, before I asked you to settle and listen, several students were wandering around the classroom. A number of you were ... (here I *briefly* detailed what I'd seen with the students wandering; the calling out; the very loud working chatter; throwing things ...)' ...

'I'm not saying it's all of you. You know we stay in our seats during class learning time. We never throw anything (even in fun!). We use partner-voices during classwork – it was far too loud before. Maybe some of you were not aware of that – some of you were ...' I didn't name the particularly troublesome students at this stage. 'Those students that were making it difficult for others to learn in our class will be meeting with me later today and with the Year 7 coordinator' (more sibilant whingeing from a small cache of students).

'Now – we've got 20 minutes to go before the bell. If you need Ms Smith's help – or mine – this is how you get it ... If you haven't got a pen, paper, ruler (etc.) we've got spares here in this box ... (page 145). If you need our help, this is how you get our help' (I explained yet again how to seek teacher help without just calling out or clicking fingers ...). 'What you need to be doing now regarding the work is ...' I gave a brief reminder of the learning task. For the rest of the lesson the students worked reasonably well. *We had started the slow business of re-habituation.*

Helpful reminder

I always take a box of materials (for students) into my new classes. It has biros (red and blue), *sharpened* pencils, rulers, lined and plain A4 paper.

I will never argue with a student about 'why' he hasn't got any materials. He can use 'the box'. If he makes a habit of not bringing equipment to class (three times in a row) then we'll have a formal one-to-one meeting to find out what's going on and offer one-to-one support. If he still continues to come to class without equipment, I'll check with other colleagues who also teach the student and we'll come up with a joint approach.

In some high schools (for example) we provide a 'table pencil case' (kept at school by the tutor teacher) it's the student's responsibility to hand it back at the end of the day.

What we don't do is argue with, or embarrass, students (in front of their class-mates) who forget (or choose not) to bring equipment to school.

After that first session together, my colleague and I sat and talked about the class together – inviting the Year 7 coordinator to join us. His admittance that this was also a challenging 'cohort' for him clearly encouraged her. She had seen my natural struggle with this class, too, and though they had eventually settled (and even got some work done) she said it was 'good that you saw what they can be like ...' Our *shared* struggle had boosted her confidence (page 175).

- We followed up the five students who were most problematic (page 119). We developed an *individual* behaviour plan for each of them in conjunction with the year adviser (page 121). These plans were based on specific behaviours the student needed to be aware of and take responsibility for – such as consciously remembering to put your hand up *without calling out* during class discussions; staying in your seat during classwork (without wandering); doing your best with the set work (start the work – and keep going). We also modified the set work for some of those students with learning needs. We reviewed these plans twice a week, briefly (at lunchtimes) with each of the students.

- We also reviewed the seating plans and reorganised the seating of the more attentional students so they wouldn't be easily distracted. They were – initially – annoyed that they couldn't sit with their 'best friends' but agreed (reluctantly) that it was probably better. We pointed out that they had plenty of time (outside class time) to be with their best mates.

- My colleague and I also reviewed the fundamental routines for classroom entry and settling (page 93). I noticed (on the first visit to the class) that students came into class *very* noisily – chatting loudly, taking a long time to settle into their seats. I noticed, too, that my colleague had got into conversations with individual students (at the classroom door) instead of a brief positive greeting to students (as they entered) and *then* focusing the whole class (page 95). It had taken nearly five minutes for the class to 'settle' (the first lesson) – even then there was significant low chatter, with several students calling out and needing reminding (or enjoying some attention?).

We reviewed the entry-to-class procedure and explained to the class group why we needed a considerate entry and the distinction between 'social time' and 'classroom learning time'. We focused on the importance of a calm, considered entry to class – settle in your seat, relaxed and focused to the front of the room. We settled on a reasonable 'target time' of two minutes. A student was appointed (for the next class period) timekeeper to see if we could reach that goal – we did, to the surprise of my colleague.

- We reviewed noise volume (of chatter) during on-task learning time. We noticed how the noise level (of students) rose significantly at that transition between whole-class teaching time and on-task learning time.

We used a simple cueing and tracking graph on the board. Firstly we discussed with the class how easily noise volume can rise with 26 people in such a small space (including two teachers). We modelled the difference between 'partner voices' and louder 'outside class voices' to some laughter. Using a simple graph we drew a vertical axis on the board where 0 = silence; 2 = whisper; 5 (and below) = 'partner-voice'; *above* five was getting too loud and 10 = House of Commons (!) On the horizontal axis I had (about three centimetres apart) time fractions of five minutes. I explained to the class that every five minutes the class teacher (or me) would give them visual feedback on how the volume of *group chatter* (while working) appeared to us. We'd use the bar chart (every five minutes) against the numbers. I added that if we (as a class group) could keep the noise level below 5 I'd award 'points' on the board. If we could get to 20 points well before the end of the class period, we would pack up five minutes early and have some 'free time'. This was an early incentive for all during the first lessons together.

- We also clarified that if any student wanted their teacher's help/feedback then they needed to put their hand up (without calling out) and we would come over to them as quickly as possible. However, we also pointed out the students' responsibility to read carefully and thoughtfully the information on the board, book or worksheet. Check the set work and ask yourself, 'What do I actually need to do now ...?' If you're still not sure, ask your classmate *next* to you (not in the next row or ...) only then put your hand up for the teacher (without calling out, thanks). This gives everyone a fair go.

While these routines may seem basic, they are essential to any sense of focus, engagement and fairness in a typical classroom period.

- We also revisited pack-up routines and exit from the classroom. I recall that on the first session my colleague and I had worked with this class, several students had bolted out of their seats as soon as the bell went. I called them back (they whinged) and we emphasised to the class 'This is *not* a detention; a few minutes and we're all away. We leave *row by row*.' 'Matt – your row first, thanks ...' From that first session we reminded the students to check the floor for any litter and, '*even if you didn't produce it* we'll put it in the bin on the way out of the classroom. We leave row by row and straighten our furniture *before* we leave.' We pointed out that *in doing this* '*we were also doing the next class a favour – thanks*'. My colleague and I would always say goodbye to each student as they left, as well as 'goodbye' to the whole class prior to 'the dismissal'.

This 'process' – these activities and approaches were developed with the whole class (and individually with more attentional, demanding and needy students) – saw a re-engaging of the students *as a group*. Many students expressed their awareness, interest and even gratitude that their teacher had clearly made an effort to 'reconnect' with them. They noticed, too, a more positive attitude in their class teacher.

She took on each of the ideas with enthusiasm and became more conscious about how she was speaking to the class as the teacher–leader, how she was actually communicating with and relating to them. She paid special attention to the language of correction and to encouraging her students' efforts.

> NB If there is no reasonable, significant response to whole-class refocusing and if you feel the class is slipping away into borderline chaos, do not hesitate to send for a senior teacher. Most schools have (or should have) clear protocols for how to cue for immediate senior teacher support in any emergency (internal phone call systems, mobile phone cueing, even sending a student – though this is less effective). It is self-defeating, even humiliating, to start pleading with a very noisy, very fractious class. It is equally self-defeating to start shouting, yelling or threatening. The 'catalytic students' will see this as the 'theatre' they were – perhaps – hoping for!

A note to senior teachers about organising classes for first-year teachers

It is disconcerting – even distressing – to give a *known* challenging class, or a class with a challenging cohort of students to a beginning teacher. This practice still occurs in some schools – knowingly, even calculated (page 138). It creates significant and unnecessary stress (at this point in a teacher's career). Not only does it create stress for that teacher, it creates stress 'along the line' because senior teachers have to intervene frequently, process and 'troubleshoot' in classes, follow up with students, organise detention, make phone calls to parents, and so on.

If a known hard class is given to a beginning teacher– in the broad equity of the timetable – then we should at least engage in supportive mentorship with those teachers in the critical first meetings with their class/es.

Mentoring a teacher's first meetings with a potentially challenging class

A senior colleague (known and respected by the students) will plan with the beginning teacher how best to conduct their first meeting with the class. The colleague mentor and first-year colleague will discuss and plan how to introduce themselves, how to settle and focus the class (page 95); even how/where they will stand (in the classroom) as they engage the students in establishing the lesson. They will also plan how they will explain and then discuss the core routines for learning and behaviour with the class (page 93); how they will team-teach during whole-class teaching time and how they will address any behaviour issues during that phase of the lesson; how they will engage and focus the class in the transition between whole-class teaching time and on-task learning time. They will also plan how they will manage the on-task phase of the lesson with particular reference to noise levels; students' movement around the room; how to give feedback and assistance to students; students who are off-task, and so on. Both colleagues discuss how to best plan and enable lesson closure and any, if necessary, follow-up of students who have been particularly disruptive during that first lesson (page 119).

Our experience has been that when such mentor-teaming is based on collegial goodwill and genuine team-teaching then the more challenging students are far less fractious in those critical first lessons than they would be if the beginning teacher were simply left to their own devices (Rogers, 2006).

> *Some senior teachers will think it helpful if they introduce the beginning teacher to the challenging class along these lines: 'RIGHT be quiet all of you! (after 2–3 minutes of loud cueing) – that's better. Now, let me introduce Miss Smith. She's a new teacher at our school. SO BEHAVE YOURSELVES ...' This senior colleague then turns to his junior colleague and says, 'If there's any problems, Miss Smith, you know where to send them!' and the senior colleague then walks out of the classroom. This sort of pathetic excuse for 'support' still goes on in some schools.*

Once the class settles the senior colleague will turn to his junior colleague and the class, and welcome them back from their holidays and say 'Let me introduce Miss Smith your new teacher this year for ...' (not making reference to the fact the colleague is a first-year teacher). He will then turn to face his colleague who will then address the class as their teacher. While his junior colleague is speaking, he will not stand at the front of the room sternly scanning the room, hands on hips, as if he is the one *really in control of the class – the real teacher*. He will show respect for his colleague by looking at them (while occasionally – briefly – scanning the class group). He models to the students what he expects of them – that at this point in the lesson they need to be facing the front and attending to *their class teacher*.

During whole-class teaching time they will observe the protocols of supportive mentoring (Chapter 10). If there are particularly difficult behaviour issues, the senior colleague will intervene. If such behaviour issues occur while the beginning teacher is engaged in whole-class teaching, the support colleague (mentor) will cue the beginning teacher, *and the class,* as naturally as possible before addressing the disruptive behaviour. The way my colleagues and I do this is through a (pre-arranged) verbal cue, 'Miss/Mr Smith (…) excuse me (…) do you mind if I have a chat with the class?' We make it *sound* and *look* as relaxed as possible – as if it is part of the normal team-teaching. The senior colleague will then address the disruptive behaviour/s and re-focus the class to the flow of teaching and then hand the class back (as it were) so it *looks* as symbiotic as possible. The practical utility of such interventions need to be discussed prior to going into the classroom (page 167).

Later that day they will debrief and discuss issues of concern and planning for the next lesson. By working directly in the classroom with the junior colleague – for the first few lessons – it enables a sense of moral support and confidence and gives a meaningful basis for collegial reflection later. Also the students will often give the new teacher respect 'by proxy' (as it were) because the senior teacher is there. In time, the junior teacher will *earn* the respect of the class, but initially – in those naturally stressful first few lessons – it will help to have the senior colleague working with them in a genuine teaming role. In subsequent lessons the senior colleague will drop into class occasionally to visit and chat with the students – to keep a 'roving brief' as it were.

This sort of initial mentoring is often part of a first-year peer-support programme in many schools.

Organisational change to support welfare/discipline at the whole-school level

Last year our school had 'one of those' grades. It was a grade 5 and heavily gender imbalanced, having 17 boys to 5 girls. The girls in the group were 'swamped'. More than half the boys were regarded as 'behaviour problems'. Two of the grade's students were integration students (special needs).

'What will they be like as a grade 6?' was the question on everyone's lips as the grade 5 year drew to a close. Gender imbalance was clearly a problem. The girls were almost *unheard* minority. These students had travelled through the primary school in the same social group – one of those typically 'hard' or 'reputation' classes. Perhaps it was time for a change?

Other grades in the school also pointed to a need for some kind of restructure. Grade 4 was small – 15 girls and 5 boys. A 'good' grade, exactly the opposite of grade 5. There was a small grade 3 – 14 children – and a small group of 15 early years.

To spread the load more evenly over the teaching staff, to avoid having the newly appointed vice principal bound to a grade and to balance the genders in the upper grades while separating the 'behaviour problems' of grade 5, it was decided to restructure the entire school into multi-age groups. This involved a great deal of discussion and meetings of the whole-school community, which was very supportive of the idea. Parents were happy to have some of the social groups rearranged. This year we have two gender-balanced grades 5-6, a 3-4, a 2-3, a 1-2, a straight early years grade and no problem grades!

The specialist timetable was arranged so that 'teams' of two class teachers have joint planning time that the vice-principal can also share in. A major part of the VP's role is to support the class teachers –especially in the 5-6 area, since that had initially appeared to be the area of greatest need.

All the multi-age groups are running smoothly. The atmosphere in the school is one of cheerful cooperation. There is growing involvement between classes. Having another pair of hands – the VP's – to call on is increasingly appreciated. A sense of teamwork is appearing among the staff members. The two grade 5-6 teachers have become largely 'self-supporting' and don't require extra support to the extent that the administration at first felt they would.

Organisational change may be just the thing to make that definable difference between 'good' and 'bad' grades, between a happy school and a not-so-happy school. In our case, it worked. Marie (Deputy Principal)

An out-of-control class: a note to senior teachers

When you hear (how can you not!) and then see a riotous class through the classroom window, you *know*. You can see the look of desperation mixed with thanks that you've arrived. This is not a 'white knight' moment. If you 'storm the citadel', *always* do it with professional grace and dignity.

In such situations my colleagues and I knock on the classroom door (it's a respectful cue), enter, walk across to the teacher and *quietly* ask (as an aside) if you can 'borrow two or three students, please'. We then turn to the class – *now* less noisy since the arrival of a senior teacher – and say, clearly and firmly, 'Excuse me, class ...' and then direct the three most 'catalytic' students out of the classroom. 'Brett (...) Nazim (...) Jayson (...) come with me now. Bring your bags.' Whenever I've done this I then walk off, and wait just outside the door – *expecting* them to come. They do; 'Close the door *quietly* behind you ...' (this to the boys as we head off).

In such cases we normally direct the students to a coordinator's office (or an interview room – if we have time) to make it clear about what we saw (regarding their behaviour) as we entered the classroom.

This firm – but respectful – directing of a few highly disruptive students 'de-catalyses' the behavioural stress points in the class. It also gives the class teacher temporary – and essential – respite from *these* students. It also gives the teacher an opportunity to regain a sense of focus with the class. The rest of the students in the class will have 'picked up the message'. This approach has to be conducted with dignity and calmness by the senior colleague.

Of course it is essential to sit with the class teacher – later – to ask how we can support them (beyond this temporary respite). We'll ask the obvious questions such as 'How long have these kind of disruptive behaviours been going on?' 'Who are the main catalysts' (ringleaders/followers)? 'What have you done – so far – to try to address any of this?' 'Any idea what these students are like in other classes?' 'Any other concerns?'

Going into a class like the one above to 'de-catalyse' has a limited 'shelf life' as a support option (important as it is). If we (as senior colleagues) have not put into place an ongoing support plan for our colleague then no amount of 'crisis-intervention' will help – in fact it may make things worse.

Any longer-term plan to support that teacher will involve some kind of mentoring support (Chapter 10). It will also need to include working with the 'catalytic students' one-to-one to develop individual behaviour-management plans (page 121).

Senior teachers and the out-of-control class

Some senior teachers will storm into very noisy, riotous classes with a loud – even shouting – voice level: 'WHAT THE HELL DO YOU THINK YOU'RE DOING!! I can hear you all the way from my office!' Several students sit back in their seats, arms folded in mock 'demurement' trying to hide a smirk. 'And don't you laugh! YES YOU! Do you think this is funny – DO YOU!? Right, you'll be the first on detention! I-AM-SICK-AND-TIRED-OF-THIS-CLASS !!'

This sort of harangue can often go on for five minutes. He then tells the class they'll all be on detention. Several students whinge. One confident student puts her hand up (he ignores her) so she says, 'But *we* didn't do anything ...' (she means the 30–40% of students who were trying to keep some sense of self-control and focus in the mayhem). The response to this student by the senior teacher is, 'You can moan all you want; I don't care ...! You're all on detention!'

The senior teacher then walks off, stridently, past the class teacher and out of the classroom as if to say, 'Well, it's clear you can't control this class! You needed me to come in and control them ...' It's hard to believe that this kind of unthinking behaviour still occurs in our schools – but it does. Some senior teachers even think such behaviour is professionally acceptable – tolerable. What is even more disconcerting is that some senior teachers may think they are actually 'helping'.

Beyond the two or three catalytic students: another note to senior teachers

You've seen the chaotic class through the classroom window; you've sensed that your colleague – now – is best right out of that 'maelstrom'. Even directing several students out of the room would make little difference.

You knock and enter and walk across to the teacher and quietly let them know, 'Mrs Smith, there's a message at the front office.' Once your colleague has left the classroom (with a returned look of bemused gratitude?) it will help to walk to the front centre of the room and calmly, firmly and clearly address the class, 'Settling down – everyone'. We tactically pause (...); a *brief* waiting for that confident expectation to register.

We cue the several 'catalytic' students ... 'Michael (...) Shannon (...) Ahmed (...) back in your seats – *now*.' This to the boys who I'd seen wandering and loudly chatting and gesturing (when I'd looked through the window before entering). On occasion, even boys standing on tables and a *'play fight'* at the back of the room.

'Chelsea (...) Alana (...) Krystal (...) away from the windows now (...) back in your seats.' Again some brief tactical pausing to convey expectation. 'Looking this way and listening – *everyone* ...'

Once the class is settled and focused (often a few minutes) we let them know what we saw prior to coming in the classroom. 'Let me tell you what I saw as I came into your class. 'I saw several students standing looking out of the window and talking to students wandering past our classroom ... *while* your teacher was trying to speak to you all. I saw several students wandering around the class chatting to other students; I saw students waving their hands and clicking their fingers REALLY LOUDLY and hassling students who were trying to listen. I saw a couple of students at the back of the classroom "play fighting". Some of you were turning round and loudly – very loudly – chatting to students behind them ... All this *while* your teacher was trying to teach your class.'

That's enough – a brief, but clear catalogue of catalytic behaviours stated calmly and clearly as we're scanning the eyes of the whole group.

What we *don't* do is, 'WHO THE HELL DO YOU THINK YOU ARE ...!! I COULD HEAR YOU ALL THE WAY DOWN THE CORRIDOR! YOU, YOU, YOU ...! (the teacher points to each catalytic student in turn). Yes – *and YOU,* out of your seats wandering around as if you owned place …!'

Tempting as such a harangue might be, it will not enable any sense of focus or concern and it certainly won't enable the potential fresh start such a class will need to pursue with their teacher later (page 141).

Some senior teachers will walk into such a class and by posture, gesture and lecture convey that – now – the *real* teacher has arrived. The one who can *really* control this class. This, too, is picked up by the students as a message that their regular teacher (who has just left) cannot *really* control their class: 'it needs *this* senior teacher to come in to shout at us and threaten us …' This message will certainly get round the school through the student 'tribal tom-toms'.

It is essential in any such supportive intervention that we follow up with the class teacher later that day to ask the essential questions. That follow-up will need to address each of the 'catalytic' students (in turn) as well and the offer of some ongoing mentoring – perhaps a fresh-start approach.

A difficult note of advice to first-year teachers

If you're having a very difficult time of it with your class; if they are very noisy, fractious and disruptive – more than 'just a few' – and *then* you see, out of your classroom window, a senior teacher staring at you in your struggle to manage the class … You see them standing, frowning – perhaps even glaring – at you. You note – as you glance through the classroom window – their constrained body language. You conclude, 'they're judging me …', 'that standing stare suggests to me that I am a failure …'. All this at nanosecond speed as you try to manage that challenging Year 5 class or 8D, 9C or 10E!

Before the senior teacher walks in and simply 'takes over' (in the way noted above – it does happen!) I suggest you go to the front of the classroom and do your best to cue the whole class – briefly – 'CLASS (…) Mr. Smith is outside… I'm just going to ask him to come in and see how we're all going with our class work today. Won't be a moment.' Leave the classroom door open.

> NB I am not suggesting for one minute that all senior teachers do the 'failing teacher glare', or the 'storming of the citadel'. Sadly, though, there are still some senior teachers who strut their seniority in this way, even believing that such behaviour is important in conveying 'the proper control message to the class'. It only undermines a teacher's leadership of their class.

I suggest that (with your heart thumping) you then go outside, into the corridor and address your colleague. 'Mr Smith, I saw you looking at our class,' (*our* class, not *my* class). 'I'd like you to come in and wander round and have a quiet chat with the students about the work we are doing today.' In other words you both pre-empt and 'define' (as much as one can) how you want your senior colleague to 'support' you. This will not be easy. As I said, your heart will be thumping, you may be a little tongue-tied. At least you will have been professional and, hopefully, pre-empted him simply walking in and shouting your class down (page 151). It is also a good idea, from time to time, to invite them to come into your class (*en passant*) when 'your class' is working well.

- It can also help to invite your head of department, perhaps even the principal, to visit one of your 'better classes' – suggest a date (rather than an *ad hoc* visit).

- Note down (in your 'diary') any positive feedback from students or parents (particularly notes). We forget, sometimes, the positive feedback our students give us.

- Never rate your ability, your 'performance', your very role as a teacher by your hardest classes, or your bad days.

If a senior teacher has shouted your class down

It will be important to speak with the senior teacher privately, and professionally, about your concerns over the way they came into 'your' class and simply took over. You won't use those words, however, ('took over'). It will help to write down your concerns beforehand so that you're reasonably clear about what it is you want to say. For example, 'Difficult as it is to share this, Mr. Smith ... when you came into 8D the other day and stood in front of the class and said (here be specific) ... I felt ...' If you felt discouraged, even humiliated, say so – 'belittled' might be too strong a word for them – even if you felt that. If you are uncertain about what to say, it will help to talk it through with a supportive colleague first.

'I'm sure you were trying to help, Mr. Smith, but what I felt was that my leadership was compromised ...' 'I do obviously value your support. What I would appreciate is this ...' You can then outline the kind of class visit you believe could assist ... the possibility of help with following up key power-brokers in the class; even support in mentorship (Chapter 10). *You are being the professional at this point* – you don't merely defer or acquiesce because of their seniority.

It's not easy to be clear, specific *and professional* about such concerns. You'll no doubt feel very nervous even asking to see a senior colleague. However, if you say nothing (but 'bottle up' your anxiety, frustration or anger) then things will probably get worse. The senior colleague may even feel he has 'helped' and may well do so again, in the same unhelpful way, should he notice your class behaving in an unruly way.

The bullying of teachers by some students

I have taken some pains, and written at some length, about this very disturbing behaviour that occurs in our profession. It is not a 'new' issue in schools. It is, however, rarely discussed in any significant way in the literature, although it is cited directly and indirectly in stress reports.

In stress reports, and newspaper reports, it is often 'hidden' under more general descriptors such as 'impossible classes', 'teachers who cannot cope', a 'stressed-out profession', 'work care claims' and 'stress-related illness in the profession'. Bullying (by some students) is a cause of great stress for some teachers, and while I do not want to suggest it is a common experience, it is certainly occurring more frequently these days. This is not an easy topic to address – particularly in print – because I do not want (in any sense) to disparage our profession.

And (like any bullying) the degree of confidence and assurance felt by victims of bullying regarding the degree to which it is *appropriately* addressed depends largely on the kind of colleague support in their school. Teachers have a right to a safe workplace.[1]

I've spoken with many teachers who have been bullied by students (and sometimes even by other teachers) (see Appendix 4). I've worked with teachers to confront the perpetrators (as we must), and sought to enable colleagues to resolve the issues around bullying behaviours, and seek to recover professional (and personal) esteem.

The education union (ATL) makes the point that the significant stress teachers sometimes experience in their workplace is also related to bullying by other colleagues: 'a persistent (and often deliberate misuse of power or position to intimidate, humiliate or undermine' (page 1). This creates excessive anxiety about addressing the issue with the senior colleague concerned lest they 'misinterpret it as hostile criticism or treat it with derision or suspicion' (ibid.).

It can create a loss of confidence, self-worth and even health-related concerns.

Most of all there is the ongoing anxiety about facing school each day due to the fear of recurrent bullying behaviour by such colleagues. In such extreme situations it is essential to get trusted colleague advice and union support.

Detailed advice on the actions one can take to stop such bullying can be found at www.atl.org.uk/help-and-advice/worklace-bullying/what is bullying.asp

Field (2010) notes, that 'teachers and lecturers have made the most calls to the UK National Workplace Bullying Advice Line since its inception in 1996 and they make the most inquiries to bully online (www.bullyonline.org). The Teacher Support Network says that teachers are four times more likely to experience stress at work than employees in other professions' (ibid)

In the sense in which I describe bullying by students of teachers I mean the calculated, intentional, selective (and gutless) *repetitive* behaviour by one (or several) students towards the teacher. Behaviours designed to specifically hurt. Most bullying is psychological – taunting; name calling; suggestive body language used to homophobically target a teacher, and so on. It is sometimes the texting; the Facebook comments that imply, demean, suggest, malign, provoke. Taunts ('subtle' or explicit) about clothing; gesticulation in body language that addresses a teacher's sexuality; sexual orientation; ethnicity/accent; the teacher's ability to teach . . . in fact almost anything. Like any bullying, the bully exercises an intentional desire to hurt; to 'prove' their social power; to draw others into their disturbed private logic about defining and proving their social place. Bullying is always about power.

Bullying is not the ill-thought, silly, stupid or attentional comment by a student; it is not the dropped swear word, or occasional sexist comment. All these are normal in the wear and tear of teaching. Bullying is a calculative, selective and repetitive *pattern* of behaviour designed to create a situation, a climate, where the bullying student ratifies their abusive social power. If left unaddressed, such behaviour will normally get worse.

The right to feel safe in a school is a right we should all expect to enjoy, and when affected by repeatedly disruptive behaviour and bullying it has to be confronted with senior teacher support.

We should never diminish bullying behaviour by implying that the teacher is 'unable to discipline effectively', or 'can't really hack it'. It bothers me greatly that *some* senior teachers (including some deputy and head teachers) see bullying behaviour by students as an issue about the teacher's classroom control and discipline rather than addressing *bullying behaviour* for what it is. In effect they say 'Well, it's their fault (the victim) because they can't manage the students'. It is attitudes like this that create the acute anxiety and stress – and reluctance in teachers to come forward and seek senior colleague understanding and assistance early in the cycle of such behaviour/s.

I have spoken with colleagues who have put up with appalling – disgusting – behaviour by bullying students but have been reluctant to 'come forward' lest they be seen as 'weak', 'ineffective' or (worse) 'incompetent'. Such colleagues (like any victim of bullying) then struggle on in a kind of degrading survivalism.

NB There are some teachers (not many in my experience) who bully students. The issue of the bullying of students by teachers is not addressed in this book. However, if there is reliable evidence of teachers who bully students, they (like any perpetrator) must be confronted with the evidence brought forward by the victim(s). The process that follows is – also – relevant when confronting adult bullies and supporting victims who are students.

Addressing the bullying of teachers

- All bullying in a school should be addressed from *the fundamental right to feel safe in one's workplace*.

- We need to address and confront such behaviours *as bullying* – and take these as seriously as we would any bullying behaviour in a school. It is no less serious because the victim is an adult (even an adult in the role of teacher). Such behaviours should also not be trivialised by senior colleagues – 'Well, that teacher does wear "provocative clothes". 'He does have a mincing gait.' 'She does have a confusing and difficult to understand accent ...'. These are some of the milder comments I've heard from some senior colleagues when unravelling and 'interpreting' bullying episodes.

- We need to make the distinction clear between one's ability and one's skill as a teacher–leader in addressing normative distracting and disruptive behaviour, and a teacher having to 'put up with' or 'cope with' calculated and repetitive bullying behaviours.

- It is important that we never convey to the victim of bullying (our colleague) that they are at fault – that they are somehow to be blamed for what they are experiencing. While some teachers clearly need help in their professional role of teacher–leader (particularly with respect to behaviour management and discipline), we should not confuse this with bullying behaviour.

- Students who bully (like all bullies) are cowardly and sneaky, yet desperate for attentional power within *their peer group*. However, they trade in 'secrecy' from adults (other teachers). They do this because they know that once their behaviour is clearly known by senior teachers that those teachers can, and will, make it stop. Bullying students, however, need the collusive support of other students in order to exercise their social power[2]. *Collusive* bullies are those students who laugh along, jeer with, or join in the 'theatre' of bullying. ('Yeah, give it to her!'; 'Yes meeeesss – we can't understand youuuu; why can't you speak *proper* English?!'). Other students in the class will acquiesce in this 'theatre' perhaps because they fear peer rejection or are anxious about being bullied themselves. Bullies are cowards.

- The issue of bullying is sometimes compounded by the way *some* senior teachers address very restless and challenging classes (page 151).

- Sometimes bullying of teachers occurs in non-classroom settings – for example playgrounds, out of school, or the world-wide graffiti board (Facebook world).

- If the teacher is reluctant to come forward to ask for senior teacher support in addressing a bullying issue in their classes then we will need to approach them as a senior teacher or supportive colleague. We do this quietly, privately, professionally.

If we suspect there a colleague who is being bullied, it is crucial we approach them. This is not easy – naturally we do not want to 'make' our colleague feel a failure or 'at fault'. We do not want to imply that the issue is that they simply cannot manage their class(es). What we need to do is help them to differentiate between what is disruptive behaviour(s) and what is bullying, and then work with them to confront and challenge the bullying students in a structured one-to-one meeting (see below).

It will be important in that first meeting to take what they say seriously. Listen, empathise first, then take careful notes. We will then need to organise and plan for an accountability conference with the principal perpetrators of (the) bullying.

The bullying of teachers: conducting an accountability conference

An accountability conference enables an adult victim[3] of student bullying to respectfully confront the perpetrator(s) of the bullying about their behaviour and to expect clear assurances that such behaviour will stop, and do so within a process of supportive review with a senior teacher. This process gives a necessary voice to the victim of bullying while also giving appropriate right-of-reply, as well as consequential due process, to the perpetrator(s).

When I speak about 'confronting' a student about their bullying behaviour I do not mean we are nasty, peevish, verbally domineering (although such is tempting!). I mean we respectfully – but firmly, resolutely and seriously – confront the student about what they have said, done or implied that constitutes bullying behaviour.

- We call the bullying student to account for their bullying behaviour – we also give the student due right of reply.
- We call on the student(s) to assure the teacher (the victim of their bullying) that these behaviours are wrong and totally unacceptable.
- We make clear that these behaviours will stop and direct the student/s to redress what they have done.
- We seek to re-engage the student to their responsibilities, to own their behaviour within the rights dynamic of the school (page 113).

Planning the meeting

It is crucial to plan any such meeting thoughtfully with the victim of bullying beforehand. As well as detailing when and where the bullying occurred, the senior teacher will need to get the facts of the bullying *behaviours* clear – on paper. Dates, times, specific (and typical) examples of what the bully did, said, suggested (the non-verbal bullying), texted, 'twittered' or 'facebooked'.

Obviously we can't plan for every contingency in conducting such a meeting. There may well be tears shed at the actual accountability conference, or angry (and occasionally) offensive outbursts by a teacher or student. The senior teacher will need to discuss with the teacher concerned beforehand what to do if tempers flare or emotions get strained. Some bullying students will become belligerent, some will deny that their behaviour is *bullying* and a few will say nothing (see later). Many students do apologise and change their behaviour when teachers work to re-engage them.

Accountability conference

- Have the details of the bullying behaviour clearly transcribed before the meeting.

- Discuss beforehand with the teacher concerned how the senior teacher's role will operate in conducting, mediating and arbitrating due process during the meeting between the teacher and the bullying student, and how best to work towards an appropriate outcome.

- The difficult part of any such meeting concerns how the teacher (the 'victim') will respectfully confront the bullying student about their behaviour and the effect such behaviour has had on the teacher, other students, on the teaching and learning (in class time) and, crucially, *how such behaviour(s) affect the fundamental rights of respect, safety and fairness.* It will be essential to plan beforehand what the teacher is likely to say at the meeting, and how to deal with the student's right of reply.

- The bullying student's presence at such a meeting is mandatory. Allow a good half an hour to forty-five minutes for conducting the meeting.

- A 'circular' seating arrangement is preferred – not too close in seating proximity.

- The senior teacher (as facilitator) will open the meeting by making it clear – *briefly and specifically* – why this meeting has been called.

   The tone is serious, respectful and formal. 'I have called this meeting (this to the student) because of what's been happening in 8D ...'. At this point the senior teacher (referring to the printed notes) will read out the most typical and frequent bullying *behaviour.* If the student butts in, 'But I was only joking when I said that he's a poofter!' The senior teacher will clearly point out to the student that they'll have their opportunity to have their say later. 'Over the last few weeks, in 8D, you've frequently been saying things like (be *specific* and refer to the list) ... and making gestures like ...' (the senior colleague can also 'mirror' the typical bullying gestures to the student – this will need to have the teacher's permission beforehand). The emphasis at this point in the meeting is to briefly, specifically and clearly outline the *bullying behaviours* to the student.

The most difficult part of such meetings occurs when the senior teacher then asks the class teacher to make clear – to the student – what has actually been going on regarding the student's bullying behaviour. At this point the teacher will face the student directly, and address the student (by name): '... This is what you have been doing/saying (or texting) to me – or about me ...' Be specific, brief, clear and succinct. The teacher will make it clear:

- the effect that such behaviour has had on the teacher's *right to respect and fair treatment*

- the effect such behaviour(s) have had on the teaching and learning in class time (Bullying always affects others, not only the victim.)

- that this behaviour (point to the list, without rereading it) has to stop: 'What will you do to make it stop?'

The teacher will have discussed with the senior colleague how 'best' to phrase the language and how they will then deal with the student's possible right of reply.

- While it might sound (to some teachers) unreasonable to extend a right of reply to a student who has been bullying, it is important – not least because *it is a right*. Most students when asked, 'What do you have to say about all this ...?' will discount, minimise, shift blame or lie:

  - 'I wasn't the only one! Others were saying stuff too!'

  - 'I was only joking!' (very common) 'I didn't mean nothing.'

  - 'Anyway, she's not a good teacher; she's boring. And the other kids in class say so too – it's not just me.' (These kinds of comments *may* have a bare and skewed 'truth', but are bent to serve a *bullying purpose*).

It is essential to address, confront and *reframe* these typical excuses:

  - 'Maybe you thought it was a joke when you said (suggested or texted) ...' Here we briefly – and specifically – confront the bullying *behaviour* '... however, that kind of language is never a joke; *ever*. That language is sexist, arrogant, hurtful (cruel or disgusting, or ...) *because* ...' (Here we give a brief reason why such language or behaviour or gestures are hurtful, sexist, racist or cruel, or ...)

  - 'Even if other students said ... (be specific) *you are responsible for what you do and say* ...' It will also help to briefly explain that you (the senior teacher) will be speaking to other students as well. At the moment you're concentrating on what *this* student has been doing/saying.

  - 'Even if you don't like this subject ... or Mr. Smith's teaching ... There is no excuse for doing/saying ...' (Here again we need to be brief and specific about the bullying behaviour).

- Some students will 'go silent'. Perhaps they are thinking that in claiming 'their right to silence' (they've seen the police shows) then they won't implicate themselves, nor can they 'really be held accountable'; after all they haven't admitted anything – *yet.*

My colleagues and I find it helpful to *let the student know what we think they are probably saying to themselves,* and then confront these possibilities and outline the expected student response.

'You're not saying anything, Jayson ...' Always use the student's name (allow for some 'silence' and 'take-up'). 'Perhaps you're saying it was all a joke when you said/did/texted ...' (be specific). 'It's never a joke to say such things ... What you said was hurtful, cruel, nasty ...' (use apposite descriptors relating to the behaviour). 'These behaviours are bullying – you have been bullying Mr Smith ...'

> The challenge in confronting bullying behaviour is to address and confront the bullying behaviour and to do so respectfully but with due seriousness. This is not 'merely' disruptive behaviour. We are dealing with *repeatedly* hurtful behaviour(s). It is tempting to want to attack the student ('You arrogant, disgusting little b____d!') Remember the difficult maxim – address the behaviour rather than attacking the student.

The meeting needs to progress to:

- A clear understanding that the student is responsible for their if behaviour, *'You own your behaviour.* This meeting has been your opportunity to be clearly aware of how hurtful your behaviour has been towards Mr Smith ... What can you do *now,* and in class, to make things right?'

- 'The right thing to do is, of course, to apologise and accept responsibility.'

  Some students will apologise straight away, some (collusive bullies) will even be unaware of how hurtful their behaviour has actually been. Some students refuse to apologise, or even acknowledge their behaviour. It is pointless forcing an apology. We make the clear point that it is the right – and fair – thing to do and leave them with that expectation. We also make clear what the consequences of such continuing bullying behaviour.

- Most importantly we direct the student to assure the teacher (and the senior teacher) that the bullying behaviour will cease. We will need to re-emphasise the central due rights – *the right to feel safe; the right to basic respect and fair treatment; the right of the teacher to teach* ('without having to put up with behaviours of the sort we've been discussing in this meeting').

  Some students say, 'Yes, we'll stop doing/saying/texting ...' We need to also ask what they will do *instead* so that the teacher will be reassured they can teach without having to put up with those behaviours. *'What will you do* to show basic respect towards your teacher in class /in school ...?'

If the student can't (or won't) suggest, or indicate, where and how they need to change their behaviour, we will need to make clear *what behaviours need to stop, and what sorts of behaviours need to start* in their responsibilities as a member of that class group. It can help to write these behaviour expectations down for the student.

● It is essential that the teacher, as the adult, communicates to the student that they extend goodwill for the immediate future between teacher and student. The process of repairing and rebuilding will need to be communicated in good faith from the teacher, within shared expectations relating to these essential rights and the responsibilities (the school's behaviour code).

● We make it clear that the student knows that there will be a review meeting (in a week's time) to see how things are going in 8D (or wherever the context of bullying has been occurring). We hope, of course, that the student in question will take serious and thoughtful note of what has happened at this meeting. We also need to let the student know that if there is no meaningful change in their behaviour then their parent(s) will be contacted and there will need to be a *formal meeting about this bullying behaviour*. On occasion, the outcome of such a meeting may need to clearly indicate formal expulsion as a consequence of repeated bullying behaviour by the student/s (particularly where the parent/s have been intimidating or threatening). This, fortunately, is rare.

The earlier we address any bullying, the stronger the likelihood that there will be a workable, even a positive, outcome for the teacher (and the student(s)).

Isolated serious episodes

If there has been an isolated ('one-off') episode of verbal assault or threat made to a teacher then we would normally call a formal meeting between the student(s), the teacher, a senior staff member and the parent(s) or caregiver(s). We would follow a due process similar to that of an accountability conference.

Collusive bullies

Those students who enable and support the 'theatre' of bullying also need to be called to account. It is advisable to speak with each of the collusive bullies separately (not in a group).

● Make clear what has been going on, in the context of the bullying towards the teacher concerned (classroom or playground). Be specific and clear about their *behaviour* – have the details (etc.) recorded. Ask the student, '*What do you know about this* …?' Point out that we are aware that they have been 'laughing' along with the homophobic comments such as

.... That they have 'cheered', jeered', 'clapped' and 'whistled' along with ...'. Such behaviours (by the colluders) enables the bullying student to believe that what they're doing is OK, that they (the other student(s)) are legitimising the bullying of their teacher.

- The teacher will ask 'How do you think this kind of behaviour makes me feel? How do you think it affects my right to teach?' If they don't (or won't) answer, we need to tell them. It is important that this is said calmly (though not without emotion, obviously). Again we address the *bullying behaviour*, we don't 'attack' the student.

When student(s) protest that it was just a joke (etc.), deal with each disclaimer or discounting of their behaviour, as noted earlier (page 160).

- Ask each student (in turn) what they will do to stop such behaviour and enable their teacher (and their other classmates) to enjoy a class where:
  - *we can enjoy the right to feel safe* (without having to put up with behaviours like ... Here we refer to the list again.
  - *we can enjoy the right to respect* (without having to put up with behaviours like ...)
  - *the teacher can teach* (without having to put up with behaviours like ...).
- Let each student know (in turn) that we will be meeting in a week's time to review their behaviour.

As I said, this is an unpleasant aspect of school behaviour to have to address. On most occasions, early intervention will stop such behaviours if there is adequate and ongoing support for the teacher in question. That support has to both address and respectfully confront the bullying behaviour while seeking to rebuild teacher–student relationships.

We're not asking either student/s or teacher to 'like' each other – we are expecting respectful and civil relationships. We expect the students to *own their behaviour* and be responsible for what they say and do. We need to work with the teacher to so lead and engage their classes that this is the most likely outcome. Often an ongoing mentoring support will go a long way to realising that essential aim.

Notes

1. Christine Stewart (2009) (Australian Education Union) has made the very important point that while challenging behaviour from students is the risk factor, there is 'now a recognition that *the safe workplace is a right, not an added extra* ... this principle is not always implemented ... our challenge now is to make it happen.'

She further notes that Worksafe Victoria now trains its inspectors to consider risks to psychological health as well as physical injuries.

Farewell To Arms: *Australian Education News*. Issue 8. November 2009.

2. It is important to note that there are many students who get very anxious when they see a teacher being *bullied*. Many students feel uncomfortable about speaking up (or out). Some (thankfully) will report the bullying by students (of a teacher) to a senior teacher. I have also had students (and parents) share their concerns in letters about 'what is going on in 8D or 9C'. We need to takes their words seriously as part of the overall evidence when confronting bullying students and supporting victims.

3. The term 'victim' is always difficult, in terms of a word sufficiently common in understanding and usage (rebullying). It may easily conjure up images of someone 'at the mercy' of another; a 'helpless' person. Consult any thesaurus and, used as a noun, the word *victim* often carries meanings relating to *sufferer* (with associated meanings of 'dupe', 'stooge', 'charlie', 'sap', 'patsy'). When used as a verb, however, we now see the bullying *behaviour* – to 'victimise'; 'persecute'; 'exploit; 'maltreat'; 'discriminate'; 'prey upon' and even 'terrorise'.

I have chosen to use the term *victim* as someone undeserving of such behaviours – *and not at fault*.

Mentoring support for professional development in behaviour leadership

What this chapter will explore and develop:

- The nature and benefits of colleague mentoring and coaching
- The practical development of mentoring and peer-coaching in behaviour leadership practices and skills
- How to give supportive colleague feedback
- Modifying, developing and changing one's behaviour leadership practice, with particulare reference to core skills

The benefits of mentoring

For many years now I have been involved in mentoring support in schools – *elective* mentoring for professional development. The particular area of mentoring that my colleagues and I engage in is focused on behaviour leadership – particularly the skills inherent in positive discipline practice (Chapter 7).

One can go for years – in our profession – without having the opportunity for feedback and constructive advice based on *direct classroom observation* through supportive collegial teaming. This 'teaming' includes options such as team-teaching, peer-coaching, peer-support groups and professional development *directly linked to the skills of behaviour leadership* in classroom (and non-classroom) settings.[1]

My role in such mentorship has focused particularly on peer-coaching – enabling colleagues to reflect on their typical, *characteristic*, behaviour-management practice and to utilise such reflection as an opportunity for ongoing professional development. The basis for such reflection involves a form of team-teaching that involves the mentor working with their colleague directly in the classroom – in part as 'observer', in part as 'coach'. And then, later, using shared feedback for professional self-awareness, reflection and change.

Professional self-esteem

In developing any mentoring relationship with a colleague, the aim is always to support a colleague's professional self-awareness (of their teaching, management and discipline). Making time for considered professional reflection is never easy in our busy teaching week. However, if we value professional development that includes such mentoring, we can create time-opportunities that enable colleagues to support one another. Such support can enable the kind of relaxed 'collegial structure' that mentor-teaching can occasion for professional reflection and professional development. This mentoring, by its very nature, needs to be based in *elective*, mutual trust.

The mentoring model discussed in this chapter is based on the concept of 'peer-coaching' – *learning within the context of one's direct teaching experiences*. In this sense the mentoring emphasis is concerned with supporting a colleague's self-awareness about their management and discipline by team-teaching with them – in their classrooms. We can then see, hear and experience something of *their* normative experience as they seek to lead, teach and manage their students. Until we see, hear and experience the dynamics with a given class group – *with* their teacher – it may be difficult to enable and support a colleague's professional self-awareness and reflection about their characteristic behaviour leadership.

The mentoring approach explored in this chapter will normally develop within a whole-school professional development focus. Colleagues are encouraged to see the possibility, and value, of working with a trusted colleague – one-to-one in the classroom. In such a whole-school approach the mentors will have been carefully 'selected'. Such colleagues are acknowledged by their peers as those with whom one would take a professional risk, and trust, to work with in their classroom, and one to whom they would be willing to trust for professional feedback.

Mentor–colleague pairs need to be able to build and sustain a positive, purposeful, professional and collegial relationship. Their ability to reflectively and empathetically listen is crucial to their role. The mentor's ability to motivate and encourage through their own modelling – as well as giving constructive feedback – is also essential in building confidence in the mentor–mentee relationship. The last person one wants as a mentor is the teacher who exudes the kind of hubristic 'confidence' that says, 'I don't have any real problems with behaviour management; I'll show you how to do it ...'

Beginning a mentoring journey: an invitation to professional trust and risk

Inviting a colleague into one's classroom (on a reasonably regular basis) carries some natural 'risk' and anxiety, as well as trust. When a teacher decides that a mentorship option has *considered* professional value, they will meet with a colleague mentor to *discuss and develop how it might work for them*[2].

The 'mentee'[3] meets with their 'mentor'-colleague to clarify and discuss:

- Why the mentee has chosen to work with a mentor-colleague – what *they* hope to gain from this partnership.
- The viability, value and utility of a collegial mentoring relationship.
- Timetable slots for the mentee and mentor to work together with a given class group (this is always a challenge) – how many sessions will we be able to (initially) sustain? (4, 6, 8?)
- What mentoring involves practically – basics such as how the mentor-colleague will be introduced to the students in the mentee's class (page 168); where the mentor-colleague will stand/sit during whole-class teaching time in relation to their mentee-colleague; how (and if, and why) the mentor might intervene in any discipline or management situations, if necessary, in the mentee's class; at what points in a lesson the mentor will team-teach with their mentee-colleague (so as to model particular aspects of teaching, management or discipline.
- How, and when, feedback will be shared – the nature and utility of feedback from the mentor to mentee (the 'coaching' aspect). As the coaching aspect

is an essential feature of such mentoring, colleagues discuss the *mutual* nature of observation and feedback within a team-teaching context.

- How we might use such feedback for ongoing professional development with our mentee-colleague – particularly when addressing the skills of behaviour leadership, discipline communication and student engagement in learning (page 171).

- Such mentorship can also extend to one-to-one behaviour interview sessions with students (page 119).

In any mentoring process it is that opportunity to *learn from that context* that is integral to the mentoring journey. I've sat in on many one-to-one sessions between a teacher and a student with problematic behaviour. By teaming in this way colleagues can 'feel' (as well as see and hear) how to manage in such contexts in a more considered and positive way.

Introduction of the mentor colleague to the mentee's class

When a colleague introduces a fellow teacher (the collegial mentor) to their class, (at the beginning of a lesson) the students are naturally inquisitive – perhaps (at times) 'suspicious'. 'Why is this *other* teacher in *their* class today?' (see page 32)

It will help if colleagues discuss beforehand not just where they will stand (at the front of the classroom) but also how the class teacher will introduce their mentor-colleague during the establishment phase of the lesson. (In an early years class I sit next to my colleague at the front of the classroom).

We find it helpful to say something like, '... Mr Rogers is here with us today looking at teaching and learning in a number of classes in our school. He is interested in how we all learn together here in our class.'

Normally at this point the class teacher steps aside, as it were, and the mentor-colleague resettles and refocuses the class. We try to make the symbiosis of such team-teaching look as 'relaxed' and 'natural' as possible. Then – when the students are settled – the mentor colleague greets them 'formally' ('Good morning / afternoon') and asks the class what they 'are working on ...', 'what they're learning together *at the moment* (with their regular teacher)'.

I have frequently worked in subject areas well outside my normal 'teacher comfort zone' as a mentor–teacher – maths, science, chemistry, foreign languages (French, German, Italian, Indonesian, Japanese, etc.).

At this point in the lesson I am inviting the students to share with me as the 'other teacher'. This gives the mentor an opportunity to engage with the whole class and to 'model' the sort of teaching/behaviour leadership that mentor and mentee will discuss later. At this point in the lesson the mentee is standing to one side 'watching' their mentor-colleague as well as casually (and incidentally) 'watching' their class from the front of the classroom.

After 10 minutes or so of working with the class, the mentor-colleague will 'hand back' whole-class leadership to their colleague, with a cue such as 'Mrs Smith will now discuss what we'll be working on in class today ...' The mentor-colleague then 'steps aside' and the regular teacher re-engages the class.

During *whole-class teaching time* the mentor-colleague is (normally) standing at the front of the classroom 'teaming' with the class teacher. When the class teacher moves into the transitional phase (between whole-class teaching and on-task learning time) the mentor and mentee would normally move around the room engaging/supporting and – where necessary – disciplining students. Even here (at this point in a class period) the mentee and mentor have opportunities to incidentally 'observe' one another.

NB It is important to stress, yet again, that there is no concept of 'superior'/'inferior' in any such collegial 'mentor'/'mentee' relationships. This is a professional collegial relationship based on professional trust and focused on shared aims/objectives. The mentor will work with, and alongside, their colleague (much as a good coach would) and use their direct classroom observations (later) as a means of shared reflection, professional dialogue and skill development. The observation and feedback elements are crucial to behaviour-leadership *awareness* for the mentee. They also provide a basis for conscious review and behaviour change in a teacher's behaviour leadership practice.

Raising behaviour awareness in mentor-coaching

Some teachers may be unaware of their typical – or *characteristic* – management and discipline behaviour. For example, during whole-class teaching time a teacher may be struggling – somewhat – with a 'restless' Year 9 class. Several students are distractedly chatting while the teacher tries to gain whole-class attention and focus. Some students are calling out; others are a little too kinaesthetically active in their seats (fiddling with water bottles and 'loud' pencil cases); several students are chatting (seemingly ignoring their teacher). The class teacher seems unaware that she is pacing up and down at the front of the room and that her overly raised voice (and 'pacing') actually telegraphs a corresponding 'restlessness' in his students. She is also unaware of her characteristic discipline language, such as an overuse of the 'interrogative form' as she seeks to settle the class – 'Can you please stop talking?!' 'Will you all PLEASE face the front and listen ...?. She also seems unaware that when she individually targets distracting students she is, again, overusing the interrogative form – 'WHY are you calling out Adam ...?', 'And you – yes, you two – Damien and Bilal – ARE YOU SUPPOSED to be talking now?'

She is also unaware that she uses frequent negative directions such as *'Don't* lean back like that in your seat ...', *'Don't* talk while I'm talking ...', *'Don't* call out ...' (page 97) Most of this behaviour (of course) arises from frustration and (in the emotional moment) is hardly open to any self-awareness in the immediacy of the moment! I also need to stress, here, that many teachers don't *mean* to be negative in their discipline, and yet that is often what comes across in language and often tone and manner.

During on-task learning time the class teacher also seems unaware of how she enters a student's 'personal space'; of how she often picks up students' workbooks without asking ...[4] or how she asks students *'why* they aren't working; *why* they haven't got their pens, rulers' (page 110); *'why* they haven't started their work yet' (*'Are* you supposed to be wandering around the classroom ...?'). If a student is 'wandering' – purposelessly as it were – a brief, quiet, *direct* question is more appropriate, 'Jayson (...) you're out of your seat. *What* are you supposed to be doing at the moment?' A direct question ('What?' ... 'When?' ... 'Where?' ... 'How?') helps to focus responsibility back to the student.

NB The *unhelpful* use of interrogatives – in behaviour leadership language – has been discussed earlier (pages 95, 97).

When a teacher is under the *normative* daily pressures of day-to-day teaching, they may not be aware of their *characteristic* management and discipline, language and behaviour. What mentoring can do is assist colleagues to be more *professionally self-aware* regarding how they use corrective/discipline language. Because the mentee-colleague has invited their mentor-colleague to team with them in their classroom, the mentor is able to observe the mentee-colleague's *characteristic* behaviour leadership (expressed in some of the deceptively 'small' ways noted earlier) and give feedback to their colleague based on direct, classroom observation.

It is this *awareness raising* that is an essential feature of professional reflection, review and opportunity for change.

Team-teaching as mentoring

The mentoring model my colleagues and I engage in is based on a team-teaching approach. The mentor is introduced by the mentee-colleague (the host teacher) with a general introduction along these lines – 'Mr Rogers is a visiting teacher and he'll be working in our classroom this morning. He's interested in how students and teachers work together to support positive learning ...' (or words to that effect). The classroom teacher then steps aside (at the *front of the classroom*) and the mentor-colleague leads the class and invites the students to share what they are learning in that subject. For example, addressing the class, the mentor-colleague (the 'visiting' teacher) will say something like, 'I want you to share with me what you are studying, at the moment, in French (or science, or English, or maths or chemistry, whatever the subject topic). I want you to remember I'm not a French teacher, I'm an English teacher (...). Hands up, thanks – without calling out – and please give me your first name ...'.

At that point – in the establishment phase of the lesson – there is very often calling out by several students; or students may be talking while I seek to engage class discussion; or a student walks in late (sometimes with a 'grandstanding' entrance). I've had many students – in challenging classes – walk into a class and see the other teacher there (myself) and say, 'Who are you?!'. Several students could be distracting others with a 'loud' pencil case or water bottle. This phase of the lesson gives the mentor-colleague an opportunity to both engage the class and exercise the sort of behaviour leadership they will discuss with their mentee-colleague later. After, say, 10 minutes or so of engaging the class (by discussing what they are learning in that subject) the mentor-colleague will hand back the 'formal extension' of the actual lesson to the mentee-colleague – 'Thanks, everyone ... I'll now ask your teacher to share with you what we're working on today ...' At this point in the progress of the lesson, the mentor-teacher will stand to one side and the mentee-teacher then leads/teaches the class.

All these elements of teaming (during whole-class teaching time) need to be thoughtfully discussed, prior to both teachers going in to the classroom. Later – during the on-task learning phase of the lesson – teacher and mentor-colleague will move around the classroom (encouraging and supporting students, giving feedback, etc.) and both colleagues will return to the front of the classroom for lesson closure.

Later that day, mentor and mentee will reflect on, and review, their shared experience. A key feature of their reflection will involve supportive feedback.

Colleague feedback

Colleague feedback can assist in raising awareness of what they *characteristically* do and say in management and discipline situations. I emphasise 'characteristic' (yet again) because I am not talking about the 'bad-day syndrome' that we all face. Tiredness, frustration and the stress and 'busyness' of our teaching day, do – at times – contribute to the overly snappy voice, ill-thought comment or ineffective way in which we sometimes address behaviour issues.

When the mentor is giving feedback to their colleague – after a classroom visit (over tea or coffee) – the emphasis is always focused on *descriptive feedback* as a precursor to any suggestions about considering new skill repertoire, or any suggestions about changes in a colleague's practice. Before entering into any mentoring relationship, it is important to discuss the nature and purpose of mentoring feedback. The fact that this mentoring model is elective will mean that the mentee-colleague can initially see benefit in such a professional mentoring journey. In *any* mentor-coaching relationship, supportive feedback should not appear judgemental – feedback is primarily a means to *professional self-awareness* and *self-reflection*. Within such shared colleague discussion, mentor and mentee explore shared understandings as a cue for appropriate change.

When giving feedback the mentor will focus only on observed teacher *behaviour* and language in the classroom (rather than on suspected 'motives', 'temper-ament', personality or attitudes of one's colleague). Giving, and receiving, colleague feedback (particularly when it relates to less-than-effective or ineffective teaching practice) is never easy. We are, after all, raising sensitive issues concerning the professional role and 'ability' to lead, teach and manage.

Feedback will address *both* the positive behaviours and the unhelpful behaviours in our colleagues' practice.

Perspective taking

Imagine you are in the position of your colleague and you are on the 'receiving end' of feedback about your teaching and your behaviour leadership. That perspective taking *itself* is the harbinger of care – it will enable us in that creative tension between giving *useful and descriptive feedback* and *being sensitive to our colleague's professional (and personal) esteem.*

The feedback will be *descriptive* in form, in order to raise – and heighten – profes-sional self-awareness:

- 'Were you aware that ...?' – here the mentor briefly focuses on *characteristic* aspects of their colleague's leadership behaviour observed in the lesson.

- 'Do you often hear yourself say things like ... (be specific) during whole-class teaching time?' – give examples.

- 'Were you conscious that ... ?' (specify), ' ... aware of ... ?' (specify), 'Do you often notice ...?' (specify) – For example, if a colleague is not aware that they *frequently* use interrogatives, and negatives, in discipline contexts, mentor feedback becomes an important feature of ongoing professional awareness and can enable potential skill development. 'Are you aware you frequently say things like "*Are you* calling out ...?", "*Why are you* ...*", "You *shouldn't* be talking now should you ...?" – particularly during whole-class teaching time.'

Some colleagues will still not be aware of the unhelpful nature of such language until the mentor-colleague highlights some *contrasting* management language – or approach – *and why* the *contrasting* language is a preferred form of discipline language. Again, when we highlight a *preferred* language approach (in discipline), and a *preferred manner*, we are not merely indicating a personal preference but are referring to school-wide preferred practices (Chapter 7 and Appendix 3).

A secondary question can help to sharpen or focus the contrasting self-reflection – 'Are you aware of the *effect* that such language has …?' (be specific as to what has been observed in language/approach in given behaviour/discipline interventions and student responses/reactions). A 'why' question (as above), as a characteristic feature of corrective language can easily invite unnecessary procrastination and argument with students.

For example, if a teacher paces up and down during whole-class teaching time, with frequent interrogative cueing to the whole class ('*Will you* please be quiet and listen?' '*Can you* stop talking …?'), they may also be unaware that their overly kinaesthetic movement is telegraphing corresponding restlessness in the more kinaesthetic students. If the teacher's tone of voice is overly *earnest* it only adds to the 'request feature' of one's tone and manner within language cueing. Particularly so if their characteristic voice level is high and loud – and I'm not talking about *shouting*; shouting is always counterproductive. There are times when we need to *raise* our voice – briefly – for effect, often to raise attentional awareness with a louder class group. The infrequent (and necessary) use of a *raised* voice can be effective. It is also worth noting that when enabling a restless class to settle and focus, *directional* language is to be preferred over 'interrogative cueing' (page 95). When we use interrogative forms such as, '*Will* you please be quiet and listen?' '*Can you please* stop talking …?' we are, in effect, making a request. *Directional* language, expressed confidently and respectfully – with some brief tactical pausing – is more appropriate for whole-class cueing – 'Looking this way, thanks …' a brief *tactical pause* (…) as the teacher scans the class group. Scanning also enables the teacher to be aware of how they are 'coming across' to the group *at this point* as they cue for settling and focus. It enables – brief – relational eye contact across the students.

We may need to repeat the whole-class cueing, calmly and firmly to the class but relaxedly (how 'simple' it sounds on paper!) 'Looking this way and listening, thanks.' 'Thanks' is to be preferred to, say, 'Stop talking and listen *please*.' 'Looking …', 'Listening …' are the key verb(al) imperatives. As noted above, it is not a *request*. The teacher will often need to address distracting and disruptive behaviours *while* they are cueing the class to settle. These interventions need to be brief, positive and focused on the disruptive *behaviour*. 'Dean (…), Brett (…) you're chatting. Looking this way and listening, thanks.' Here the teacher is using a brief description/direction. If several students are chatting, fiddling/restless or calling out, the description/direction is focused on the group – ' … several students are calling out (…). Eyes and ears this way. Thanks.' *Brief* tactical pausing (…) by the teacher helps the students to register/focus on what the teacher is saying *at that point* (page 35). When the class is settled, listening (or at least 'attentionally focused'), *then* the teacher will briefly thank them and 'formally' greet the class to indicate that '*we've now* begun …' (page 96).

I have worked with many colleagues who have tried to settle a noisy, restless class by speaking *through* – or *over* – restless student 'noise' – often beginning with an overly loud 'GOOD MORNING', followed by several loud 'requests' such as 'Can you *please* stop talking and listen …?', 'Will you *please* be quiet and listen!' I believe we should only 'formally' say good morning/afternoon to the whole class *when* the class has settled and focused to their teacher at the front of the classroom. Obviously we greet students verbally (and non-verbally) *as they enter the classroom*. This is essential whether in a classroom, a drama workshop, a hall or even outside conducting a Phys. Ed. lesson/activity.

When initiating and sustaining *whole-class attention and focus,* it is essential that the teacher communicates a sense of calmness, positive engagement and expectation to the group (page 103). These skills (of whole-class cueing/settling/focusing) can be discussed with the class teacher based on the shared classroom teaming in the mentee's class. These skills will also have been modelled (even in very challenging classes) by their mentor-colleague during their team-teaching sessions. The mentee-colleague (the host teacher) will also have seen their mentor-colleague's normative struggle with their own class, yet also observed how their class responds to the 'new' teacher.

Supporting behaviour-leadership change

Descriptive feedback becomes the basis for the next stage in the mentoring journey. Colleague feedback is utilised as the basis for suggested, or necessary, changes in behaviour leadership and discipline practices. In any discussion of management and discipline practice it is the framework of *school-wide preferred practice in discipline and management,* rather than a mentor's personal discipline/management preferences (or 'style'), that are the basis for any discussion on discipline skills (See Chapter 7 and Appendix 3).

Some of the aspects of a mentee's characteristic management behaviour may appear to be 'small' when taken individually, but taken together they can have a significant effect on student behaviour, engagement and cooperation. I have worked with many colleagues who have seen a significant change in student responsiveness, and cooperation, when their discipline language moves from 'don't …' to 'do …' – 'Hands up without calling out – thanks …' rather than 'Don't call out' – from 'No, you can't because …' to 'Yes you can when …' or 'When … then' (conditional/'choice' language). Moving from negative to more positive 'conditional' language can be a significant feature of behaviour leadership change for some teachers. Of course, language is *always* mediated by our characteristic tone of voice, manner and relational intent. Students will read our *intent* and *relational manner* as significantly as they 'hear' our language (the actual words). Aspects of teacher leadership behaviour, like characteristic loudness of voice usage, 'timbre' and clarity, proximity awareness and body language awareness (e.g. 'open hand' rather than 'pointing finger'), can also be supportively reflected on, and refocused through mentor-coaching.

As the mentee takes on a new skill repertoire, the mentor uses ongoing feedback (and their own modelling in their colleague's classroom) to consolidate the new skill repertoire.

The existential moments that build trust

I have been in many classes (as a mentor-colleague) where I have experienced significantly disruptive behaviours *while I am teaching* (in the team-teaching context). When my colleagues see my struggle (my normative struggle) with those students who challenge, confront, argue, swear and (on rarer occasions) behave aggressively, it gives them a sense of shared experience, shared understanding and even hope. One of the most common things a colleague will say to me, after we have worked together with a very challenging class is, *'It's not just me is it?'*, *' – you saw what they're like.'* (see case example page 122)

In that 'normative struggle' with a challenging class, I am seeking (as mentor-colleague) to also establish my teacher leadership (as the 'other teacher') with this new class. Some students will exhibit their habituated patterns of behaviour whether it is repeated talking-while-the-teacher-is-talking; frequent calling-out; grandstanding behaviours; smart-alec replies; argumentative behaviours; task-avoidance/refusal ... The mentor-colleague (in challenging classes) will meet them all.

The mentor will manage and lead differently, of course. The mentee may not always 'see the difference' in their colleague's behaviour and language – this, too, will need to be thoughtfully discussed later in debriefing sessions. If the mentee suggests that the mentor's more positive response from students is merely, or only, due to the mentor's personality or 'it's just *your* way' then we will need to 'unpack' the approaches we used, the language we used – *and ask why.* We're trying to emphasise *transferable practices and skills* rather than merely 'one's personality' (pages 111–112).

By being there with one's colleague (existentially), we can (in part) see, hear and experience their 'normative' struggle. Our colleague is more likely, then, to trust us and listen to us when we share together later. It also gives a shared perspective for discussing possible strategies to engage and support the more attentionally distracting and challenging students.

Modifying and changing one's practice

When we seek to develop any changes in our behaviour leadership, the new speech, behaviour, actions – and even thinking patterns – do not always feel 'easy' or 'natural'; this is normal. The mentor will encourage their mentee-colleague to persevere with their 'new' skill repertoire until it becomes naturally 'theirs' (pages 109, 177).[5]

In any area of 'coaching', the person on the receiving end of the (hopefully supportive) coaching knows that they will improve with the experienced insight, observational feedback, modelling, rehearsal and support offered by their mentor-colleague. It is disconcerting to see a struggling teacher continue with ineffective teaching and behaviour leadership for want of some ongoing mentoring support.

I stress again, the mentee-colleague has to see both need and value in such a mentor-coaching relationship with a fellow teacher to take on such a teaming relationship (page 167). Many colleagues have noted, however, that while they were initially quite nervous at embarking on such a 'journey', they became *professionally* conscious of ineffective behaviours and learned a range of under-standings, practices and skills that enhanced their teaching and management (Rogers, 2002).

A colleague recently pointed out to me how he had noticed that his wandering around the room *while* giving whole-class directions had an unsettling effect on whole-class attention. This was not something he was consciously aware of before the mentoring journey. He subsequently became more focused on how to *thoughtfully* give whole-class instructions and how to 'calm', focus and better engage his class (following supportive collegial feedback from 'his' mentor). A 'small' (deceptively small) change in this aspect of his overall behaviour had a surprisingly positive effect on the class group and – correspondingly – on his confidence and on his professional self-esteem.

When developing any mentor-coaching in a school, it is crucial to stress that it is a feature of one's *overall professional development* – it is not a way of identifying 'struggling teachers' ('All teachers who are struggling with behaviour management and discipline are to report to the conference room after school today – we will assign you a mentor …!'). Any invitation to engage in mentorship has to be *elective* (even when invited) and it should always be linked to professional devel-opment within *whole-school preferred practices in behaviour leadership*.

Mentor-coaching, as discussed here, is a labour-intensive feature of professional development and colleague support. For some teachers it is the most effective form of support – until someone can actually see, hear and experience *with their colleague in the classroom reality,* there may be a mismatch between what they hear in a meeting or an in-service event or read in a book. A trusted mentor can see, specifically, (at least for a time) what their colleague's experiential reality is actually like. Any ongoing mentoring will need to be buttressed by wider –

generalised – opportunities for collegial sharing (such as peer-support groups, page 15). In our faculty and team meetings we do not always have the time – or opportunity – to share professional concerns and needs in depth.

There will be a time in the mentoring journey where mentor and mentee will have to 'disengage'. After four, six, eight, ... sessions we need to enable our colleague to generalise their behaviour leadership practices and skills within normative school-wide professional development opportunities. We will still be available to meet with them in out-of-class sessions as need, and opportunity, dictate. There is a small percentage of teachers (in our experience) who – even with long-term mentoring support – see no significant change in their behaviour leadership practice. This issue of concern is addressed later (pages 203, 204).

One's ongoing teaching and behaviour leadership practice can always benefit from colleague mentoring. I encourage you to consider how you might develop and utilise such a process in your school.

Mentoring: practising and developing skills

It's one thing to hear – or read – the description of a skill; it's quite another thing to realise that skill in daily practice – no matter how clearly contextualised that 'hearing' or 'reading'. When we seek to speak and act in ways outside our natural experience, or 'comfort zone', the words don't always seem right when *we* say them. Under the normative emotional pressure of the typical context in which we want to try out that skill, it will probably *feel* different; this is normal. We may well experience some initial stress as we seek to *tactically* ignore (for example), or reframe negatives into positives (from 'Don't call out ...' to 'Hands up, thanks ... one at a time.'). What may seem deceptively easy (on paper or at the staff workshop or in-service event) is another matter in a busy, fractious, classroom. There, our emotions are immediately engaged – our need to say and do *something*.

My colleagues and I find it helpful to practise these skills in a safe setting – several colleagues together, actually practising in an empty classroom (with no possible student audience, at the end of the school day).

By physically standing up *as if* one is addressing a fractious class or individual, one can recognise a 'script' and then practise the emotion and physicality – the tone of voice, the eye-scanning, the assertive manner. This is particularly helpful for learning assertive language. In such role-plays we actually use a written script to *re*-cognise; *on the spot* as it were. We can re-practise several times *and* ask for immediate feedback from our colleagues on how we come across ... This role-play opportunity can form a very powerful learning adjunct to the mentoring programme and to professional development generally.

Scripted role-plays

In any such role-play it is important to 'script' the role of any 'disruptive students'. Otherwise, if we give our colleagues licence to 'play the role of the disruptive student' some teachers will, cathartically, call up their worst behaviour memories (!) For any such role-play to be constructive, and useful, and yet stretch the emotional reality, it needs to be scripted. Each teacher in the group playing the role of distracting/or disruptive students has a small cue card that details what they are to do and say:

> 'You are a distracting student – call out while the teacher is teaching. Say "Miss – we did all this last year!" – then stop. Wait for 10 seconds and call out again (whatever the teacher does) and then say, "Why do we have to do this Miss?" After that, whatever the teacher says or does, role-play a dutifully attentive student.'

A few teachers will have similar cards detailing 'how to chat (while the teacher is teaching)'; 'how to come in late to class'; 'how to fiddle with a loud pencil case'. The colleague playing the role of teacher doesn't know which teachers in the room are playing the role of distracting/disruptive students, though they know there will be behaviours such as calling-out, chatting while the teacher is teaching, incidental distracting behaviour and – say – lateness. The other teachers are playing the role of cooperative students. They are listening, paying attention and (if they do ask a question) are putting their hand up without calling out or clicking fingers (they'll wait to be cued by the person in the role of class teacher). It is helpful to have only two or three students distracting, at first, to enable the 'teacher' to get into the spirit and 'feel' of the role-play.

The role-play can be stopped at any time by the facilitator to reassess, to give immediate feedback to the teacher in role and even ask the teachers playing the role of students how they felt (as students responding to 'a teacher').

There are three phases of a lesson we build in to such role-plays:

- entry to, and settling, of a class group
- dealing with the early distractions and disruptions during whole-class teaching time
- dealing with distractions and disruptions during on-task learning time.

Personality or professionalism?

'It's not just *me*!' I sometimes hear colleagues saying (about a given skill or practice) that they can't really take it on board because it's 'not them'. They have a perception that their personality or temperament somehow precludes the sort of good practice that enables positive teacher leadership (page 111).

Does it need a particular 'personality':

- to organise one's classroom place and space to maximise teaching and learning?
- to use positive corrective language (where possible)?
- to address distracting and disruptive behaviour in a way that minimises unnecessary confrontation? (page 105)
- to have a framework of thoughtful interventions when managing distracting and disruptive behaviour? (page 108)
- to organise a curriculum, units of work or individual lessons that *reasonably* cater for the students we have to work with?
- to regularly, and thoughtfully, use encouragement and descriptive feedback to our students.

The list could go on ...

My response to the 'it's just me; that's how I am ...' response (often an avoidance and discounting response) is to suggest that if you continue as *that kind of you* it will have a detrimental effect on your leadership of a class and its individuals as well as any positive working relationship. If *the me* I am, at present (as a teacher), is clearly not enabling me to teach, lead and manage myself and others, then I need to consider (thoughtfully and *supportively*) those aspects of 'me' – in professional role and relationships – that need to be addressed and changed.

Practising new behaviour leadership and discipline skills

During *any* practice, whether in a 'safe' setting like role-play, a peer-support group or in a real-time classroom setting, we are seeking to convert not only our 'old' verbal repertoire and leadership behaviours, but also our old 'involuntary' *emotional habits* to a more voluntary state. Those old *habits*, developed over countless exchanges with students, may well need thoughtful reappraisal.

When we decide to consciously reappraise our discipline language – for example – there will be some cognitive dissonance between 'old' and 'new' *feelings* about the new skills repertoire. The new language skills may well feel less 'comfortable' than the old language skills we've been using (even if those skills and approaches were less effective). There will be natural mistakes, miscueing even mistargeting, when we're developing a new repertoire. We need to acknowledge this – it is normal.

Fine-tuning a skills repertoire

As we fine-tune and develop our behaviour leadership skills – particularly in the dynamic setting of the classroom – we will continue to fine-tune *within the overall purpose of such skills* (page 109). We'll need to have discussed what we mean by 'good practice' in our behaviour leadership – practices and skills *work together* to inform and delineate what is good in our daily practice. Utility *and* moral purpose also need to inform any discussion about 'good' practice. Any core practices (and attendant skills) also need to be directed to the fundamental aims of school-wide preferred behaviour-leadership practice (see Appendix 3).

Is what I *characteristically say and do*, when I lead and discipline students likely to enable them to be aware of their own their behaviour in a way that is safe and respectful, and acknowledges and affirms the rights of others? And is the way I lead likely to build a positive and workable relationship between teacher and student, and student and student?

One can hardly engage in any mentoring for behaviour leadership without an acknowledged framework of *preferred* practices within a school. It is within a *shared* framework of preferred practices that mentor and mentee alike set aims, give feedback review and fine-tune their personal practice.

- Is what I am *currently* doing reflecting school-wide preferred practice and skills (Chapter 7 and Appendix 3)?
- How consciously comfortable is the new skills repertoire I'm developing?
- Where do I specifically need to fine-tune, adapt, modify or change my current practice?
- How do the actual skills – particularly the language skills – *feel* in the dynamic of the new repertoire I'm developing?
- Is my modified practice enabling a more positive working relationship with my students? How?
- How 'differently' are students responding to my leadership in the light of the conscious reappraisal of my practice? For example, do I notice any difference in how I am settling and focusing the class during whole-class teaching time (in the light of past experiences with this class)? What are the differences?
- Is the mentoring journey – and the changes I'm adopting – enabling me as the class teacher to be more relaxed and consciously positive as a teacher–leader?

Developing new skills in the area of behaviour leadership

Whenever we reflect on aspects of our teaching and behaviour leadership – particularly in the area of actual skills – it can create natural discomfort, even anxiety. If we have seen a need to modify, fine-tune, adapt or develop changes in our characteristic practice, we will obviously do so only if we see a need. That need may be generated by conditions or necessity – even our ongoing stress.

The skills noted in the many case studies (and in Chapter 7) are typical of those my colleagues and I work on together. The need and necessity for such skills is developed from our shared observations in classroom settings and what we know about 'good practice' (see Appendix 3).

There are several phases we normally go through when learning a new skills repertoire:

- *Understanding any 'individual skill' within wider practice and context* – for example, *tactical ignoring* is a context-dependent skill. We would normally not ignore any *repeated* calling out. We might well use *tactical* ignoring of attentional calling out *combined with selective attention* when the student does put their hand up (without calling out). See the case example on page 32. The ability to use a skill like *tactical ignoring* also requires a reasonable degree of frustration tolerance, as a teacher. If we *frequently* find ourselves saying 'children must not be rude', 'children must respect me' then typical 'secondary behaviours' will easily be interpreted as *personal* disrespect and rudeness (page 48). Such a mindset will make it difficult to *tactically* ignore some aspects of student behaviour (such as the 'secondary' behaviours noted on page 45). It may even make one's behaviour management more stressful.

- Whenever we use any language skills, we also need to be aware of our tone of voice, degree of assertion, *how intent and manner are conveyed by what we say* and the context in which we say something (the degree of least-to-most intrusive, page 105).

- *Initially the new skill may not feel right, or 'comfortable' or natural'* – this is true in any area of skill development (even the cognitive habits mentioned earlier, Chapter 4). If we're convinced that the skills we are seeking to develop *and* habituate are necessary and professionally right for our practice then we'll need to persevere beyond the natural discomfort.

'Subconsciously' ineffective to 'subconsciously' effective

Remember when you first learned to drive? Do you remember how 'stressful' it was (I crashed a car – *skilfully* on my first run!) It's all the things we have to *remember* – seat belt; handbrake; mirror; gears; indicators (before we even set off). It's *balancing a lot of small things* – each is essential. It's those 'small' skill aspects *taken together* that enable the purposeful act of driving. And remember learning to park? Doing a handbrake start? City driving?

→

When you hop in a car *today*, your mind can be on several other matters (as when listening to the radio) – all *while* you drive. And on a familiar route you may not even remember turning a particular corner. Of course, we do snap back into immediate – reactive – consciousness in any dangerous situation. Again, the skills we have learned will, hopefully, enable effective braking, swerving ...

When learning new skills there is a phase we go through in which we are 'consciously uncomfortable', before we begin to be consciously comfortable and – in time – 'unconsciously ' comfortable.

For some colleagues, to consciously change the use of directional language from 'don't ...' to 'do ...' takes time. To go from a normative, '*Don't* call out in class (please)' to, 'Hands up, thanks, if you've got a question' or' Looking this way and listening, thank you' instead of 'Don't talk when I'm teaching' will not necessarily be easy. To say, 'Yes ... when' may feel unusual if you're used to saying, 'No, you can't because ...' – in part because we're *consciously* reframing our characteristic language.

- *Remember the purpose of any skill – a language skill is not some mere technique,* it enables a more positive working relationship with our students and, particularly, to enable students to be aware of and own their behaviour in relationship to others.

- *The elements of a skill* – take the skill of incidental/descriptive cueing, as when we say to several students who are chatting at the beginning of a lesson, 'A number of students are chatting (...). It's whole-class teaching time.' The teacher says this to raise *behaviour awareness* in the group:

  - She has said, 'A number of students are chatting ...'. In this she has *described* the behaviour reality as it was.

  - Her tone of voice has been positive, expectant – she is conscious of a slight raising of the voice to initiate and focus whole-class attention.

  - She *tactically* pauses between 'A number of students are chatting (...)' and 'It's whole class teaching time' to increase a sense of *attentional awareness in all the students* (page 35).

  - She scans the faces of the students in her class – with brief, transitional eye contact to *engage that essential human contact with all the students in her class.*

  - Her posture is confident, upright and relaxed. She doesn't *sit* and cue the whole class (secondary students) – she stands during whole-class teaching time to give a visual, physical, engaging *presence*. Her manner is calm, even reassuring, as she addresses the class (page 103).

What seems like simple language cues to the class (as a group) needs the *overall* 'global set' of behaviour to communicate her sense of calmness and expectation to the group (Rogers, 2006). Any 'individual skill' has its positive, purposeful out-working within that 'global set'.

- *We need to allow, and learn from, temporary setbacks and failure* – we always encourage our students to utilise and learn from their failure; not to interpret failure self-defeatingly; so too ourselves. Language skills (within preferred practices, Appendix 3) do take time to move from *'subconsciously unaware'* through to *'consciously unaware'* through the learning phase of *'consciously aware'* and in time (like our driving) *'unconsciously aware'*. This is where our skills set is integral to our characteristic behaviour leadership.

Learning from failure

Learning from failure is only meaningful if a person actually *learns* from it – actually attends to what needs to change.

- Accept the normality of failure.
- Avoid globalising failure – e.g. 'I am a failure.' When we fail, we fail in a given *'instance'* – it doesn't define us *as* a failure.
- Know what it is that is actually unhelpfully self-defeating and ineffective in your practice. Without that awareness – and knowledge – it is hard to focus on where to change.
- Know *why* you want to fine-tune, adapt, modify or change aspects of your teaching practice.
- Seek trusted colleague support to develop some kind of plan and framework for reflection and change.
- Incidental, or class-based, mentoring is a powerful way to build professional confidence through reliable feedback and support.

When a student argues about having an iPod on in class we won't need to think, 'Now how do I *partially* agree? – how do I refocus the student/s to the rule? – how do I avoid arguing or defending? How do I *tactically* ignore the sigh, the pout, the raised eyes, the whine in their voice? – *we'll just do it*!

Notes

1. Mentoring in non-classroom settings involves areas such as playground management, lunch-time supervision, one-to-one counselling (with children),

developing behaviour management plans (one-to-one with children), mediation settings, and so on.

2. Sometimes the mentee will meet with their mentor within the context of an ongoing peer-support group (page 15). Sometimes a colleague will 'self-select' to work with a mentor – at other times a colleague might be approached by, say, a head of department.

3. I use the terms 'mentee' and 'mentor' only to delineate the 'distinction' between the class teacher ('mentee') and the mentor-colleague who teams with them in the classroom, and discusses, reflects and plans with them beyond the classroom setting. There is no sense of a mentor as one who is 'better than', nor is there any distinction of 'superior' and 'inferior' (!)

4. In feedback/reflection time I have often shared this observation with colleagues and they do not (immediately) see anything untoward in *simply* picking up a student's workbook without – say – a basic, quiet and courteous, 'Jayson … Do you mind if I have a look at your work, thanks …?' This is an occasion where the interrogative form is obviously appropriate. I have actually had some colleagues register surprise when we discuss the importance of *asking* to see a student's work. I've had colleagues say, 'Do you mean I'm supposed to ask permission to see a student's work?' It's not *permission,* it is basic civility.

5. As Breheney et al. (1996) note when addressing new ideas (behaviours, practices and skills), as well as a teacher seeking a need and being clear about why change will benefit them (and their students), they also need to develop 'positive mental images of themselves doing the new activity.'

Colleague support: auditing for stress and supporting one another

What this chapter will explore and develop:

- The normative stress of living – and working – together as colleagues
- The benefits of a school-wide 'stress audit'
- Procrastination and organising of time and pressures – the importance of planning
- The relativity of stress in the workplace
- The difficult and whingeing colleague
- The cost of giving colleague support

Auditing for stress and supporting one another

The 'little hassles'

Broken cupboards in the classroom; old, run-down toilets (not enough toilets and too close to passers-by); no curtains or blinds on those hot windows; poor or inadequate heating; lack of air-conditioning; minimal filing cabinet space; chairs that squeak and scrape!

I recently team-taught in an old science lab. The stools were high and wobbly. Every small move (multiplied by 25 students) made teacher–student communication very difficult – and the acoustics were appalling. In the twenty-first century how is it that fixing simple bottom rubbers to stools and fixing sticking windows is so difficult?

I was very concerned for my colleague. They were 'already' a challenging class – these physical/structural factors were *unnecessary* additional stressors. At the next faculty meeting we raised our concerns and – finally – the windows were fixed, rubber stoppers purchased and put on the bottom of the legs of the stools (the students helped) and decent, heavy curtains properly installed. These 'things' – seen in isolation – are 'small' in 'stressful weight', but *taken together* they can significantly affect day-to-day stress.

It is also important to be aware that weather has a significant effect on stress levels. I've taught in many schools in Australia during the very hot summer months: no air-conditioning, sometimes ineffective curtains or blinds. I've worked in some schools in Britain where the radiators create stifling heat. Auditing for stressors in our workplace (and space) means asking what we can do about physical *and* organisational stress as well as the relational stress arising out of our teaching and management role.

People just don't do things the way you do

Small things can easily upset some of us. Those colleagues who leave a defunct tea-bag strewn across the staff kitchen bench; the 'trail of mess'; cups left 'hither and thither'. I get annoyed with lazy mess-leaving behaviour. Yes, even *these* small things upset some teachers – classrooms left as a pig-sty, well hardly a *'pig*-sty' but – yes – *messy* (furniture awry; whiteboard full of ...; litter on floor; equipment not packed away ...). It's not just the mess (say my colleagues) – it's the lack of consideration for others. I can fully understand this. We are *colleagues* – we have to work in, live in and share the resources in this place. Civility, courtesy and consideration for others always helps – isn't that what we tell our students?

There are many such *irritants* in a school day – the overly loud, and sometimes frequent, loudspeaker messages; the insistent last-minute email; messy staffroom; photocopier's busy! I've italicised *irritants* – because they are just that. The problem comes when we interpret such events and situations as *inherently* stressful because those teachers *shouldn't* have left a mess like that! If our characteristic explanatory style is one of insistent demand, we'll get *unnecessarily* stressed by such irritants.

We have to accept – and live with – the reality that not everyone 'is as tidy/ organised/thoughtful/considerate as us.' (Cough smugly at this point!) Our profession is one where we need a reasonably high level of frustration tolerance ('The thousand natural shocks ...' page xii). We can moderate such irritants by raising awareness in staff meetings, but we also have to balance this with the reality of living daily with our fallibility, our humanity and each other.

Where the behaviour of a colleague (or student or parent) is *particularly* offensive – yes, we need to make our concerns known to them about their behaviour appropriately – as it impacts on us and our basic rights. We'll do this best with some considered thought, and a brave, risky attempt at a private, collegial and professional chat. It will also help to plan ahead for any such 'chat', or more formal meeting, by discussing with an enabling colleague first.

A stress audit

'Form' follows 'function' in colleague support. The function of colleague support is to attempt to meet colleagues' needs – their *espoused* needs, not merely their *assumed* needs. While there are common needs that we all share within our common humanity (Maslow, 1970), there are needs relevant, and particular, to our professional life within a local school culture.

As well as a general review of colleague support (Appendix 1), it is always worth conducting a 'stress audit' once a year with *all* staff (not only teaching staff). Staff need to know that they will have a *genuine* opportunity to raise issues of concern and that – wherever possible – *reasonable* and *possible action* will be taken by senior staff to address those concerns.

There are issues, of course, that relate to *external* mandates that will always affect normative stress in a school – external policies from the Department of Education; formal appraisals (OFSTED); student-testing 'regimes'. While we can't eliminate these stressors, we can learn *to manage their impact within our local school setting*. Leadership teams will work with their staff to effectively address and manage such external mandates more constructively *at the local level*. One obvious network option, here, is the leadership team's interaction with other schools – to raise colleague awareness beyond the local level to see what lessons can be learned and then applied at our own school.

In a stress audit, staff have the opportunity – through survey and group discussion – to:

- **Identify workplace stressors and their effect –**

  - *Physical stressors* such as 'sticking doors'; 'flickering neon lights'; those annoying stools that make such a racket in some science labs; inadequate toilets (or servicing of toilets); poor furniture in classrooms; inadequate heating, etc. Some of these issues/concerns may seem 'small' but they all have an effect on a general sense of our place and space being cared for –that we too are valued as individuals and our work and welfare are genuinely considered. Most of the structural stressors (above) require little expense to remedy – the fact that someone listens and then actually does something about such concerns enhances the feeling that our collegial voice is heard and valued.

  - *Organisational stressors* such as staff routines; communication and organisational procedures; timetabling; rosters. The questions we ask is do the current organisational procedures/processes/routines enable the fair, smooth running of the school? Are they fair/equitable? How can we fine-tune, adapt, modify or change them where they aren't? As always with any policy procedure, routine or plan we ask *what purpose does it actually serve and why?*

  - *Stressors related to behaviour issues at classroom-level* – how we address our most challenging and at-risk students; positive use of time-out and follow-up procedures with difficult students; and duty-of-care management concerns in non-classroom settings (playground, lunch supervision, bus duty, wet-day duty). The stressors related to behaviour concerns is a separate survey in itself. Disruptive student behaviour and related concerns of management are a major issue in many schools. Any surveying that addresses behaviour issues should also directly address school-wide policy review and workable and realistic practice.

- **Assess the noted stressors** in terms of the *frequency* (of stressor/s as noted); *intensity* (how much the stressor/s impact on staff and students in terms of their stressful effect); and *generality* – are *all* staff saying much the same thing about a given stressor/s?

- **Decide what can realistically be addressed** – when assessing and addressing occupational stress (whether environmental, organisational, managerial, relational) we need to ask what we can, and must, immediately address – compared to what we need to fine-tune, adapt and modify over reasonable time. Some changes will take longer (organisationally and financially) and staff need to be aware and accommodating of that reality. What they need to know is that they have been heard and that *something will be done.* The changes that take longer are normally those that require some significant change in our thinking and behaviour leadership. It is pointless simply having a well-articulated, and positively expressed, behaviour policy if we don't attend to how we address our own behaviour-leadership behaviour *in light of the aims and purposes of such a policy.*

- **Develop action plans and strategy** – any plan (even simple environmental change plans) need to be communicated to staff so they know what is actually being done and why. Policy processes, too, need ongoing updates so that staff know their reported concerns have not 'disappeared'.
- **Review any plans** – this can be as basic as checking if a colleague is happy about a light or cupboard being fixed (or effective rubber stoppers on those stools in the science lab ...) or as detailed as a policy feedback review on behaviour and discipline concerns (Rogers, 2007).

When a school leadership team *reasonably* and realistically addresses workplace stress, they act preventatively as well as supportively. Stress auditing is an essential adjunct to school-wide colleague support.

> **Therapeutic massage – available to all staff**
>
> One of those schools I work with in Australia was mindfully aware of the normative and extra stress during exam and reporting week. They employed three professional masseurs who were available to *all* staff over several days so that staff could book a relaxing and therapeutic massage (neck and shoulders).
>
> This is a 'service concept' used widely in the corporate area (I stress *therapeutic* massage). It is the first time I had heard of it in a school context. They never had that when I was a full-time teacher – we *only* had powdered coffee then, and the collegial moan-bonding of course! (the whinge ...).

Procrastination is the thief of time

'I can't get anything done! I can never find that student profile or the minutes of the meeting. I keep losing those notes ...'

Whether it's the necessary paperwork; student profiles; ongoing marking; lesson organisation and planning; finding time to speak to *that* student – if it's necessary and important then *we have to organise it*. When we bring some organisational control to *anything* (even diet and exercise – even a daily walk) we're trying to get some reasonable control over a necessary and worthwhile *routine*. A routine that minimises, and helps to manage, normative stress.

How many times with students (at school and university) have we shared the deceptively simple truth – 'procrastination is the thief of time'? If anything is important to our career, whether it be our students' learning and welfare or our own welfare, well-being and relationships, it will only happen (or happen reasonably well) if we make time for the better outcome. It will only happen by bringing some organisation and relative control to the management of time. Bit, by bit, by bit … (as I have frequently told my students) is the only way we get *anything* done.

Even if some teachers can work in an environment where their class desk (and their office desk) is piled high with a mass of seemingly disparate papers, it will be less stressful if that 'mass' is organised in some way helpful to the teacher – and also to those they are responsible to and for.

When we're surrounded by paper and deadlines it only increases our generalised anxiety, 'I should do something about all this! I can't find that …!' A constant deferring will only add to the residual anxiety.

Prioritising

There are always enough problems for one day as a teacher. It's patently obvious that we can only do one thing at a time. When we feel overwhelmed by 'it all' and the sometimes insistent inner voice says, 'do this!', 'no, do that!', 'no – *all* this has to be done …'. It's quite possible to then actually do little that is productive.

It makes sense to rank and prioritise what we have to do – particularly when there is a crisis that needs immediate attention. When there are lots of things to do, and the clarion voices call (even our own internal clarion voice), we need to order the challenges and task problems, one after the other – in order of priority, need and importance. This kind of planning will minimise stress.

So, what is most important and why? This next hour, this day, this week, month, year?

As Allen (2001) notes, 'The big problem is that your mind keeps reminding you of the things when you can't *do* anything about them' (page 23). He quotes Sally Kempton, 'it is hard to fight an enemy who has outposts in your head' (ibid.).

Our mind – our thinking – each time we glance at 'the pile', raises the stressful spectre, 'I wonder *where* that piece of paper is…?' It becomes even more stressful when we're busy or when deadlines loom. We can sometimes spend as much time worrying about it all as if we were actually to set aside an hour or two a week (and often less) to *reorganise*, and then *maintain*, the space, place, paper and electronic 'files'.

Take time, make time

We take the time and we *make* the time, to address 'the clutter' and organise the 'bits and pieces' into essential/immediate, necessary and coming up/possible/helpful. Of each of these categories we ask 'What do we need to take action on immediately? for the very soon? or those in the near, or longer, future?' These we need to commit to our diary with an *explanatory note*.

So – we bring *a basic sense of focus, order and direction* to the clutter, and from then on use a basic system of file and diary for future paper and emails that cross our path.

I would recommend Allen's (2001) very helpful book. He makes the essential point that we need to take the initial time to address 'the stuff' [*sic*] and ask the basic questions 'What is it?, Is it necessary to file (it) or should I be taking action?' If the answer is *'no'* then either 'trash it' or file it into a 'someday' or 'maybe' file. If the answer is *'yes'* then we need to ask 'What's the next action?' (regarding this paper or email or necessary task.) 'Does it need to be done right away?' Then *do it*. If the answer is *'no'* then we need to ask if we can 'delegate this or defer it.' If we defer it, we'll need to put it in the diary – if time is important. Always have a diary cue to 'flag' the coming event/activity/meeting – a bit like we do for coming birthdays and special events. I recall an old proverb, 'The faintest ink is stronger than the strongest memory.'

When we organise and file and 'date it' we feel more 'in control' as it were – even *that* feeling helps us to know we've done the best we can do *for now*.

If we've got the student profiles up to date, if we've got even a basic lesson plan, if we have jotted notes for the upcoming meeting (and filed them *for* the meeting) – we've allocated enough energy on the matter *for now* and we do not, therefore, have to worry unnecessarily ahead of time.

- Set aside some time each week – even *briefly* each day – to file, so you know you can find 'it' or 'track' it.

- Make sure the necessary bits of paper are annotated, dated *and filed*. A well-thought-out filing system takes a lot of unnecessary stress out of the plethora of paper that teachers still have to negotiate (let alone emails, efiles, etc.)

- *Can I locate and find* the essential and necessary and 'soon' information? Basic filing is the cornerstone to successful personal organisation.

- Stress is associated with lack of focus and direction. When we have reasonable and appropriate goals – and means of reaching them – it lessens the anxiety associated with a busy and *naturally* stressful profession like ours. We also *feel* better when we *reasonably* achieve our goals – this, in turn, helps our ongoing motivation. This assumes the goals are necessary or chosen, reasonable, clearly articulated and that we have the means (and support) to achieve and assess these goals.

- And even if I have taught the same lesson topic before, I'll still need to *consciously* fine-tune, adapt, modify or update even individual lessons. It's worth filing a brief reflection on such lessons (whether they went well or not – particularly if they didn't go 'well' …). By adding a brief note – when the mind/thinking is close to the event – it will help next time we teach (or review) that topic.

> *As I write this, I think how basic it all sounds. Perhaps that's the point. If you are an organised person, you'll know how helpful a good system is. If you're not then ask a colleague – who you know is well organised – and ask them how they do it. Some colleagues are super organised, even over organised? But that's how they do it. We have to find our own level of realistic organisation.*
>
> *Again – we're back to colleague support. I've learned so much – in this regard – over a coffee with a colleague.*

We get little physical work space to organise our little 'office' space at school (unless you're a senior teacher …). We often rush in and out of the little space we're given – let alone the classroom desk (there is no *personal* classroom desk if you're a secondary teacher). When we come into the allocated team, or faculty 'staff office area' (how grand it sounds for so small a space!) we try our best to personalise it with photos, pot plants, humorous cartoons. It will help if the clutter is at least *organised* 'clutter'; even better, *minimal* clutter so we can actually work there when we pick up a pen.

I don't have a 'Blackberry' (or any other fruit-named personal, electronic device). Many colleagues do. I am told it can help in the daily onrush of 'information'. I still carry a notebook though – just to jot, record, note – and then file it later on.

- If you have to *keep* moving things on your desk together in order to get at *anything,* it's time for a clean-up and a reorganise (am I knocking over 'things' each time I search for something on my desk?)
- If you are frustrated at having to *keep* going through lots of bits of paper to find 'the necessary bit' or 'the essential bit' then it's time for a reorganise.
- If a spasm of annoyed pain runs across your face every time you sit down at your des, *it's time.*

Planning – it does save time and reduces unnecessary stress

At the edge of the forest, on a rather hot day, a man is stripped to the waist, sweating as he repeatedly hacks away at a tall tree with his axe. He curses and he swears – his axe is making little impression on the tree trunk. From

→

a distance another man – walking through the forest – notices the fellow's unprofitable energy and frustration.

Coming alongside the sweating man – who has temporarily paused from his labour – he greets him. He says, 'I see you are struggling. The tree is hard, friend. I see your axe is very blunt – it may well be the cause of your problem. Perhaps stop awhile and sharpen it.' Wiping his brow, the other man says, 'Damn it, I haven't got time for all that!'

If we make time to declutter, focus, file, organise and prioritise, we'll actually 'save time'. Step back a bit, reorder and refocus.

What's your para-ergon?

Teaching is a profession that can 'eat up your life' – and more. There is always more you can do – more planning, marking, organising. It's important to have a *para-ergon*.

When I was studying theology one of my professors said that in the busyness of life we all need a 'para-ergon'. (I was studying New Testament Greek at the time).

Para is the Greek preposition for 'alongside'; *ergon*, the noun for 'work'.

We all need something alongside, and instead of, our work to keep us sane – to refocus and to reengage the creative and imaginative soul within us. A *para-ergon* is not merely a second glass of red (even a good Australian red), it is something that takes our mind – and the week's creative tension – into another place. A hobby, a pastime, an activity for enjoyment and a refreshing of the mind and spirit. It may be as pedestrian as a favourite armchair, a good book and a mug of tea (that's mine) or as industrious as a county walk over the weekend.

What's your para-ergon?

First impressions?

I walked into the secondary staffroom. I was visiting the school (for the first time) to meet up with some senior teachers. I'd got there early so I asked the secretary where the staffroom was so I could get a cuppa, suggesting I could meet up with the principal when he was 'free'. I wasn't invited to get a tea/coffee though, I was shown where I could wait and was directed to the staffroom *if* I wanted a coffee.

I found the staffroom, walked in and saw several teachers sitting down reading newspapers, some working. No one said hello. I could have been a supply teacher, or new teacher to the school on their first day.

I reached for a cup – to make a drink – and took the minimal risk of sitting down and saying hello to one of the staff. Suddenly I heard a strident 'Hey –that's *my* cup, thank you!' How could I have known? – it looked ordinary enough. I turned to face the stern voice and apologised. I sought a civil response 'Good morning. My name is Bill, I'm a visiting teacher.' No smile from the stern voice. 'There's cups for visitors in that cupboard'. He pointed; ahh – foam cups.

I've worked in schools where the first impression – at the front desk – is positive, warm and welcoming. They *offer* you a tea or coffee. They assure you of when, whom, where. You *already* feel better.

I don't have a problem with ...

You come out of a particularly challenging class period. The students have been noisy, chatty – hard to settle and focus. You did your best – all up.

You enter the busy staffroom. Sipping a cuppa you sit with some colleagues – you pass a remark that you've just had 8D. They (surely) can see the careworn face, the sigh, that bit of 'angst' in what was a passing comment. One of your colleagues says, 'Oh, 8D – I don't have any problem with them.' Do you then feel you want to share any more (or at least with *him*)? Even if it's true that *this* colleague has no problem with 8D, this 'throwaway' line can be really demotivating to a colleague who is struggling. It is hardly likely to create confidence in seeking out a colleague's help.

Teachers can often be quite self-critical, and highly comparing: 'Is it *just me* then?', 'How is it they can cope and I can't? – *What's wrong with me?*'

'No one cares about me!'

Actually Bruce had said, 'No one gives a sh-t about me!' I'd approached him, sitting alone – wan and disconsolate in the staffroom. We got talking about one of his very challenging classes (I'd 'heard' them a number of times as I passed Bruce's classroom – Room 17). He said again, 'No one cares.' I said, 'I care; that's why I dropped in for a chat' I mooted the name of his head of department. He reluctantly agreed that he was 'OK' too. Bruce had got into the habit of speaking this way when stressed. It took some time to encourage him to reframe and start to say things like 'Well – there are those here in this school who do care and do know (really know) what it's like to teach here.'

When we're stressed it can be easy to latch on to *the most permanent and pervasive causes or explanations of our stress*. 'No one cares ...', 'All the students in 8D are ...'. When we easily, and frequently, use pervasive explanations ('all', 'never', 'everyone', 'can't', 'won't'), such language has an emotional affect and effect (page 51). When we use more context-specific language, '*some* students in 8D are very challenging, most are reasonably cooperative ...'; 'it's difficult *but with help* it's not *so* difficult ...'; 'it's tiring *but it's not impossible* ...' This kind of reframing is not some kind of language trick. When we more consciously, and *realistically,* reframe how we explain our stressful reality, such language enables a more realistic perspective to which the more optimistic possibilities seem possible (page 56). 'It's tiring *but with the planning and organisation I'm doing with my colleague(s) it's not so tiring. I feel more focused, more in control.'* Attitude, practice and support, *then,* reinforce each other in self-enhancing ways.

As we began to talk, Bruce reluctantly acknowledged that yes – perhaps – his head of department (and even 'you') were supportive (by that he meant we were approachable, we'd listen and we'd help as much as we realistically could). I suggested the possibility of mentoring (Chapter 10) and we began an elective collegial journey of risk and trust which slowly saw a change in attitude and a renewed, more positive leadership relationship with 8D. (See the case study on page 32.)

Open doors, closed doors

As in all schools, there are a number of staff who accept more readily a second pair of hands working in their rooms than others. Some staff members like the idea of another person helping out with creative writing, taking a literature or maths group, working on a computer in the corner with a child or two, or whatever – just generally being part of a team of two people teaching together.

Then there are those who would rather keep the door closed or, if you are to help, would prefer that the group you are working with be withdrawn. That's OK, but you don't really want it to stay that way. The school's policy is towards team-teaching and open doors. So how do you get around this? Tread softly, be patient and positive, and be *around*! Be the floating staff member; I try to get *them* used to me first. I pop in daily (probably drive them nuts at first!), make a point of talking to them, try to get to know them better in the staffroom and corridors, take a real interest in them as people, engage them in discussions about children in their grades, look at and discuss their students' work with them (always focusing on the positives), involve them in team-planning sessions, keep offering help, continue taking the groups out but offering plenty of feedback and discussion about their progress, take their grades (for something they say they are not good at) while they are in the room, and be ever watchful for the time when I can say 'I'll help you with that. You'll need someone else to get through it all.'

It's possible to open seemingly closed doors, but it's important to be prepared to be patient, positive, somewhat persuasive and pretty persistent! There can be real 'pay-offs' in getting to know the people behind the doors better. Most

→

people really *do* have something special to offer to the life of a school, given the chance or the encouragement.

Margaret
Primary school senior teacher

Dot and square – a metaphor for the relativity of stress

Imagine, if you will, a drawing of a square about the size of this sheet. Just a square, four lines – 'empty', except in the centre is a dot. A clearly visible *dot*.

When I've drawn an empty square and a central dot on a whiteboard in class-rooms and asked students what they see *in* the square, they invariably say they see the dot. 'What else?' I ask. 'A dot.' It's as if the only thing they can see, or *focus* on, is the dot – *at the expense of the white space within the bounded square.*

This, of course, is a visual metaphor. It is also a metaphor about conceptual reality; it *focuses* relativity. I often use this metaphor to illustrate contrast, relativity and focus in regard to stress. Sometimes all we see and feel – in our daily reality – is the stressful experience, situation, relationship, circumstance, and so on. We don't 'see' the supportive colleague or friend; we don't remember the many good days, when we've had successful lessons; we forget the responsible and cooperative students; we forget others' kindnesses. All these, and more, are like the *larger 'white space'* as relative to the stressful *dot*. Stress – like the dot – can appear to dominate the white space.

Obviously it is foolish, even dangerous, to deny the dot (the stress – its triggers, its antecedents, its reality, its demands its effects). We have to confront and address those things that occasion stress in our lives. The problem comes when we *overfocus* on the dot and 'forget' the white space.

The white space in this metaphor 'contains' the good and positive things in our lives: our loved ones, the many good and positive things we've done – and do – in our teaching practice. It is the colleague support we give and *receive*. It is those people who enable us to cope and gain a new, a better, more confident and realistic perspective on ourselves.

The white space is often 'larger' (in reality) when actually compared to the dot – if we will take the opportunity and time to enable the possibilities that the white space affords us.

Sometimes colleagues will say the dot is too big! Our response is: how can we increase the 'white space'?

In the metaphor, we seek to minimise the dot dominating our perspective; the stress is obviously there, *so is the wider – and present – support.*

Humour in colleague coping

'*We can bear to be human because we can laugh.*'

Nicholas Bentley, 1957

'*People like laughter,*' *answered Father Brown,* '*but I don't think they like a permanent smile. Cheerfulness without humour is a very trying thing.*'

G.K. Chesterton, 1981

I recall sitting at a staff meeting discussing some particularly difficult – and verbally aggressive – parents. The principal had recently faced a threatening and abusive parent yelling at him in front of the school at the end of the day. He had handled it remarkably calmly *and professionally.* Now, at the staff meeting, we were reviewing policy and practice. A couple of staff had put together a clever – humorous – song about the 'parent episode'. As they sang their ditty it helped revisit and *reinterpret* a stressful experience (at the time).

The shared humour had a buffering effect – not just for the principal but for all of us. It was a way to 'let-off safe, healthy steam' (as one colleague put it). He went home that day feeling better – all the staff did.

We didn't need Freud to tell us that humour is a coping mechanism; ask any teacher. We *feel* better, less stressed, when we can see a funnier side to things. The apt *bon mot*, the in-house jokes, farce, even satire are all 'coping mechanisms'. 'Our laughter is with some pain fraught ...' (Shelley: *To a Skylark*, verse 9). 'Laughter has a physiological function as well – it defuses tension, lifts the mood, buffers shared stress and can enable a re-orientation of the stressful experience' (Goleman, 1996).

Victor Frankl, a Viennese psychiatrist (interned in the concentration camps of Dachau and Auschwitz during the Second World War), saw all the horrors; the terror and worst abuses humankind can inflict on humankind. He also saw – in those same camps – the power of human love and the affirmation and dignity of shared support. He also notes that '*even there*' humour was, at times, possible.

To discover that there was any semblance of art in a concentration camp must have been surprise enough for an outsider, but he may be even more astonished to hear that one could find a sense of humour there as well; of course, only the faint trace of one, and then only for a few seconds or minutes. Humour was another of the soul's weapons in the fight for self-

preservation. It is well known that humour, more than anything else in the human make-up, can afford an aloofness and an ability to rise above any situation, even if only for a few seconds.

V.E. Frankl, 1963 (page 62).

Humour (with colleagues and students) is always to be distinguished from sarcasm, cheap shots, 'scoring', 'shafting' and malice. These have no place in our professional life and need to be challenged in student and teacher alike. What Aristotle, in a chapter on 'social tact', calls the 'humour' that 'wounds' the feelings of the person who is being made fun of. This is something, he says, 'which the witty man will not do ... for ridicule is a form of abuse or slander ...' and 'what one man detests in the way of humour another thinks delightful.' ' The buffoon can never resist a joke sparing neither himself or anyone else, provided he can raise a laugh, and saying things which even a man of taste and intelligence would never dream of saying and would not even listen to ...' (*Nicomachean Ethics*, Book 1, Chapter 8 – Thompson, trans. 1969).

Colleague support

Colleague support will only find its valued expression in a school when such support meets the espoused needs of colleagues. Staff – all staff – need to have the opportunity to share what those needs are. Some needs are common to all:

- *The need for assurance* – that we're on the right track, or the 'best track at the moment'.

- *The need for psychological safety* – staff need to 'feel safe' in school. The central issue of rights, such as the *right to feel safe* and *the right to respect and fair treatment*, are relevant for all staff. This need is crucial in situations where there is a crisis, say a student effectively holding the class to ransom.

- The need for advice and for support – moral support and practical support.

- *The need to know how to do something better* – or different, as need or context necessitates. Learning new skills, or fine-tuning and adapting one's skills, are essential to our professional well-being and development. Ongoing professional development that is realistic and practical and that addresses our needs is an essential aspect of colleague support. Elective mentoring, though labour-intensive, is a powerful way to meet such a need (Chapter 10).

Form has to follow function; the function of colleague support is to meet our fundamental human needs and our professional needs. We need to review our 'structures', 'forms', 'processes', 'organisational structure/culture in that light. Such 'structures' and 'forms' and internal policies will derive their *supportive function* from a collegial-needs analysis, normative team-feedback and stress audits (page 187).

Teachers who are struggling in their teaching and behaviour leadership need to have the assurance that if they approach senior colleagues for assistance then it will be given without censure. Conversely, staff need to be assured that if a senior colleague is made aware that a teacher is clearly struggling (beyond bad-day syndrome) that *it is normative practice in our school* that they will be approached professionally, privately and offered whatever support can reasonably be given. We should never allow a colleague to suffer the degrading humiliation of repeatedly stressful classroom experiences – whatever the precipitating cause.

NB There is a difference between a colleague clearly struggling with teaching and behaviour-management issues, and a teacher struggling with personal issues that are affecting their day-to-day teaching.

There is also a difference between the above and a teacher whose behaviour (we may suspect) is inappropriate or unprofessional and has been for some time.

There are naturally sensitive areas. In every case we need to address what we see and what is reported, as well as the perception our colleague brings to any professional discussion. We need to do so with the professional dignity that also allows a colleague the right of reply and the opportunity for support (page 203).

These professional conversations are never easy but we do have to appropriately confront inappropriate and unprofessional practice when normal, and reasonable, opportunities of colleague support have been resisted, ignored or refused.

Such colleagues have to be called to account and their practice challenged and reviewed when it consistently ignores school-wide policy and practice.

A supportive colleague culture will also pay particular attention to the needs of first-year teachers and supply teachers.[1]

Colleague support cannot merely be 'mandated'

Colleague support should not have to depend on the reciprocity of goodwill alone. The anomaly is that the very thing we all need, that is central to our professional and personal coping, cannot simply be 'forced' or mandated.

This is particularly so where changes in policy and practice are necessary to an individual's teaching practice or a whole-school commitment to change. As Fullan (1993) notes, 'The more complex the change the less you can force it' (page 21). McLaughlin (1990) makes the salient point that ' we cannot mandate what matters to effective practice' (page 15).

While we cannot mandate colleague support – as such – we can provide for, and enable, its likelihood through those 'forms', 'structures', 'organisational processes', teaming and sharing opportunities and mentoring options. We can hardly mandate an individual's heart and mind – their loyalty, commitment, morality or even their goodwill and civility! Without these features of collegiality, organisational support has a limited soul let alone a meaningful utility (see page 16). Commitment to an 'ecology' of support depends on how a community of individuals chooses to operate and how it is encouraged to operate in terms of mutual regard, collegial goodwill and professional respect.

Collaboration

What characterises cultures of collaboration are not formal organisation, meetings or bureaucratic procedures. Nor are cultures of collaboration mounted for specific projects and events. Rather, they consist of pervasive qualities, attitudes and behaviours that run through staff relationships on a moment-by-moment, day-to-day basis.

Help, support, trust and openness are at the heart of these relationships. Beneath that, there is a commitment to valuing people as individuals and valuing groups to which people belong.

Fullan and Hargreaves, 1991 (page 48)

Concord

According to Aristotle, concord is not merely an acquiescent agreement – it is the effort we make to have 'pretty much the same ground to stand upon ... and directed to what is both just and expedient.' He warns that those who work against concord, 'invariably want more than their share in such advantages as may be going, while at the same time shirk as much as they can of the trouble and experience of public service. And while each hopes to secure these advantages for himself, he keeps a critical eye on his neighbour to prevent him [sic] from gaining them.'

Aristotle: *Nichomacean Ethics*, Book 9, Chapter 6

Sound familiar? Have you ever been in a school like that? He adds that those who 'want more of their share', who 'shirk ...', who 'keep a critical eye on (their) neighbour' end up creating a situation redolent of 'discord; everybody trying to make everybody else do his duty, but not doing it himself'. (ibid.)

The cost of giving support

You want to break – just 10 minutes that's all. A cup of coffee, a chance to clear your thoughts before your next class. In walks a colleague – to the faculty staffroom. 'I've been looking for you, can I have a chat ...?' Already you see their 'look' – that 'hunted' (even haunted) look. The ill-concealed spasm of anxiety and, behind it, a reaching-out in hope. You ask yourself, 'What will I have to do now?', even before they have started their 'chat'. There is a 'cost', an undeniable cost in the giving of colleague support. Not the occasional reaching out, but the ongoing needs of some colleagues. We give of ourselves – our time, our thought, our energy and our goodwill. It's when it's frequent – seemingly every hour of every day. We, too, have demands on our time; we, too, have our own needs. Yet there are others who depend on us – a little too much at times. There are colleagues who seem to need constant 'propping-up' and assurance. We sometimes wonder 'if they'd only make a genuine, more sustained, effort ...'. I have sat with many, many senior colleagues who speak about having to put out 'behaviour spot fires' – time and time again – and often with the same teachers. I know, I remember.

I recall reading a major report on teacher stress some years back, referring to 'staff factions', 'teacher laziness', 'incompetence', 'abuses of the system ...'. The report was headed ' Hell is other teachers'. It sounded like something Sartre might have said in one of his novels. I've certainly felt that! And yet schools are – essentially – relationships among people. They are not merely 'systems', 'organisations' or bureaucracies.

John Mortimer (1986) has said the world is 'roughly divided between nurses and patients'.[2] Within any school, there are complex relationships between person-alities and 'structures'. The demands of policy, curriculum, addressing behaviour concerns and the constraints of time all affect our daily interactions with one another. There are those colleagues who give unstintingly of their time, energy and goodwill. They, too, speak of their stress in that giving; of balancing the desire to give without creating, at times, unhelpful and (even) irresponsible dependency in others.

Some colleagues will give support out of duty, some out of practical utility, others out of their good nature and personality – or all three. There are natural tensions inherent in that giving – we need to acknowledge that as a normative reality. And – a word to those who give – remember that we too have a life, we too have needs for support.

We simply cannot be available to everyone all the time, nor can we (or should we) be able to satisfy all the demands made on our time by students or colleagues. While this is patently obvious in a reflective, calmer, moment, in the busyness of a teaching day it is so easy for a caring senior colleague to get drawn into trying to solve everyone's needs. We have to be able to say, 'I've heard ... but I'll have to wait before I can get round to ...' If it's something that needs to be *done* (in timetabling, fixing a broken light, an item to raise at a meeting), it will need to be recorded (somewhere) to actually *remember*. Well, I have to record anyway – I can't rely on memory alone.

When we do seek to help others with concerns and problems, it is more effective (though more labour-intensive initially) to help them to solve the issue or concern and to face their challenges. This is why mentoring can be a more helpful long-term option for behaviour support than frequently putting out classroom 'spot fires'.

Self-interest and the difficulty of balancing

Self-interest is not the same as selfishness. Ours is, naturally, a demanding and stressful profession. It is also a *caring* and *giving* profession. We can *always* do more for our students and our colleagues; always – as time and demand persist. But we too have a life. We have our own needs, our loved ones beyond our professional life. If we let it, if we accede to those constant demands in our profession to the detriment of our own welfare (and our loved ones), we will not be acting responsibly. Difficult as it is, we sometimes have to say 'no' – thoughtfully and professionally. One of the reasons we have teams in a school (formal and '*ad hoc*' teams) is to *share* responsibilities, duties and the necessary demands of our profession.

Yes, we sometimes have to go the 'second mile', but I've seen colleagues 'burned out' by giving in – and giving over – to the next demand, and the next, and the next – from students, a colleague, a parent. I have done it myself at times. There is a cost. I have seen well-meaning, incredibly caring, colleagues 'burn out' because they had tried too hard to 'do all', and 'be all' 'for all'; *all the time*.

This is a profession where we can always do more – if we choose. Teaching, if you let it, can easily eat up a lot of your life for a lot more than is fair to you or your family – *more than a fair share* of our time and effort.

We have a life outside our profession. We don't – normally – have to be at school at 7.00 a.m. – and go home at 6.00 p.m. *every day*. While it can be helpful to get in early to organise and be well prepared, and then – perhaps – do the lion's share of marking at school before heading home, we have to realistically balance our life between home and school.

Ours is a profession where our shared humanity is the integrating feature of our shared existence as a local learning community (a school). We too, though, have to balance our needs (and those of our loved ones who were not called to teach). Teaching is our profession – *it is not our life*.

Unsolicited advice and 'Job's comforters'[3]

It is rarely received well – *unsolicited* advice I mean. We're given answers before we asked; assumptions are made when our story is not known; we told when we haven't even been heard.

'What you need to do is …', 'Why don't you just …?', 'What you should/ shouldn't do is …', 'I'd *never* do that …' When a colleague *merely* tells or moralises or judges, we feel inadequate, and even 'judged' (though that may not be their intent). If a colleague is sharing concerns about, say, a difficult class or student, it rarely helps when the other colleague says things like, 'Well I don't have any problem with …' (page 196), or 'all you need to do is …!'

Most of us don't like someone else *telling* us how to do our job. It's even more annoying when it's from someone you don't easily respect. Listen first, then try to understand – then explore how best you can help directly, or link your colleague to another's enabling support.

The difficult – but necessary – interview

For those of us in senior positions who do have to speak with colleagues about 'performance-related issues' we are in difficult emotional territory. Some of the colleagues we need to speak with will be very anxious at the thought of such an 'interview' – or even 'the brief chat'. Other colleagues will be annoyed – some will think that *any* fault lies in others, not them. Some will become withdrawn, unco-operative; others sarcastic even bombastic. Perspective taking is crucial – how would you feel in a similar situation? They are, after all, our colleagues.

- Be well prepared beforehand with the facts of the issue/s, circumstance/s, concern/s.
- Tune into how they might be feeling – without patronising them. Acknowledging their feelings does not mean we validate all they say. Explain why you have called this meeting and explain the why – *in the context of their 'job description' and the school's preferred policy and practices*. It will help to have this written down, and have a copy available for them.
- *Always* invite their right of reply.
- Avoid being sidetracked from the essential and the necessary areas of concern and focus. Some colleagues will not respond cooperatively even when such an interview is conducted with professional probity and supportive right of reply. Some colleagues will deny their inappropriate or unprofessional behaviour towards students or colleagues. Some will simply 'go silent'.

  Some teachers are actually unaware (some are aware but deny) that their 'sense of humour' (as they call it), their snide comments and put-downs, are actually intimidating to students (or fellow colleagues). Such behaviours are not merely inappropriate – they are offensive and unacceptable and must be challenged. Schools should have due process to enable such difficult collegial 'interviews'. There are colleagues whose practice is characterised by persistent laziness and indifference to students' needs. Their professional obligations (let alone goodwill and even civility) betray any meaningful commitment to school-wide practice.

We need to focus their attention to where their behaviour is clearly working against rights, responsibilities and professional obligations. We do this respectfully, firmly and professionally. We need to have clear, reliable information before we embark on an interview. It will help, obviously, to have a senior colleague 'sit in' (particularly if mixed genders are involved). With the facts clear, we should not resile from professionally confronting such colleagues and calling forth their responsibilities and necessary restitution to those they have hurt.

● Always follow up with a review meeting to progress any suggested (or required) plan or review procedures.

● Most of all we need to be consciously aware that we engage procedural fairness in this sensitive area.

The difficult and whingeing colleague

When discussing these skills and practices (Appendix 3) I come across colleagues who will say 'been there...', 'done that, 'doesn't work ...'.

In such meetings, with colleagues who whinge, it is important to refocus to the reason why certain behavioural leadership practices are the professional expectation within our school (page 42). Why it is necessary to have *shared core routines* for classroom teaching and behaviour; why we need a common, school-wide, commitment to *shared plans* such as *a classroom discipline plan* (page 92) or, say, a common duty of care plan for playground supervision or lunch supervision.

While we cannot directly change others, we can influence them within our shared values and our collegial practice. When we meet the common whinges, and complaints, we need to offer support and – at times – challenge our colleagues' assumptions and viewpoints. We do this within a *shared philosophy and practice* based on sound pedagogy and sound psychology. The practices discussed in the case studies, and particularly Chapter 7 are typical of what is meant by *shared practice*. (See Appendix 3.)

Differences of opinion – and points of view – are important in a healthy collegial culture. Such differences are acknowledged and even affirmed in collegially supportive cultures. We have to compromise at times, and compromise that enables a desirable and worthwhile objective is good. However, where compromise results in abandoning our core values, principles and objectives as a school it is a betrayal of our mission. Acceptance of the reality of compromise should not acquiesce to those colleagues who actively and purposefully divide and dissent; who work against the school's mission, its aims and its practice (Rogers, 2002).

Frequent and pervasive whingeing, carping and moaning can be destructive. It is often symptomatic of an unsupportive collegial ethos. The frequent moaning and complaining is, for some teachers, an effort to validate their own feelings of frustration. It often comes across, though, as if 'someone else should fix what is wrong in the school'; they are not responsible.

In a supportive collegial culture, differences are aired, within an ethos of civility and collegial respect. As one senior colleague said, 'It's not that we never disagree, never argue, never dispute. When we do, we do it clean, fair and open.'

In another school a colleague describes it as 'non-competitive here, everybody has the opportunity to talk about what does and doesn't work and why. There's no back-biting here. Yes, we'll argue things out – but we're not bitchy' (ibid.).

The typical comments – you may have heard these or said them?

- *'Been there, tried that, done that ...'* – what *exactly* did you try? What did you *actually* say?, How *long* did you try? I've worked *directly* with teachers in countless team-teaching sessions (in their classroom) who will say they 'did' or 'said' a certain thing only to under-report (the 30 times they said 'Shh!!', or '*Why* are you calling out!') or over report, 'I *always* try to be fair ...' (then you see them railing at a student over a minor behaviour issue like lateness, or not having equipment ...)

- *'I've got no time for all this* planning' – If we make time now we'll 'save' it later, and use our time more profitably. Planning is also likely to enable us to *focus on what we are actually trying to achieve* and how we might go about achieving any of it (page 189 and Chapter 7).

- *'It will never work!'* – well, let's try. Together.

- *'Sounds good, but ... well ... I'm just one of those people ...'* – you mean a special case? No one denies that facing up to issues of stress in our profession is a challenge. No one denies that change (in attitude and behaviour) is difficult – particularly in the area of behaviour-management skills. It may be that our excuses are a way of avoiding the need to decide; to take action. If something is clearly not working for us, it is in our best interest (and that of our students) to work at change. It is possible to 'condition' ourselves, you know.

- *'I can't help my feelings ...'* – very few of us can. What we can do is learn to understand and utilise our feelings rather than letting our feelings decide, by themselves, what we should or shouldn't do. Learning to choose *how we think* about things is a very helpful starting point.

- *'It's hard to change'* – it is. It's not impossible though – if we choose to, and if we know *where* and how to change, and if we have support. Colleague support will always help. The rest is the exercise of will, of time and effort.

- *'It's fate ... Those other teachers are lucky!'* – we make our 'luck', we make our 'fate' by what we do or fail to do.

- *'Nobody here cares ...'* – nobody? Really? Who have you asked? Are you prepared to seek out *one* colleague at your school who you could take the risk of working with? Support is based on reciprocal trust. When we isolate ourselves, not only do our problems seem worse (than they actually may be) but we'll feel worse as well. There is no virtue in being a collegial isolate. While we should not force a colleague to accept our support, we should be sensitive to awareness of needs in others and offer support.

- *'I can't get organised'* – ask someone *how*.

- *'You don't know* that *student;* that *class ...'* – I do.

- *'But I'm bound to fail'* – we're not bound to fail; though we will – not every time, on every occasion. What do we tell our students about failure? We don't blame them or criticise them – we teach them that failure is a normal part of the learning process. It depends on how we define and interpret and, then, what we do about failure. If we start out by saying 'I *must* get it right first time ...' we'll feel worse (much worse) when we fail. We'll also be easily discouraged and may feel like giving up or giving in.

- *'I can't be assertive ...'* – it's a skill; it can be learned.

- *'It's so difficult, so tiring, so much to do'* – yes – 'the thousand natural shocks that flesh is heir to ...' (page xii). What minimises the difficulties, the stress and the tiredness is the planning (page 189), the practices (Appendix 3), the daily enabling. These increase confidence and give that sense of shared connectedness as professionals.

The very hard word

There is a small percentage of teachers who by dint of personality – and temperament – and by repeated proofs of their inability to lead, manage and teach students, and to manage the multi-demanding nature of our profession are better counselled out of the profession. Our profession is clearly not suited to everyone. It is not merely a matter of 'degrees intelligence'. Our daily work involves social and emotional intelligence; the ability to think on one's feet; the need for a high degree of 'frustration-tolerance'; the desire to make a genuine difference to the lives of young people; the desire to learn 'on the job' – to be a reflective practitioner; the willingness to be part of a team. These are all essential attributes in our profession and more important than one's IQ or university marks. The overly demanding, overly vigilant personality, the very non-assertive, very anxious and non-vigilant personality will find teaching very stressful.

Having worked with many senior colleagues who have the unpleasant – but necessary – task of making such professional issues, obligations and options clear, I know *how stressful this is for all concerned.* It becomes more unpleasant when 'performance review' procedures are entered into.

While some teachers will leave the profession with rancour, anger and blame, others – thankfully – will realise they have made the best decision for their health, their well-being and future career prospects.

Notes

1. Supply teachers are sometimes the 'forgotten' colleagues in a school – 'babysitters'. They may well be covering challenging classes. They need considered, conscious support from their arrival to our school; a 'teaching-buddy' they can call on; a decent map; 'bell times'; even an introduction to the class, particularly the challenging class. See Rogers (2003).

2. Sir John Mortimer – the English barrister, novelist and playright. (See Rumpole and the Goldern Thread. Peguin. 1983, page 221).

3. *Job's comforters* comes from the Biblical account of a 'good' man who suffers intolerably. He never claimed perfection – just that he was a reasonable man – doing his best, but suffering acute loss of family and ongoing physical and psychological suffering. Several friends come (three in particular) to give advice as to why he suffers so much in his physical, mental and spiritual anguish. The most common thread – in their 'advice' – is the trite, pious (and theologically unsound) view that suffering is accounted for by sin. In a world where so much human suffering seems to have no reason at all this is 'the unkindest cut of all (!)'. (Julius Caesar, Shakespeare – you know, in the speech by Marc Anthony ...)

Conclusion

This has not been an easy book to write. Each case example of very challenging class(es) and challenging students – particularly the section on bullying of teachers – brings back painful memories; I feel it as I write. Thankfully in almost all these situations there were collegially positive outcomes. These balance – well balance (thankfully) – the remembered and resolved stress.

We choose this profession; we choose to *be* a teacher. In that choice we also recognise the *naturally* stressful nature of the profession. With a realistic mindset, colleague support and experience – along with the planning, practices and skills noted in this book – we can utilise that necessary stress, that *motivating* stress, to do what we chose to be. We can also better recognise and manage the more wearing aspects of stress in our profession if we recognise that we chose, and choose, to be a teacher.

We have to live in a world in which the human family have to live with the ambiguity of partial power, partial knowledge and partial freedom. We also have to live with and cope with the natural – and impositional – stresses that daily life and work bring.

If we characteristically moan about those stressors and easily blame our feelings of frustration, anger and anxiety on others – or our situation – we'll feel worse than we need to. If we demand that others should – must – be as we say then we'll not only feel worse but we'll also find our work and relationships more stressful than they need to be.

Before we choose to lead, teach and manage others we need to be able to manage ourselves – good and bad days alike.

Others can (and thankfully do) encourage, guide and support us – however, *we still have to manage ourselves*, our thinking, our emotions, our behaviour.

There are many practices, approaches, strategies and skills that can address and enable this area of our life. Some are dealt with in this book – particularly as they apply to our professional life. I have chosen approaches, strategies, practices and skills that my colleagues and I seek to build into our teaching practice. The central message of this book is that we need to balance the managing of self with the management and support of others.

I encourage you to remember that our moods, emotions and behaviour are all also inextricably linked to how we rate, perceive and talk to ourselves about our daily stress. I further encourage you to ask what can *reasonably* be done to effectively address the stress we experience in our professional life at school. That balance between stressful demands and coping resources will need to involve our colleagues. This needs to involve that creative tension between individual respon-sibility, accountability and colleague support. When we feel comfortable enough to share needs, concerns and problems with our colleagues – within a climate of professional trust – we will find the solutions we need to fulfil what we exist for as school communities.

It is my hope this book will contribute positively to that process.

Best wishes.
Bill Rogers, Melbourne, February, 2011

APPENDIX 1

COLLEAGUE SUPPORT: A FRAMEWORK FOR A SCHOOL-WIDE SURVEY

The nature of our collegiality is a crucial feature of our school culture – it shapes the social and professional fabric of our life at work and our life *in* our work.

The following questions invite colleagues to address what they understand – and seek to address – in terms of both informal and the more 'formal', 'structural' aspects of colleague support.

1. What do you understand 'colleague support' to mean for you?

2. What do you note as the benefits, and value of colleague support:

    a) as an individual?

    b) as a member of a grade or faculty team?

3. What do you regard as the *essential features* of a collegially supportive school?

4. In what ways do we express colleague support here (in our school) – such that we enhance and enable our teaching practice and our behaviour leadership practice?

5. a) What 'formal' structures/processes/'ways-of-doing-things'/policies do you find particularly supportive? In what ways do you find such 'formal' expressions of support enabling to you?

    b) In what way could those 'formal' aspects of support enable you to do your work better as a teacher–leader? (For example the school's behaviour policy; the use of an 'individual discipline plan'; the organisational planning for core routines in the establishment phase of the year (Chapter 7).

6. How does collegiality and teamwork operate in our school? Do staff have opportunities to develop and pursue professional concerns and engage in purposeful problem-solving here?

   a) Whether in their 'formal' teams or opportunities for informal support groups – how?

   b) How are the needs of struggling teachers met? (And how do we respectfully identify and offer support to struggling colleagues?)

   c) How confident are you of approaching a senior colleague for support in the areas of your teaching practice? Your behaviour leadership and discipline? What could improve those professional links to identify needs and opportunities for support?

7. If you were struggling with a challenging student/s or a challenging class, how would you seek colleague support? How confident would you be of receiving a positive and enabling response? If not, how can we improve the support offered to colleagues struggling with behaviour/discipline/leadership concerns? If colleagues choose (or refuse) not to come forward for support, how best can/should we approach them with the support needed?

8. What are the areas that need immediate redress regarding colleague support in our school? And why?

9. Do you have any suggestions about how we could develop/improve the colleague culture of our school? Please share those with us.

10. Do you have any other concerns about colleague support in our school not addressed by these questions? What are they? Please share them and we will do our best to respond – directly and personally wherever we can – please let us know.

APPENDIX 2

HELPFUL EXERCISES

There are helpful exercises for the deep-muscle tissue – that area of our body difficult to access 'voluntarily'. I've found these helpful – they're found in many exercise manuals. As with any exercise, if you're none too fit then you know you should always check with your doctor.

- Lie flat on your back (on a blanket rather than a hard floor). Gently arch the middle section of the back. Gently raise the torso from the raised middle section by about the width of a hand – say 10 centimetres – and then slowly lower the back, breathing slowly and regularly.

- Another lying-down exercise – flat on the back. Lift one arm about 15 to 20 centimetres slowly – then let it gently arch (no contortions). Let it drop. Do the same with the other arm and then try each leg (no arching – just gently lift 15 to 20 centimetres) then let it drop.

A half-a-dozen repetitions and a cup of tea afterwards (!)

APPENDIX 3

THE CONCEPT OF 'PREFERRED PRACTICES' WITHIN A WHOLE-SCHOOL APPROACH TO BEHAVIOUR LEADERSHIP

The concept of 'preferred practices' relates to a **school-wide consciousness** about the way we – as teachers – characteristically seek to lead and manage student behaviour (bad-days notwithstanding!) Even on our bad days our leadership can model respect as well as normative fallibility.

The term '**preferred**' is deliberate – there are some behaviour-management practices we prefer (when it comes to management and discipline) because of certain values we hold. **Core values** such as mutual regard, mutual respect and dignity of the individual give a focus and direction to our management and discipline practice. In relating our preferred practices back to our core values we also give **meaning** and **purpose** to why we discipline the way we do (our **characteristic** practices). Management and discipline practice, then, becomes purpose-driven, not merely task-driven.

Preferred practices also imply whole-school commitment to *skilled* discipline and management practice.

Preferred practices

Within a whole-school plan for behaviour management, teachers agree to common behaviour management and discipline practices at the classroom level and 'duty of care' level (outside of classrooms) and take **active** responsibility for management and discipline. These preferred practices do not delimit a teacher's own sense of professionalism and contextual management and discipline. They, rather, enhance such professionalism and increase the sense of **shared professional consistency across the school.**

● Each teacher will establish and clarify **classroom rules responsibilities and consequences** based on a year-level framework. These will be developed with the students in the 'establishment phase' of the year. At secondary level these *core* rights, responsibilities and rules are discussed at tutor/form-group level and then fine-tuned/adapted by subject teachers.

● The teacher will also establish the **core routines** necessary for the smooth running of classroom learning – entry to classroom; settling for whole-class teaching time; appropriate seating plans; cues for questions/discussion; appropriate movement around classroom; how to fairly get teacher assistance in learning-task time; appropriate noise levels; pack-up, clean-up and an 'orderly' exit from classroom (page 92).

● The school-wide **3Rs** (rights, responsibilities and rules) will be the **basis** for corrective, consequential and supportive management/discipline, and those **3Rs** will be expressed in the *student code of behaviour*. At primary age level, these 3Rs can be developed within a **classroom behaviour agreement** (see Rogers and McPherson, 2008).

Aims of management/discipline

The aims of all management and discipline are to: enable the student(s) to own their behaviour, and be accountable for their behaviour; to respect mutual rights and to do so within the context of workable relationships with other students and their teachers. The core rights are: the right to feel safe; the right to learn (without undue distraction or disruption); the right to respect and fair treatment. These rights entail responsibilities by all, and education and leadership protection by all teaching and support staff (page 113).

Teacher will consciously discipline within these aims in order that the primary business of the classroom (teaching and learning) can take place and that the safety and well-being of students are protected.

● When correcting/disciplining students, teachers minimise *any* unnecessary confrontation (in management and discipline) – i.e. undue criticism, sarcasm, ridicule, embarrassment, public shaming, and so on. Unintended, hurtful communication by a teacher should *always* entail an apology.

● When developing and utilising corrective discipline we consciously address the:

  ● 'Language of discipline' – giving some thought to words and meaning within our typical, **characteristic**, discipline language (Chapter 7)

- We balance 'language of discipline' with 'language of encouragement'

- We utilise a least-to-most intrusive intervention approach when managing and disciplining individuals and groups; becoming 'more intrusive' only as is necessary (pages 105, 108). This means becoming appropriately assertive where necessary (it does not mean becoming hostile, mean-spirited or verbally aggressive).

- In addressing distracting and disruptive behaviours, we keep the focus of our discipline addressed to the 'primary behaviour' or 'primary issue' and avoid arguing or debating 'secondary behaviours' or 'side issues' (wherever possible) (page 45).

  Where necessary we direct the student aside from their peers and in a heated conflict situation we always allow cool-off time (this may result in formal time-out for the student). Some behaviour consequences will need to be deferred until after 'cool-off' time. We need whole-school clarity *for all uses* of informal and formal time-out procedures (Chapter 8).

- When applying behaviour consequences we emphasise the fair, and reasonable, *certainty* of the consequences rather than merely their severity. We remember to always keep the fundamental respect intact when *applying* the consequence:

  - Establish a year-level approach to the use of behaviour consequences for common rule-breaking behaviours; emphasise reparation, restitution and reconciliation as the norm. In this sense there is a degree of seriousness in the application and kind of behaviour consequences used, relative to the degree of rights-infringing behaviour.

  - Distinguish between 'negotiable' and 'non-negotiable' consequences. Non-negotiable consequences are *school-wide* and address issues such as drugs (including smoking); bullying; aggression and violence.

  - When establishing behaviour consequences, where possible we try to gain a **relatedness** between the disruptive behaviour and the consequential outcome. Where appropriate, we should ask the student what they think they should do to address the behaviour in question. The sorts of questions we ask are:
    - What happened? (regarding your behaviour)
    - What rule (or right) was affected by your behaviour?
    - What is your 'side of the story' …? (a basic right-of-reply question)
    - What can you do to make things better? Fix things up? Repair/re-build?
    - How can I help?

  - We seek to repair and rebuild with the student beyond the consequential process.

- 'Separate' the distracting, disruptive, offending behaviour 'from' the student (particularly in the way we treat the student).

- Actively promote positive behaviours with all students through verbal, relational and appropriate symbolic encouragement. Consider the range of possible 'incentives' and public recognition programmes (beyond academic 'achievement'). Regular use of *descriptive* feedback and encouragement by teachers, and teaching assistants, should be the norm.

- 'Exit' and 'time-out' procedures are used to enable cool-off-time for repeatedly distracting and disruptive behaviours – and any behaviours that are unsafe or potentially dangerous. All teachers (and teaching assistants and senior personnel) work together to establish appropriate year-level and school-wide due processes for exit, time-out and follow-up of any students whose distracting, disruptive or dangerous behaviour has necessitated 'exit' from the classroom – for example, **persistent** refusal to work within the fair rules and within reasonable teacher direction; safety concerns; verbal abuse; aggressive behaviour.

  Address fundamental questions with regard to time-out such as *How*?, *To whom*?, How long should the student stay in time-out? What happens when the student refuses to leave the classroom and go to the time-out area? Where do they go for time-out? What happens during time-out? On what basis do they renegotiate entry back to the classroom that day? (See Chapter 8.)

Class/subject teachers are – primarily – responsible for follow-up of time-out procedures with support of senior colleagues

- Emphasise the crucial importance of re-establishing working relationships and reconciliation between the teacher who initiated the time-out and student(s) concerned. Obviously senior teachers will often need to support class/subject teachers in such follow-up. Avoid holding grudges (tempting as that may be!). Where the relational/conflict issues are serious, use supporting mediation (from other colleagues) for resolution outcomes. Where necessary – and where possible – involve parents (case-by-case) through diaries, phone calls, parent/teacher conference (let them know positive outcomes too!).

- Clarify **roles** in the discipline/pastoral sense (i.e. of class/subject teacher through to head teacher). Establish clear communication processes for follow-through of the more serious and persistent discipline incidents. It is important that the grade teacher, or subject teacher, be **directly involved** in the follow-up and follow-through of disruptive behaviour (119).

- Emphasise collegial responsibility of duty-of-care management *school-wide* – 'relaxed vigilance' in out-of-class contexts such as corridors, playground, lunch supervision, bus supervision, after-school supervision. It will help to have a *school-wide plan* for such duty-of-care management rather than leaving it merely to professional discretion.

● Most of all, we need to build and utilise a supportive colleague culture for problem-solving and 'structural'/policy support. Colleague support is essential in the management of difficult students and students with emotional and behavioural disorders. The 'hard-class syndrome' and playground supervision are also crucial areas that benefit from focused colleague support (both moral support and organised, planned, practical support options). (See, particularly, Chapter 9)

These preferred practices, and shared expectations, need to be expressed in a common policy school-wide:

● with a common discipline framework at the **classroom** level (Chapter 00)

● a common 'duty-of-care' framework in non-classroom settings – e.g. corridors, playgrounds, lunch supervision wet-day, bus supervision.

● **due processes for consequences, counselling and individual behaviour management plans** for long-term behaviour change with students who have ongoing disruptive patterns of behaviour.

APPENDIX 4

BULLYING BY COLLEAGUES

Any bullying in the workplace is unacceptable – by any definition. Schools should have *a clear framework of rights and responsibilities within which the issue of bullying is addressed* – any bullying, by anyone.

There are those staff – even senior staff – who treat colleagues in controlling, intimidating and verbally abusive ways. This includes veiled threats, repeated snide comments, warped and sexist 'humour', picking on certain individuals, abusive emails, emotionally manipulating job requirements, and so on. Where such behaviour is intentional and repetitive, it is bullying. Behaviour that springs from an insecure, and often, controlling personality.

The NASUWT has published clear guidelines to address this issue in schools. So too has the Health and Safety executive: www.hse.gov.uk/stress

If you are confident enough to confront such a colleague, then do so – bullies are cowards and I'm always encouraged when I see a teacher professionally – and assertively – confront a bullying colleague.

This is not always an easy matter, particularly a junior colleague experiencing harassment from a senior colleague or principal. It can be difficult – sometimes – to 'pin-down' what a bullying colleague is doing or saying that you know is bullying. Bullies tend to trade in secrecy from others (apart, perhaps, from a collusive bully or two. They know that if their behaviour was open to wide colleague knowledge and display then their behaviour would be rightly and duly confronted, challenged and restitution called for.

It will be important before confronting such a colleague to talk it through first with a trusted colleague and a union counsellor. It will help in clarifying your thoughts and concerns about the bullying colleague's behaviour.

Plan what you want, and need, to say – specifics (including the nature of their behaviour; even dates/times/occasions). Note it all down clearly – before going into any formal meeting to address your concerns. Far better to address such behaviour early – with trusted colleague advocacy – than suffer the indignity of such injudicious, intemperate and clearly inappropriate behaviour. When you confront a bully with senior colleague advocacy, it's out in the open; something has to be done and will be done.

In more severe cases the NASWUT notes that schools should give a commitment to advise the perpetrator of abuse of legal actions that might be taken against them. In addition there should be a clear, school-based, protocol for monitoring incidents, including taking into account equality and anti-discrimination implications, which may relate to the duties to promote equality on the basis of gender, race and disability. (This protocol would work for students as well.)

See also www.teachersunion.org.uk and www.teachernet.gov.uk

Bibliography

Adler, V. (1989) 'Little control – lots of stress'. *Psychology Today*, April, pp 18–19.

Allen, D. (2001) *How To Get Things Done – the art of stress-free productivity*. London: Penguin.

Baars, C.W. (1979) *Feeling and Healing Your Emotions*. New York: Logos International.

Barr, K. (2008) 'Pain, pain go away – outsmarting chronic pain so it doesn't cramp your style.' *Psychology Today*, March 1st, pp 56–57.

Bentley, N. (1957) *How Can You Bear to be Human?*. London: Penguin Books.

Bernard, M. (1990) *Taking the Stress Out Of Teaching*. Melbourne: Collins Dove.

Bernard, M. and Joyce, M. (1984) *Rational–Emotive Therapy with Children and Adolescents: theory, treatment, strategies, preventative measures*. New York: John Wiley and Sons.

Braiker, H.B. (1989) 'The power of self-talk'. *Psychology Today*, December, pp 23–27.

Breheney, C., Mackrill, V. and Grady, N. (1996) *Making Peace at Mayfield – a whole-school approach to behaviour management*. Melbourne: Eleanor Curtain.

Brighouse, T. and Woods, D. (1999) *How To Improve Your School*. London: Routledge.

Bronson, L. and Todd, G. (2009) *Overcoming Stress: a self-help guide*. London: Constable & Hunter.

Burns, D.D. (1989) *The Good Feeling Handbook*. [in Braiker, op. cit.]

Cade, J.F. (1979) *Mending the Mind: a short history of twentieth century psychiatry*. Melbourne: Sun Books.

Chesterton, G.K. (1983) *The Penguin Father Brown (Stories)*. London: Penguin Books.

Colarelli, S. (1989) 'A Smile's a Smile ...'. *Psychology Today*, March, p 44ff.

Coopersmith, S. (1967) *The Antecedents of Self-Esteem*. San Francisco: Freeman.

Davies, S. (2006) *The Essential Guide to Teaching*. London: Pearson.

De Bono, E. (1986) *Conflicts: a better way to resolve them*. Harmondsworth: Penguin.

Department for Children, School and Families (2007) *Safe to Learn: embedding anti-bullying practices in schools*. London: DCSF.
[NB Without being critical of the DCSF, bullying needs to be addressed not just from an 'anti-bullying' stance, but from a *'pro-rights' stance*: fundamentally the right to feel safe in schools].

Dobson, K.S. (ed.) (2010) *Handbook of Cognitive Behavioural Therapies*. New York: Guilford Press.

Dreikurs, R (1968) *Psychology in the Classroom: a manual for teachers*. New York: Harper & Row.

Dreikurs, R. Grunwald, B and Pepper, F. (1982) *Maintaining Sanity in the Classroom* (2nd edition). New York: Harper and Row.

Edwards, C. (1977) 'RET in high school'. *Rational Living*, 12, pp 10–12.

Ellis A. and Harper, R. (1974) *A New Guide to Rational Living*. North Hollywood, California: Wilshire Book Co.

Elton Report (1989) *Discipline in Schools, Report of the Committee of Inquiry*. London: Her Majesty's Stationary Office.

Etzion, D. (1984) 'The moderating effect of social support on the stress-burnout relationship'. *Journal of Applied Psychology*, 69 (4), pp 615–622.

Festinger, L. (1957) *A Theory of Cognitive Dissonance*. Stanford, California: Stanford University Press.

Field, E. (2010) *Staffroom Victims*. Australian Education Union Newsletter (April issue).

Fox, B. (2010) *Power Over Panic*. Melbourne: Penguin Books.

Frankl, V.E. (1963) *Man's Search For Meaning*. New York: Simon & Schuster/ Gulf & Western.

Fullan, M.G. (1991) *The New Meaning of Educational Change* (2nd edition). New York: Teachers' College Press.

Fullan, M.G. (1993) *Change Forces – probing the depths of educational reform*: London: Falmer Press.

Fullan, M. and Hangreaves, A. (1991) *'Whats' Worth Fighting for: Working Together For Your School*. Toronto: Ontario Public School Teachers' Federation.

Galton, M. and MacBeath J. (2008) *Teachers Under Pressure*. London: Sage Publications.

Glasser, W. (1986) *Control Theory in the Classroom*. New York: Harper and Row.

Glasser, W. (1991) *The Quality School: managing students without coercion*. New York: Harper and Row.

Goleman, D. (1996) *Emotional Intelligence*. London: Bloomsbury.

Grant, A., Townsend, A., Mulhern, R and Short, N. (eds) (2010) *Cognitive Behavioural Therapy in Mental Health Care* (2nd edition). London: Sage Publications.

Graves, R. (1955) *The Greek Myths*. (1966 edition The Folio Society, London.)

A Guide to Risk Assessment of Violent and Abusive Behaviour: A guide for leaders and managers. www.teachersunion.org.uk 08/6/2008.

Halonen, J.S. and Santrock, J.W. (1996) *Psychology: contexts of behaviour*. Chicago: Brown and Benchmark.

Hamlet (1988) William Shakespeare: *The Oxford Shakespeare* (Oxford World Classics) Oxford: Oxford University Press.

Hobfoll, S.E. (1998) *Stress, Culture and Community: the psychology and philosophy of stress*. New York: Plenum Press.

Horney, K. (1945) *Our Inner Conflict*. New York: Norton.

House (1981) in Russell et al. (1987), pp 269f.

Hunter-Corsch, M., Tiknaz, Y. Cooper, P. and Sage, R. (2006) *The Handbook of Social and Emotional and Behavioural Difficulties*. London: Continuum Publishing.

Huxley, A. (1976) *A Brave New World*. Penguin Modern Classics. Middlesex: Penguin Books.

Johnson, D.W. and Johnson, B.T. (1989) *Leading the Co-operative School*. Minnesota: Interaction Book Co.

Jones, P. and Tucker E. (eds) (1990) *Mixed Ability Teaching – classroom experiences in English, ESL, Mathematics and Science*. Rozelle, NSW: St Clair Press.

Kennerly, H. (2009) *Overcoming Anxiety: a self-help guide to using cognitive behavioural techniques*. London: Constable & Robinson Ltd.

Kounin, J. (1971) *Discipline and Group Management in Classrooms*. New York: Holt, Rhinehart & Winston.

Kyriacou, C. (1981) 'Social support and occupational stress among school teachers'. *Educational Studies*, vol. 7, pp 55–60.

Kyriacou, C. (1986) *Effective Teaching in Schools*. Oxford: Basil Blackwell.

Kyriacou, C. (1987) 'Teacher stress and burnout: an international review'. *Educational Research*, vol. 29, no. 2, June, pp 146–152.

Langer, E.J. (1997) *The Power of Mindful Learning*. New York: Perseus Press.

Langer, E. (2000) 'Do stop thinking about tomorrow'. *Psychology Today*, March/April p 26.

Lazarus, R.S. and Folkman, S. (1984) *Stress: appraisal and coping*. New York: Springer.

Lowe, J. and Istance, D. (1989) *Schools and Quality* (an international report). Paris: OECD.

Maslach, C. (1976) 'Burned out'. *Human Behaviour*, September, pp 6–10.

Maslow, A.H. (1970) *Motivation and Personality* (2nd edition). New York: Van Nostrand Reinhold.

Maultsby, M.C. (1977) 'Basic principles of intensive rational behaviour therapy: theories, goals, techniques and advantages' in Wolfe, J.L. and Brands, E. (eds) *Twenty Years of Rational Therapy*. New York: Institute for Rational Living.

McEwan, B. and Boyce, T. (2010) *Stressed Out! The powerful biology of stress*. The Australian Broadcasting Commission (ABC) Radio National Program *All In the Mind* 3th March 2010. [Professor Bruce McEwan is a neuroscientist and a neuro-endocrinologist. Tom Boyce is professor of Paediatrics and Interdisciplinary Studies at the University of British Columbia in Vancouver]. See http://www.abc.net.au/rn/allinthemind/stories

McGrath, H. and Noble, T. (2003) *The Bounce Back Resiliency Program*. Melbourne: Pearson Education.

McLaughlin, M. (1990) 'The rand change agent revisited'. *Educational Researcher*, Vol. 5, pp 11–16; quoted in Fullan, M.G. (1993).

Merson, J. (2001) *The Science and Politics of a Global Crisis: stress, the causes, the costs, and the cures*. Sydney: ABC Books.

Miller, A. (1996) *Pupil Behaviour and Teacher Culture*. London: Cassell.

Montgomery, B. and Evans, L. (1984) *You and Stress: a guide to successful living*. Melbourne: Thomas Nelson.

Morgan, D. P. and Jenson, W. R. (1988) *Teaching Behaviourally Disordered Students: preferred practices*. Toronto: Merrill Publishing Co.

Mortimer, J. (1986) *Character Parts*. London: Penguin Books.

Myklehun, Reider, J. (1984) 'Teacher stress: perceived and objective sources and quality of life'. *Scandinavian Journal of Education Research*, vol. 28 (1), March, pp 17–45.

Noble, G. and Watkins, M. (1988) 'Teachers' work: morale in public education', *Education Australia*, issue 2.

O'Brien, T. (1998) *Promoting Positive Behaviour*. London: David Fulton.

Ornish, D. (1999) *Love and Survival*. New York: Harper Collins.

Otto, R. (1985) *Teachers Under Stress*. Melbourne: Hill of Content.

Parkes, K.R. (1986), 'Coping in stressful episodes: the role of individual differences, environmental factors, and situational characteristics'. *Journal of Personality and Psychology*, vol. 51, no. 6, pp 1277–1299.

Pratt, J. (1978) 'Perceived stress among teachers'. *Educational Review*. 30, pp 3–14.

Robertson, J. (1998) *Effective Classroom Control: understanding teacher–pupil relationships* (3rd edition). London: Hodder and Stoughton.

Roffey, S. (2004) *The New Teacher's Survival Guide to Behaviour*. London: Sage Publications.

Rogers, B. (2002) *I Get By With a Little Help: colleague support in schools*. London: Sage Publications.

Rogers, B. (ed.) (2002b) *Teacher Leadership and Behaviour Management*. London: Sage Publications.

Rogers, B. (2003) *Effective Supply Teaching*. London: Sage Publications.

Rogers, B. (2004) *Behaviour Recovery: school based programs for students with diagnosed (and undiagnosed) behaviour disorders*. London: Sage Publications.

Rogers, B. (2006) *Cracking the Hard Class: strategies for managing the harder than average class* (2nd edition). London: Sage Publications.

Rogers, B. (2007) *Behaviour Management: a whole-school approach* (2nd edition). London: Sage Publications.

Rogers, B. (2007) *Classroom Behaviour: a practical guide to effective teaching, behaviour management and colleague support*. London: Sage Publications.

Rogers, B. (ed.) (2009) *How To Manage Children's Challenging Behaviour* (2nd edition). London: Sage Publications.
This book has a range of essays written by teachers in the UK, NZ and Australia sharing how they work with very challenging children and classes.

Rogers, B. (2011) *You Know the Fair Rule and Much More* (Major third edition). Melbourne: Australian Council for Educational Research.

Rogers, B. website www.billrogers.com.au

Rogers, B. and McPherson, E. (2008) *Behaviour Management With Young Children: crucial first steps with children 3–7 Years*. London: Sage Publications.

Ruddock, J. (1991) *Innovation and Change*. Buckingham: Open University Press.

Russell, D.W., Altmaier, E. and Van Velzen, D. (1987) 'Job-related stress: social support and burnout among classroom teachers'. *Journal of Applied Psychology*, May, vol. 72, no. 2, pp 269–274.

Rutter, M. (1981) 'Stress, coping and development: some issues and questions'. *Journal of Child Psychology and Psychiatry*, 22(4), pp 323–356.

Rutter, M., Maughan, B., Mortimer, P and Ousten, J. (1979) *Fifteen Thousand Hours: secondary schools and their effects on children*. London: Open Books.

Sacks, O. (1991) *Awakenings*. London: Harper Collins.

Safran, S.P., Safran, J.S. and Barcikowski, R.S. (1985) 'Differences in teacher tolerance: an illusory phenomenon?' *Behaviour Disorders*, pp 11–15.

Schopenhauer, A. trans Hollingdale, R.J. (1976) *Essays and Aphorisms*. London: Penguin Classics.

Scott Peck, M. (1990) *The Road Less Travelled*. London: Arrow Books.

Seligman, M. (1970) 'On the generality of the laws of learning'. *Psychological Review*, Vol. 77, pp 406–418.

Seligman, M. (1975) *Helplessness – on depression, development and death*. San Francisco: W.H. Freeman Press.

Seligman, M. (1991) *Learned Optimism*. Sydney: Random House.

Selye, H. (1975) *Stress Without Distress*. New York: Signet.

Selye, H. (1978) *The Stress of Life*. New York: McGraw Hill.

Smith, M. (1981) *When I Say No I Feel Guilty*. Toronto: Bantam Books.

Sprinthall, R.C. and Sprinthall, N.A. (1974) *Educational Psychology: a developmental approach* (2nd Edition). Massachusetts: Addison-Wesley.

Stewart, C. (2009) Stress busting. *Australian Education Union Newsletter* (October issue)

Tavris, C. (1982) 'Anger defused'. *Psychology Today*, November.

Thody, A., Gray, B. and Bowden, B. (2000) *The Teachers' Survival Guide*. London: Continuum Press.

Thompson, P. et al. (2003) in Galton and McBeath (2008).

Thompson, J.A.K., trans. (1969) *The Ethics of Aristotle* (*The Nichomachean Ethics*) by Aristotle. London: Penguin Classics.

Trotter, R.J. (1987) 'Stop blaming yourself (the research of Martin Seligman). *Psychology Today*, February, pp 31–39.

University of Melbourne (1989) *Teacher Stress in Victoria – a survey of teachers' views*. Applied Psychology Research Group, Ministry of Education.

Walker, L. (2008) *The Essential Guide to Lesson Planning*. London: Pearson. [This is a short but comprehensively helpful book on that essential topic *lesson planning*. We can't shirk this core feature of formal teaching and learning. This book gives clear, sensible, practical and realistic advice to busy teachers.]

Wehrenberg, M. and Prinz, S.M. (2007) *The Anxiety Brain: the neurobiological basis of anxiety disorders and how to effectively treat them*. New York: W.W. Norton.

Willis, S. (2010) 'Teacher Education: The challenges ahead'. *Professional Voice*, Vol. 5, Issue 2.

Wilson, B.L. and Corcoran, T.B. (1988) *Successful Secondary Schools: Visions of Excellence in American Public Education*. London: Falmer Press.

Wilson, P. (1985) *The Calm Technique: Meditation Without Magic or Mysticism*. Victoria: Penguin Books.

Woodhouse, D.A., Hall, E. and Wooster, A.D. (1985) 'Taking control of stress in teaching'. *British Journal of Educational Psychology*, 55, pp 119–123.

- www.acas.org.uk

- www.atl.uk/help-and-advice/workplace-bullying/what-is-bullying.asp

- www.beyondblue.org.au

- www.bullying.com.au

- www.bullyonline.org

- www.hsebooks.co.uk

- www.hse.gov.uk

- www.hse.gov.uk/stress The HSE (Health and Safety Executive) has produced management standards for employers and their representatives.
  On 3 November 2004, HSE launched the Management Standards and tools to help employers and employees work together to prevent excessive work-related stress. HSE's stress website at www.hse.gov.uk/stress will help organisations meet their existing duty-of-care and their duty to assess the risk of work-related stress.
  The standards define the characteristics, or culture, of an organisation where stress is being managed effectively. The 'toolkit' consists of a survey and continuous improvement model which enables organisations to compare themselves with others.
  For more information see HSE's publication *Managing the Causes of Work-Related Stress: A step-by-step approach using the Management*

Standards HSG218 (Second edition) HSE Books (2007) ISBN 978 0 7176 6273 9.

- www.mind.org.uk A national charity for people with emotional and mental health issues.

- www.stress.org.uk (The Stress Management Society is a non-profit organisation dedicated to helping people tackle stress).

- www.teachernet.gov.uk

- www.teachersupport.info (08000 562 561) The Teacher Support Line – formerly Teacher Line – is a free information, support and counselling service for all teachers (including trainees). It is a 24-hour (every day) service that encourages and supports teachers to develop solutions to the problems they wish to share.

- www.teachersunion.org.uk Email: nasuwt@mail.nasuwt.gov.uk

- www.workcover.vic.gov.au

- Career transition – moving out of teaching can be stressful. For guidance and support in this area, including details of one-to-one coaching and workshops on how to prepare for your next career move, contact helen@ challengingideas.co.uk or phone 07946 475531.

Index